D1440048

Administering Britain

Brian Smith graduated in Politics at Exeter University in 1959.
He obtained an M.Sc. at McMaster University in 1962 and
worked for the Acton Society Trust for a year before joining
the staff of the Department of Government at Exeter in 1963.
He spent a year in Northern Nigeria in 1965-6 and was seconded
to the Civil Service College from 1970 to 1972. He became
Senior Lecturer in Public Administration at the University of
Bath in 1972. He is author of *Regionalism in Britain*, vols. 1, 2
and 3 (1964, 1965), *Field Administration* (1967) and *Advising
Ministers* (1969) and has contributed to the journals *Public
Administration*, *Administrative Science Quarterly*, *Political
Quarterly*, *Political Studies*, *Urban Studies*, *Social and Economic
Administration* and the *Journal of Local Administration
Overseas*. He obtained a Ph.D. from Exeter in 1970 for a study
of field administration in Northern Nigeria.

Jeffrey Stanyer read Philosophy, Politics and Economics
(1955-8) and the B.Phil. in Politics (1958-60) at Balliol College,
Oxford. He joined the academic staff of Exeter University in
1960 as Research Fellow in Local Government, and became a
lecturer in Government in 1962. He is author of *County
Government in England and Wales* (1967) and *Understanding
Local Government* (to be published in this series in 1976)
and has contributed to the journals *Public Administration*,
Political Studies, *Social and Economic Administration*,
Parliamentary Affairs and *The Advancement of Science*.

Studies in Public Administration

This is a new series designed to introduce the reader to the study of the different aspects of public administration. Unlike most literature in this field the series will not be directly linked with the study of business administration. The readership foreseen for the series includes administrators, whether or not they are studying for professional exams, students of political science and related subjects, as well as the general reader seeking a more informed appreciation of the key role of the administrative process in political decision making.

The series is edited by F. F. Ridley, who has been Professor of Political Theory and Institutions in the University of Liverpool since 1964. He is Chairman of the Joint University Council for Social and Public Administration, has been Chairman of its Public Administration Committee, and he is a founder member of the European Group of the International Institute of Administrative Sciences. He is also Chairman of Examiners in British Government and Politics with the Joint Matriculation Board. He is Editor of *Political Studies*, and his publications include *Public Administration in France* (with J. Blondel), *Specialists and Generalists: A Comparative Survey of Professional Civil Servants* (Editor), and *The Study of Government: Political Science and Public Administration* (in preparation).

Volumes published so far are:
The Management of Welfare – R. G. S. Brown; *Techniques and Public Administration* – Maurice Spiers; *Administering Britain* – Dr B. C. Smith and Jeffrey Stanyer.

Forthcoming volumes in the series are provisionally entitled: *The Study of Public Administration* – Professor David Murray; *The Policy Perspective* – Dr W. I. Jenkins and Dr G. K. Roberts; *Comparative Administration* – Professor F. F. Ridley; *Governmental Planning* – Professor P. Self; *The State, Administration, and the Individual* – Michael Hill.

Brian C. Smith and
Jeffrey Stanyer

Administering
Britain

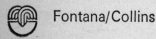 Fontana/Collins

First published in Fontana 1976

Copyright © Brian C. Smith and Jeffrey Stanyer 1976

Made and printed in Great Britain by
William Collins Sons and Co. Ltd, Glasgow

Contents

Introduction

This book arises out of its authors' experiences as teachers of 'public administration'. For several years we jointly taught a course with this title to undergraduates studying political science at Exeter University, and jointly and separately we have taught and examined students from both central and local government in this and related subjects.

At the present time, teaching public administration is a difficult process because there is no single textbook which serves as an introduction to the whole subject and presents the beginner with a defensible conceptual framework. It is easy to put together reading lists for detailed topics – for instance, on the growth of management training in the civil service, on proposals for the reform of local government and on relations between Parliament and public enterprise. What is not so easy is to get students to look at the subject as a whole. Though there are books whose titles appear to claim that they are about the system of public administration in Britain, on examination this proves to be un-justified. Most are about central government only, and some consider only part of that.

This situation has two results. First, the study of the way Britain is administered becomes fragmented into a series of isolated investigations of detailed topics whose coherence with and relevance to each other is often unclear. Secondly, public administration becomes confused with the study of central government, or worse, the civil service departments. Yet, as this book shows, many important topics occur at all levels in the British system of government – and often in those of other countries – and to study them in only one type of institution is to miss significant aspects of a comparative understanding.

Writers of textbooks on modern government always face one important problem: the system is changing in detail every moment and in substance at frequent intervals. It is clearly impossible to capture the phases and moods of a changing system in a textbook.

The search for instant contemporaneity, however, is not the most important aspect of any academic study of society; being continually up-to-date is much less vital than having a proper perspective on its general problems. This perspective we call an 'approach', though others might prefer the phrase 'conceptual framework'. An approach is simply a set of expectations – about what is important, what ought to be especially sought, what dangers may entrap the unwary, what relations the different parts of the study bear to each other, the reasons for stressing some topics and not others, and many other similar points.

We have therefore taken as our starting point the difficulties we have found in the subject when trying to teach undergraduates and public servants with the aid of traditional textbooks. One major problem here is that developments in recent years have produced a divorce between public administration and the other social sciences, including political science where it rightly belongs. This lack of harmony arises largely from the traditional methods of studying public bodies in isolation from the rest of society. Public administration has suffered from the rigid application of certain common-sense distinctions. As a field of study it has been defined by distinguishing, first, between society and government, second, between politics and public administration, and third, between public and private administration. There has also been an emphasis on the uniqueness of each country's system of government, which has hindered the growth of comparative administration, the lack of which, it will be argued, has restricted the study of individual systems of public administration.

The second major problem is a substantive one. The most important defect in the traditional literature, and in virtually all recent books on public administration, is that there is no proper consideration of the overall system – the pattern or structure of public bodies and the relations between them, and between them and the rest of society. It is not simply that there are many topics that appear in each of the different geographical levels and functional sectors of a system of government, or that each level is treated separately; more fundamentally, the structure of the whole system – the pattern of relationships between distinguishable parts – is completely ignored. Even when aspects of the overall structure are considered, such as in the study of central-local relations, there is often a failure to give equal weight to both sides of the relationships.

We have therefore devoted considerable space both to subjects which blur the harmful distinctions mentioned above and to the structure and functioning of the overall pattern, with particular reference to the distribution of activities between different types of public body and different geographical levels of government, and to the 'end-on' nature of the processes of government. We also concentrate on the fundamental aspects of all systems, irrespective of where they occur – organization (in its geographical and functional dimensions), manpower and control.

Our exposition, therefore, moves from the most general considerations, which create the main features of the overall structure, to a more and more detailed examination of its individual parts. We have also tried to present our ideas forcefully and without too many qualifications and hesitations, as the book is intended for both the layman and the new student of British government and administration.

Chapter 1
General Considerations

Public administration is an activity, a set of institutions and a subject of study. It is easy to identify the first two, as the activity occurs in the institutions, and these may be listed in such a way that the list provides an ostensive definition of the category. Few would argue with most of the bodies included in the list – central government departments, local authorities, public corporations, are all obviously part of the system of public administration of Britain, as are their counterparts in other countries. Only a few types of organization are difficult to allocate – for instance universities, mixed enterprises and organizations controlling professions.

The main problem for the student of public administration lies not in the subject matter but in the subject itself. For the discipline or field of study has been traditionally conceived, and still generally is, in such a way as to radically distort the perception of the activity and the institutions. One of our main aims in this book has been to try to offer an alternative conception of the subject of public administration – one which does not lead the student to perceive the institutions and the activities wrongly and, more significantly in a tactical sense, as boring subjects of study.

The difficulties involved in the study of public administration are partly historical in that they can be traced back to the early years of the study of political science and to the traditional political theory that preceded it. But they can best be understood in terms of a series of fictitious distinctions which seem to dominate the research and writing in the field, even if they would be formally rejected by teachers of the subject.

The distinction between those institutions which are thought of as 'political' and those which are thought of as 'administrative' dates back to the late nineteenth century, when a normative difference between policy and administration was developed in order to try to remedy, for instance, the corruption of American government at all levels. This distinction was itself an alternative to the doctrine of the separation of powers.[1]

Both the doctrine and the distinction were essentially normative concepts in that their intellectual function was to divide up the activities of the state or political system into categories and allocate them *a priori* to different people, in order to promote certain values. The processes of government were thought of as linear in the sense that they were arranged in a straight line, beginning with political activities, leading to legislation, which was then administered by an executive and a number of public bodies and adjudicated by the courts.

Every one of the distinctions embodied in this 'linear theory' of the processes of government has been seriously challenged in the post-war years. For instance, in its late-eighteenth-century formulation, it required a distinction between the legislature and the executive; this was descriptively so inadequate that it was replaced or supplemented by a distinction between the executive and the administration. This distinction seems still to dominate much of present-day thinking about government generally. For instance, general textbooks on individual states which attempt to review the whole of the political system (in modern terminology) usually taper away into a very brief discussion of the administrative apparatus (civil service, public corporations and local government in British vocabulary), and one suspects that students of British, American, French, etc., government rarely consider the administrative apparatus of those countries in the same detail that they consider parties, pressure groups and elections.

A second source of the present unsatisfactory state of studies of public administration is the fact that the literature is dominated by contributions from practising or former administrators. This is much less true now than it was in the inter-war years, but the journal *Public Administration* bears testimony to the weight of the 'practical man' contribution from 1923 to the end of the Second World War. The perspective of the practical man has been trebly unfortunate: first, because the conception of administration as a routine, clerical rule application process has been promoted; secondly, because public administration has been seen as completely distinct from other forms of large-scale organization (business firms, etc.); and thirdly, because it has been seen patriotically as a phenomenon unique to each country.

We therefore wish to challenge the distinctions which have

traditionally determined the description of the subject matter of public administration, the concepts used and the problems investigated.

The distinctions are:

> government/society
> politics/public administration
> private/public administration
> Britain/other countries

If these distinctions are blurred or abolished then it is no longer possible to conceive of public administration in a mechanistic fashion as a set of discrete institutions, sometimes related to each other. Instead, one's starting point must always be the overall pattern as a complex system.

Society and Government

The distinction between the social and the governmental is an analytic, not a descriptive, one. Thus the behaviour of public servants and those who hold authority in a political system is social behaviour as well as official behaviour. Modern political sociology rightly refuses to see the distinction between society and the political system as anything more than a heuristic device to further understanding of social reality. One of the advantages of the comparative approach to social and political systems is that it has drawn attention to the varieties of behaviour found in different situations and made it easier to avoid treating the categorization too seriously.

This point may be illustrated in a number of ways. For instance, the behaviour expected of and encountered in public officials differs from one culture to another; these differences cannot be attributed to the governmental system or to factors endogenous to the institutions of public administration themselves, but appear quite simply as patterns of behaviour common in that society. Thus 'corruption' and appointment of public servants according to particularistic criteria (family and kinship ties, for instance) rather than universalistic ones (qualifications, experience, etc.) are normal in some governmental systems because they are normal in the societies in which these systems exist.

The study of decentralization also generates many good examples of the importance of not drawing too rigid a distinction between society and government. The recent troubles in

Northern Ireland illustrate how social conflict can permeate the whole of a governmental system and produce patterns of behaviour – for instance, in respect of public service appointments, local government, education and housing – quite distinct from those found on the mainland even though political institutions were formally very similar.[2]

The point appears in a less clear form when the relationship between social and political forms of organization is considered. K. C. Wheare has called the British constitution 'government by committee',[3] and it is noticeable that in Britain as opposed to France there is a marked tendency to allocate governmental authority to a corporate body rather than to an individual. Thus in both countries regional institutions in the machinery of economic planning began as corporate authorities, but while in Britain these have maintained their position, in France the system quickly developed into one with power concentrated in the hands of a regional prefect – thus repeating the pattern found at departmental and communal levels in French government, just as the British system repeats its local and national pattern. Personalized authority in Britain is relatively rare; the roles of Secretary of State for Northern Ireland during Direct Rule, the regional commissioners during the Second World War, and the commissioners under the *Housing Finance Act, 1971* are unusual creations.[4]

Others have speculated about such factors as the relationship between family structure and attitudes to governmental authority, contrasting the United States with Germany. Left-wing critics of conventional democratic governmental systems have argued that the system of public administration embodies and reinforces the power of the ruling class or establishment in society generally.

The point may be put in a more dramatic, though fictional, form by considering the interactions between individual public servants and individual citizens. When a supplementary benefits officer deals with an unemployed Irish labourer, this is an interaction between two socially distinct types, which fact will likely influence the form the relationship takes and the outcome of the decisions. In other words, where a society is socially divided on grounds that are easily recognized by members of the society, interactions between members of distinct groups will be treated simply as such, irrespective of the ethics of the public service.

Good examples of this can be found in police-immigrant relations and indeed in the ways the police treat members of the middle class as opposed to the working class. One of the effects of the growth of middle-class active protest movements from Suez onwards has been to bring home to more articulate and powerful groups the facts of police behaviour under stress. The influence of society on police behaviour is also shown in the USA by the problems faced by the FBI in civil rights cases in the Deep South. FBI agents in the south are often southerners, or have been resident in the south for a considerable time; they acquire or share some of the attitudes of the white society in which they live and thus may not be trustworthy in civil rights cases.

This failure to place the system of public administration in its wider context reflected an excessive concentration on services as technical or professional operations and a too ready acceptance of formal or official descriptions of the tasks or roles of different types of public servants. Because formal descriptions are in effect prescriptions, public administration has also suffered from pious moralizing which has prevented proper attention being paid to the behaviour of public bodies and their members.

One of the consequences of this wider viewpoint is that the study of public administration requires a knowledge and under-standing of all the social sciences – that is, all the subjects con-cerned with social behaviour, including economics and geography as well as sociology and social psychology. The interdisciplinary nature of the modern study of public administration is something that is more apparent and more pressing in some parts of the subject than others.

Politics and Public Administration

The distinction between politics and public administration was a central part of the linear model of the governmental system men-tioned earlier. Its most elaborate exposition was found in the writings of the American reform movement where it was intended to be a distinction which would *a priori* determine the roles of political parties and elected people on one hand from those of appointed personnel on the other. It should therefore be seen as an attempt to defeat the corruption and inefficiency that was (to middle-class observers) endemic in municipal and state ad-ministration in late-nineteenth-century America.

It also drew its inspiration from models of business behaviour current at the time[5] – or believed to be current at the time – and this is nowhere better illustrated than in the city manager system which was founded on the proposition that policy making and execution can be rigidly separated in the institutional system of a local authority.

Since that time the distinction has been shown to be unworkable on many occasions, but it still keeps reappearing in different verbal forms. People have tried as substitutes 'routine' and 'non-routine', 'programmed' and 'unprogrammed', 'partisan' and 'non-partisan', etc. The latest of these attempts – by the Maud Committee in 1967 – testifies to the fatal attractiveness of the idea to those who make recommendations about the structure of public institutions.[6]

Amongst the first to challenge the distinction between politics and administration were the left-wing critics of bourgeois government. The concern of socialist parties for the biases they felt that senior civil servants would show against left-wing policies when they finally won power led to studies of the 'representative' nature of public administration.[7] It is easy to criticize the logic of representation as defined in these studies but this is to miss the point – civil servants wield political power and are a vital part of the political system of a country. In other words, civil servants have political as well as technical roles, and any account of public bodies which does not take this into consideration must be regarded to that extent as defective.

The rigid separation of politics and administration is a mistake peculiarly likely to be made by practical men writing about public administration. It has become part of the normative code of public employees in many Western countries, though usually in conjunction with a confusion of 'political' and 'partisan'. It is also a peculiarly middle-class and conservative mistake in that it derives from a view of the employment situation which reflects the conditions in white-collar, professional and administrative occupations rather than in traditional working-class jobs.

But the actions of public bodies often look very different to those who are subjected to them. What appears to the civil servant as a neutral technical action in the pursuit of his official duties may appear to the object of his attentions as arbitrary and discriminating, or as an action in the pursuit of political values which the subject rejects. The increasing role of the state and other social changes have brought the middle class into more frequent contact with the lower levels of the state apparatus. The attitudes of activists in Shelter, the Child Poverty Action Group and civil rights movements are closer to the attitudes of the militant working class than to those of the civil servants who have written about public administration in the past.

Perhaps the major contribution to the destruction of a simple dichotomy between politics and administration has come from those who have studied the government of developing countries. In these, close relationships between politicians and public employees and the obvious permeation of general political as well as partisan considerations into the administrative structure of government combine to make the Western distinctions here particularly misleading and inappropriate. To insist on the categories of Western public administration in Africa, South-East Asia and Latin America is only to make disguised evaluations.

Once the distinction has been challenged in an alien context it becomes easier to see that the approach to more familiar governmental systems needs to be modified. It is true to say that in textbooks on public administration there has been a great neglect of field administration, and this stems from the belief that field officers carry out routine tasks with no discretion. Once one comes to study colonial administration, however – or communist systems – it immediately becomes obvious that field officers, particularly the generalists, are of prime political significance, and this leads us to look at our own field administration system with new perspectives.[8]

This is not to deny that the student of public administration should be concerned with the technical activities of public officials; on the contrary the study of public administration requires a familiarity with the nature of the public services which different types of public body provide. But this is another source of difficulty within the subject.

Private and Public Administration

The belief that there was a fundamental distinction between public and private large-scale organizations was as strongly argued by public servants as it was denied by the creators of the new literature on management. The authors of general books on administration usually claimed that their ideas were applicable to all organizations at all times, and often specifically mentioned public bodies.[9] But there was usually a strong bias towards private industry and commerce in that the language used and the problems studied were of particular salience in those types of organization, and this provided some ammunition for civil servants and local government officers who wished to resist the claims of management writers to be able to tell them how to do their jobs. There is a natural resentment at this sort of treatment, but perhaps also a certain desire to maintain the mystique of public administration as a profession.[10]

Several factors have combined to destroy this as a viable attitude since the 1930s. First, the Second World War led to the introduction of many non-career civil servants into Whitehall, from other public bodies and from private enterprise and the universities. After the War many did not remain in the civil service but returned to their former occupations, thus providing a group of people with direct experience of both central administration and other types of organization.[11]

Second, in recent years there have been deliberate attempts to introduce businessmen and others into the civil service for short periods. Though the numbers are not great as yet, this is another source of staff able to make personal comparisons between the different spheres of activity – public and private. We might add to these the senior civil servants who have in recent years left to join private companies.

Third, one of the effects of the nationalizations of the 1940s and the general extension of governmental activity was to bring what had previously been private administration and organization into the public sector. Those who experienced both or studied both were then able to make direct comparisons between the two. It soon became clear that a change in legal status did not necessarily involve a change in organizational problems and behaviour.

Fourth, there has been a growth in the public employment of professions which are not restricted to the public sector but can and do find jobs in private organizations. This is particularly true of the field of specialized administrative techniques, such as personnel management, work study, O & M, and operational research. In some cases these techniques are used by firms of management consultants, and some of these have come to specialize in public administration. Thus there is an increasing knowledge of public bodies by outsiders.

Lest the above be misunderstood let us reiterate that the problem does not lie in the distinction as such but in too rigid an interpretation of it. There are differences between public and private organizations which it would be wrong to ignore. But the differences between the two types are much less than those between different types of public body and, for that matter, between different types of private body. To treat each as a homogeneous class is to ignore vital differences between many individual organizations.

Therefore it is no longer possible to act as though the literature on private management or administration is irrelevant to the study of public bodies. This fact has been reflected in a number of books which seek to interpret management literature in terms of the problems and characteristics of public administration. We do not attempt to follow these by giving a general account of organization theory or management science (call it what you will) but take what we regard as a more fruitful line – by using specific concepts, approaches, or conclusions when and where they are relevant.

There are good reasons for this. First, there is no such thing as *organization theory* or *management science* as a coherent and defensible body of concepts, to which the title of 'theory' can be attached. The greatest problem is to distinguish between good and bad in management literature, and this cannot be done in a short space. Briefly, our view is that recent books on management and public administration fail to do this properly because of the lack of a proper understanding of the nature of much management thought.

The second problem is to adapt the general ideas in organization theory to the specific circumstances of public administration. Indeed, as public bodies differ so much among themselves this is only a part of the general problem of adapting to distinguishing characteristics of all types of organizations. This again is more difficult than many recent books explicitly allow, though the failure to integrate management thinking with the discussion of institutional arrangements within the public sector is implicit testimony to it.

Our approach is less difficult to implement. By choosing ideas which, within their own limitations, are capable of a degree of acceptance, or for which there is some good evidence, as and when problems to which they are relevant occur, one solves the problem of 'good and bad' and of appropriateness at the same time.

Britain and Other Countries

We have already found it necessary to refer to the experience of other countries in order to illuminate some general point. This is because certain sorts of phenomena are more obvious in other societies and other systems of government. It is often the case that if one is interested in a particular topic it is necessary to study empirically countries other than one's own.

This has two advantages. First, it feeds back into the study of one's own system and often leads to the discovery of the phenomena in question, even if in an attenuated form. Sometimes this takes the more dubious shape of a demand for the importation of new political or administrative institutions, such as a Conseil d'état or an École Nationale d'Administration (two French institutions often admired in Britain). But at least the realization that one's own governmental system does not embody a natural or universal organizational pattern is of great help in its study. Much of the call for new administrative organs can be treated as pious moralizing – a form of the 'other man's grass' – but this is not necessary; the realization that a system contains and lacks certain specialized institutions when compared with other systems is very important.

It is tempting to try to make a rigorous comparison of a set of countries, chosen according to some defensible criteria, but this is not in fact practicable, partly for reasons of space, but mainly because the level of knowledge relating to individual countries varies so much that one is comparing the non-comparable. This mistake was made by the Maud Committee[12] when they sent one of their members on a whirlwind tour of several overseas local government systems to gather material to use in comparisons with the British system. A general condition of useful systematic comparison is that the same sort of things are known about each of the countries entering into the comparison. Unfortunately this cannot be achieved in public administration because the relevant studies have not been carried out except for a very few countries and then in a very patchy manner.

The second advantage of comparative analysis is that it enables one to develop a vocabulary and set of concepts which are not tied to the substance of the system in one particular country. It is well known that the language one uses in academic exercises and in everyday life can exert a great influence on the nature of think-ing. Simply to break away from the words used in any one country (something the 'practical man' approach can never do) is an advantage in the long run, even if, as can easily be argued, in the short run mistakes are made in the choice of vocabulary.

We have not attempted to make a rigorous comparison of a number of countries. Instead we have chosen the method which may be called 'comparative reference'. This involves reference to the experience of other countries as and when appropriate and practically possible. This has the disadvantage of leaving the vocabulary of the study dangerously close to the language of one particular country, but it also has a number of practical advantages.

First, it makes it unnecessary to devise some way of rigorously selecting the countries entering into the comparison. There are no obvious criteria for selection that are not open to serious logical objections, and even if there were, they might yield a set of countries about which there were varying degrees of knowledge, which would destroy the usefulness of the comparison.

Secondly, the illustrations can be chosen to suit both the needs of the writer and the knowledge available of a given system. In effect, one must take the right material from wherever it can be found. Sometimes this will lead the student to unfamiliar or exotic countries, but this cannot be avoided. However, the main focus will be on the British system of government.

The Analysis of Systems of Public Administration

So far our comments on the study of public administration have been largely negative: we have been concerned to avoid certain common distinctions which have plagued many approaches in the past. But before we consider more positive ideas in the subject we must look again briefly at one of the points made in the Introduction.

Many past studies have made the mistake of confusing public administration with the civil service and central departmental administration. Several books whose titles would lead one to expect a discussion of the whole system of public administration are found to have omitted local government, public corporations, field administration and bodies with uncertain or unusual status.[13] In a sense this is a serious error. Not only does it lead students and others to ignore a large part of the system itself, but more significantly it leads to failure to appreciate that there exists a *system* of government, of which central administration is only one part. The pattern of interactions and relationships between separate elements – the structure of the system – can never be studied properly from the point of view of only a small part with highly specialized characteristics.

Our first positive step therefore is to outline the considerations relating to the study of the system of public administration in a country as a *system* or *structure*.

Second, one must recognize that public administration differs as a subject from most other areas of the social sciences, including political science, in that it is essentially evaluative. By this we mean that judgements of good and bad and prescriptions of right and wrong are not marginal but central in the subject as conventionally conceived. (A political scientist might urge the creation of a new political party halfway between Labour and Liberal or between Liberal and Conservative, but he would be likely to regard this as an aspect of his role as citizen.) In this respect the subject is similar to social administration and general management thinking. A value-free public administration is possible but would be in many ways very different from the traditional subject.

GENERAL FEATURES OF SYSTEMS OF PUBLIC ADMINISTRATION

The description of systems of public administration which precedes any analysis can best be conceived as a set of rules with the following contents.

First, certain rules prescribe the role of government generally within a society – what counts as a public activity and what is regarded as suitable for public responsibility – and these may also indicate what is to be treated as 'administrative' rather than 'political'.

Second, other rules determine what are counted as public bodies and what forms these can take. Each system will assign those types that it recognizes to a particular constitutional status or role within the overall structure.

Third, there will be rules allocating responsibility for specific governmental activities to individual bodies or types of body. These allocation rules have two dimensions: some are concerned with the distribution of functions between centralized and decentralized bodies, whilst others relate to different types of body at the same geographical level. Neither of these two dimensions has any logical priority, but in practice they intersect in characteristic ways.

Both sets of rules do not have a once-for-all application but may be used repeatedly. Later we will draw attention to the phenomena of multiple decentralization and repeated internal differentiation of functions in public institutions.

Fourth, the flow of business within and between public bodies must be regulated so that the potential conflicts and discontinuities a complex system contains may be controlled as far as possible. We conceive of all public bodies as being 'end-on' to others, and having a place in the major flows of public business. At least three major dimensions of interaction can be detected within such systems: there are the lateral transfers of matters between different bodies at the same general level in the system; there are the vertical transfers between bodies at different levels; and there are the temporal patterns created by the flow of business through time.

Fifth, public activities inevitably involve money, and thus a system of public administration will contain processes by which money is taken from taxpayers and turned into goods and services. This flow of funds creates another aspect of the overall structure – one of vital importance in modern systems in which a large part of personal incomes is taken in taxation and in which many people are dependent on the state for necessities of life.

Sixth, the system of public administration is linked in a variety of ways with the rest of the system of government and with society. Business flows between it and them, just as it flows within the system between different bodies. Some describe this as system-environment interaction, and the flows as inputs and outputs of the system.

THE NATURE OF ADMINISTRATIVE THOUGHT

A striking feature of the twentieth century has been the growing importance of large-scale, complex, formal organizations. This importance may be quantified in terms of their impact on many aspects of social life, and is reflected in the growing number of discussions of what is variously called 'the administrative component' or 'managerial activities' in these social groupings. Public bodies have not been exempt from this trend, and in one sense the growth of public administration mentioned in a later section is simply an illustration of this modern development in the social structure.

The phenomena associated with the awareness of this development we will refer to as 'the management movement', and the large body of literature it creates generically as 'administrative thought'.

The writings comprising administrative thought arise from a variety of sources and are intended to fulfil a number of intellectual and practical functions. They are confusing in their number and variety, and in the approaches they embody. Thus, rather than attempting a close study of these writings we focus attention on a few of the crucial problems of administrative thought in public administration and use relevant ideas wherever they can be found, thereby avoiding the tremendous problems of finding a defensible overall approach to administrative thought which would deal with all the organizational problems of public administration.

Recent years have seen a great increase in the number of books and articles with titles similar to 'management in public administration'. It is not only the public domain that has attracted attention; many types of private organization have been singled out for special consideration. Relevant articles are to be found in such journals as *The Local Government Chronicle*, *Public Administration*, and the *Journal of Management Studies*.

At a more practical level many professional bodies, especially those whose members may be employed in public administration, have been active in promoting courses for their members and undertaking investigations of problems as they relate to their particular expertise. At the official level the movement is reflected in the appointment and work of committees of enquiry such as those on the civil service, the management of local government and local authority social services.[14]

The chief difficulty with these books, articles, courses and investigations is that of distinguishing between good and bad. No doubt many of them are of value, but they give rise to certain puzzles since two assumptions underlie the modern approach to the problems of internal organization of formal corporate bodies. The first is that there is a theory which has a very general applicability to all types of organization which can be characterized as 'formal', 'complex' and 'large-scale'. The second is that there are specific and special problems associated with each type of organization (and, it may be argued, each individual organization) which make the transfer of the general ideas more than a mere formality. This assumption states that it is neither desirable nor easy to apply general ideas and principles to particular cases in a straightforward or mechanical way.

Both these assumptions are in marked contrast to the *practical man approach*, which has been the traditional way administrative thought has been generated, especially in public administration. This approach distinguishes between management the *activity*, management the *group of men* and management the *subject* or *discipline*. All large organizations display the activity referred to indiscriminately as 'managing', 'administering', or 'organizing'. Usually there is also a recognizable group of people (at the 'top' of the organization) for whom this activity constitutes the major part of their working life, and who are often referred to as 'the management'. The subject *management* is therefore basically the study of the activity, but in practice it is often the study of the role of the group of men called 'the management'. The latter cannot, however, be understood properly without an understanding of the relevant characteristics of the activity.

The best clue to the nature of the activity itself is given by the terms normally used in relation to it – typically 'control', 'co-ordination', 'reorganization' and 'supervision' – all of which imply the existence of other activities which are their objects (e.g. there can be no co-ordination without something to co-ordinate). These latter may be called the primary or substantive activities of the organization – in the case of a steel works they produce the steel, in the case of a restaurant they provide food and in education authorities they provide teaching. Management and administration are therefore parasitic or secondary activities in relation to the primary activities which form the *raison d'être* of the organization.

The distinction between primary and secondary activities is reflected in the use of the word 'administration' in public administration. Sometimes the word is used to refer to one or more of the primary activities of a public body as in 'the administration of a pension scheme' or 'traffic management schemes'. These are obviously the primary activities of the relevant public body, and within that body there will be a role for those who control and co-ordinate the service-providers. This distinction, or rather the failure to make it rigorously, has bedevilled discussions of the role of the administrative class of the civil service – a role which is only partly managerial rather than substantive.

In addition to being parasitic the activity of management has two further important characteristics. The first is that it is one of the means by which 'top values' (those of owners or leaders) are diffused throughout the organization. This is a particularly significant characteristic in public administration. The second is that it is a relatively self-conscious activity in that those who undertake it think about what they are doing and formulate rules to guide themselves and others. Frequently it gives rise to a large amount of paperwork which embodies the rules, principles and working devices which are part of the operational managerial code of the organization and which attempt to prescribe the correct behaviour for members of the organization. This is the most elementary form of management literature or administrative thought.

Many people who are or have been members of large organizations in a senior capacity have felt that their experiences and the rules they have formulated in the course of their working life have a wider relevance and importance, and have sought to justify presenting them to a wider audience. Thus principles evolved in a particular organization become generalized and offered as a contribution to the management of all organizations of the same type. This is the genesis of traditional literature on the administration of types of organization, including local government and the civil service; it is written by serving ministers and council members, permanent secretaries and town-clerks – though rarely by those low down in the organizational hierarchy.

Some practical men have gone further and attempted to generalize their experiences to all organizations, irrespective of time and place, not simply those with which they are personally familiar.[15] Others, including academics, have tried to find a common pattern in thinking about diverse types of organization, and thus create an administrative science – or organization theory as it is often called when seen as part of the social sciences.[16] The latter have also made direct contributions to the development of management thought as organizations have become increasingly a field of study for several of the individual social sciences.[17]

Thus both practical men and academic social scientists have contributed towards the creation of a new subject called variously 'management' or 'science of organizations', as well as some of the names mentioned above. But when this general subject has been created the question arises of how the principles, concepts, or ideas may be applied to the special circumstances of types of organization which are not necessarily the same as those which originally contributed to its development. To answer this question is to attempt to transfer the corpus of general thought to the chosen category.

Writings about management in public administration therefore arise in two distinct ways: one by generalizing from particular instances and the other by particularizing from general ideas. The two distinct categories exist side by side; though formally they are about the same sort of thing, they differ in a great number of important respects. The older tradition can be illustrated by articles in the journal *Public Administration*, particularly volumes from the 1920s and 1930s. In local government its best exposition is in *Municipal Administration* by J. H. Warren.[18]

The new approach is best illustrated by writings on the use of specialized administrative techniques in the public service. These, which are sometimes called 'management services', have been developed very largely outside public organizations, but obviously have a great use in the public sector when and where the conditions for their fruitful employment are fulfilled. In local government a good example is *Operational Research in Local Government* by R. A. Ward.[19]

The existence of two sources, and therefore two types, of management in the public services, causes a certain tension within the literature and may puzzle those who come to an allegedly new subject with a knowledge of the old. For instance, the title of the Maud Committee – 'management of local government' – gave it a nominal connection with the new approach. Yet anyone familiar with the literature of the 1930s and 1940s will be conscious of a sense of *déjà vu*, as the Committee's Report dealt with problems of committee systems (number, sequences, size, etc.), common services, generalists in the local government service, and the role of the elected member, to take but a few examples.

Unfortunately it has to be admitted that the management movement has not made a great deal of progress in British public administration, as committee reports and the new-style textbooks on public administration testify. Recent thinking is obviously an advance on the generalized personal experience of civil servants and local government officers, but the difficulty is that outside the sphere of specialized administrative techniques there is little that can easily be transferred. There are basically two reasons for this state of affairs.

The first is that the general subject must be a body of knowledge, both factual and contextual, which will prove valuable to those who are responsible for the proper conduct of the organization and for ensuring reasonable behaviour within it. The body of knowledge should, for instance, aid those who have to take decisions about organizational matters; it is a guide to effective managerial behaviour. But to achieve this aim it must be more than something which is just possibly useful; it must in fact be something which stands in the same relation to management behaviour as do physics and chemistry to engineering, and as engineering does to the building of a particular bridge.

Whatever other characteristics the ideas normally called 'organization theory' have, it is quite clear that they do not have this indisputable practical value. This can be shown quite simply by looking at the diversity within the set of ideas given this title. The existence of incompatible traditions, between which a justified choice cannot be made, is sufficient evidence.

The second reason for the lack of progress of the management movement in British public administration is that even where ideas are defensible in their own terms they are often irrelevant to the problems of public administration. For instance, at the highest level in both central and local government, the system in Britain is one of government by committee. To think managerially about the problems of organizing a committee system would require drawing on a literature which dealt with such matters as the size, frequency of meeting, and method of composition of boards of directors; the role of sub-committees in private management; the relations between the lay members and the full-time staff – none of which exists in a form easily usable by the student of public administration.

To illustrate this point in a more concrete form, let us consider the relationships between minister and permanent secretary and between permanent secretary and assistant secretaries within his ministry. We appear to be dealing with relations of super- and sub-ordination, and there is a large and growing literature on leadership and supervisory styles. For instance, the new patterns of management described by Likert involve supervisors who carry out their role in a particular way. But we do not even know whether the relationships we are considering are properly described as ones of supervision, let alone ones to which Likert's prescriptions apply. For Likert draws much of his evidence from the behaviour of foremen as front-line supervisors, and we do not know whether minister/permanent secretary relations can be assimilated to this.[20]

The second assumption – that there are always problems of applying general ideas to *types* of organization – can also be extended to argue that there are always special problems in the application of ideas to individual organizations. The practical use of academic management concepts in an organization is a matter of skill; we are moving from *saying* to *doing*, and this can never be a mechanical or routine matter. If the main assumption and its corollary are true, then the problem of management in public administration is one of identifying the distinguishing characteristics of public bodies, of types of public body within the general category, and of individual organizations such as departments and local authorities. An incidental consequence of examining this assumption is that it leads to a helpful discussion of the problems of evaluation and prescription in public administration.

Distinguishing Characteristics of Public Administration

Many aspects of public organizations are shared with some private organizations, but the study of public administration is not particularly concerned with these. For instance, it may be assumed that literature on the technicalities of filing systems is relevant to public bodies. Supervisory styles in coal mines also present familiar problems, even though these are now publicly owned. What is needed is an identification of the salient features of the public sector in order that the problems of adaptation to these can be discussed.

It may be noticed that the exercise on which we are here engaged is unnecessary in the traditional approach, because the practical man automatically adapts to the salient features of his type of organization. It is because no such implicit adaptation takes place that an explicit account is necessary. It is particularly helpful to those who are familiar with, or expert in, general management thinking but do not have more than a superficial understanding of the distinctive characteristics of the type of organization under review.

Many of the main ideas in general management thinking have been developed in private commercial and industrial organizations or have been derived from academic studies of capitalist enterprises. Despite the effort to universalize them they still bear the marks of their origins. Where they have been developed or applied in public bodies these have often been of a commercial or industrial nature – government arsenals, the post office, etc. Though the present tendency is to minimize the differences between public and private administration, there are some contrasts which are important, relevant, and which ought not to be obscured.

First, in public administration the free buying and selling of goods and services is largely absent. Thus the provision of goods and services by public bodies is usually dictated or strongly influenced by factors other than those of a cost-receipts analysis. The importance of these other factors varies considerably from service to service. They are at their least important in the trading services, but even there they are not entirely absent (i.e. transport). In many local authority services receipts are non-existent and thus ordinary economic calculations can play no part.

As a general rule, the equivalent of *demand* for public services is determined by statute and the nature of the things demanded. For instance, the 'demand' for public education is determined by the Education Acts, just as the 'demand' for cash payments is determined by a variety of Acts which prescribe what categories of person are entitled to what payments. The situation is further complicated by problems of interpretation and by problems of access and desire on the part of citizens. Thus what public bodies experience as demand for their goods and services is fundamentally different from the experience of many private bodies.

It is easy to exaggerate the importance of the profit motive in private enterprise, but the comparison of costs of an operation with the receipts it will bring in provides a straightforward guide to decision making, particularly in the lower levels of the organization. In fact public bodies are still searching for a substitute as an anchor to rationality in their behaviour.

Second, public bodies are expected to be accountable to non-members of their organization. At its most elementary, public accountability simply requires that public bodies give an account of their activities to other people and provide a justification for what has been done in terms of other people's values, in a way that private bodies do not. In fact public bodies are expected to pursue aims determined by other people rather than by themselves. In general they are expected to show higher standards of conduct than those of the ordinary citizen. The word 'expected' has two meanings in this context: something may be expected in the sense of morally prescribed or in the sense of thought to be probable of occurrence. The difference between the two may be considerable, but it is a characteristic of a modern public administration system that the organizational structure attempts to bring them together.

Merely giving an account is not usually thought sufficient; it is also expected, in both senses, that if the account is not satisfactory in the eyes of non-members, remedial and punitive action may follow. It is generally thought better to prevent rather than put right wrong-doing by public officials; thus one of the functions of the pattern of public organization is to try to create responsive administration.

The difficulty with public accountability, apart from the problem of finding practical methods of ensuring it, is that aims prescribed by outsiders may be conflicting and imprecise. Public bodies are expected to pursue multiple goals and meet multiple standards; hence the problem of distinguishing good and bad is particularly acute and hard to solve.

Third, public services are generally provided under the imperative of equality; that is, public bodies are expected to treat everyone equally – something that may be hard to define in positive terms, but which is often easy to recognize when it is violated. It is most striking in the cash benefit services, and indeed in any service where the output is directly measurable. It is at its least clear where the standards of service provision are defined in relation to a set of factors which may point in different directions. Equality is especially important in decentralized administration, for any division into separate areas can lead to differences in the treatment of individuals, which are thought to be unjustified by them or by others.

The imperative of equality makes certain demands on a system of administration in that it puts a premium on stability, consistency and accuracy, which are less important values in many private enterprises. It may be noted that the general effect of the demand for equality is similar to that for accountability: it orients public administration towards external aims and values rather than internal ones.

The above general characteristics of all or most types of public administration are not sufficient by themselves to provide the basis of management thinking. It is necessary to go further and describe the special features of broad types of public body, then more specific types within these categories, eventually arriving at the individual organization. As part of our more positive approach we give as examples (and examples only) the case of decentralization and, within that category, local government.

DISTINGUISHING CHARACTERISTICS OF DECENTRALIZED ADMINISTRATION

Decentralization exists for a variety of reasons, the most important being that many public services are defined or characterized in such a manner that territorial organization is implied by their nature. The origins of decentralization lie in the *technical* characteristics of the services or public activities themselves. By *technical characteristics* are meant the activities specified by the definition of the service, and the intellectual rationale underlying them. These can be illustrated from road building and maintenance, tax collection, police and fire services, social security payments, and immigration control. In each case it is obvious that the alternative to decentralized organization and provision of these services is not centralized administration but provision by peripatetic officers of the centre who would spend most if not all of their time away from their central office. This is the form of provision adopted by small centralized bodies and by area authorities within each area if not further decentralized.

The above fact can be regarded either as of supreme importance or as trivial. It may be considered trivial because the main concern of the study of decentralization is not to contrast it with centralization, but to compare the different types of systematic and stable decentralized organization with each other. Many of the reasons advanced for decentralization merely indicate that some systematic approach is desirable or necessary; they do not distinguish between the forms it may take.

From the central point of view, decentralization may be a more efficient and more adaptable way of providing public services, as well as a source of information about the impact and reality of government. From the point of view of the individual, it may be more convenient in terms of accessibility, and more certain and intelligible because more predictable – both ways of reducing the 'costs' of being governed. Also, through decentralization an area may obtain institutions that in some sense suit its requirements and which can symbolize any feelings of area identity or separateness.

However, decentralization always contains dangers for the functioning of the overall system of government. It is a source of inefficiency, inequality and non-accountability; it may contribute to a weakening of the territorial integrity of the state and reduce the ability of the centre to pursue the aims it has set itself. The special problems of management of decentralized systems then relate to the organization of area authorities in ways that reduce the likely occurrence of adverse effects rather than beneficial ones.

The following paragraphs set out in brief form some of the most important features of different types of decentralized administration in the form of characteristics which have been valued at some time or another by one or more people.

(a) **technical efficiency** In all public (and other) services there are various relationships which determine how efficiently and effectively the service is being carried out. We have noted that in the public services the problems of measurement are acute, but in principle it is possible to make some estimate of the standards achieved in service provision by different public bodies.

(b) **equality** As all decentralized arrangements involve the use of discretion, each contains within it a potential for creating differences between areas; indeed the point of decentralization is partly to produce such differences as a result of the adaptation to the facts of spatial variation. But the differences between areas may be divided into two groups – justified and unjustified from the point of view of the individual. Unjustified differences will be referred to as inequalities.

(c) **adaptability** From the point of view of the overall system the most important form of adaptation is not to the physical environment but to the social system, and particularly to those aspects which will be called the values and perceptions of local people, that is, people resident in an identifiable part of the country.

(d) **recognition and protection of separate identities** If the system makes a special attempt to adapt to diverse values – to a separate culture or national/regional identity – then the extent to which the diversity is protected is a feature of decentralization. The demand for protection of cultural diversity may be centrally or locally inspired, but it will be related to the next characteristic, usually in a negative manner.

(e) **national unity and the security of the state** Decentralized arrangements may be used to promote the security of the state, to protect its territorial integrity, and to enhance national unity. This is a traditional function of government and one which varies in importance from time to time and from place to place. It is at its most acute in the governmental system of empires; an imperial system of government is necessarily a decentralized one and one always threatened by separatism – threats which may be internally and externally created.

Though certain forms of decentralization seem to be dangerous in many circumstances, it can also be argued that the adaptation mentioned above is often a source of strength to a regime. This will be recognized as a familiar argument in discussions of the situations in which the federal solution is the most viable and appropriate one.

(f) **accountability** In this context accountability has two distinct meanings. Public authorities in an area may be accountable both to the area (in some sense) and to authorities at a higher level in the system of government, particularly the national government. Thus decentralized bodies may have to justify their actions to two different types of person. The two types of accountability may therefore be in conflict if the values and perceptions of those to whom the account is owed differ. In fact it seems likely that this will occur if decentralization succeeds in promoting adaptation and differences between areas.

Accountability to the centre may be called *responsiveness* in this context and it is a feature of all forms of decentralization though its significance differs considerably from type to type. It is a problem which has perhaps been reduced generally with the rise of modern means of communication.

(g) **participation and democracy** Decentralization may involve greater lay participation in governmental activities, both in quantitative terms and also qualitatively through the introduction of different types of people into the machinery of government. Participation in this sense is not the same as democracy in its traditional meaning, but the underlying reasons are not unrelated. Clearly the various forms of decentralization differ markedly in this respect. This subject raises the problems of autonomy, self-government and self-determination for areas which are only parts of states.

(h) **other central purposes** Decentralization may be used to promote other purposes of the centre, but these tend to vary greatly from time to time and from place to place. A currently significant purpose is that of development – economic, political, and social – both in western countries and in the Third World.

The interpretation of the above and any other relevant factors (such as cost in time and money) must be that they are *variables*, that is, characteristics whose values change systematically. Assessing decentralized organization is therefore a matter of applying the variables as standards and bringing them into a common focus in a given set of circumstances.

It can be seen how these characteristics of decentralization provide the distinctive features to which management thinking has to adapt. But each form may itself have further distinctive features which are also relevant to the development of rigorous administrative thought specially suited to it. Take local government as an example. Local authorities are not only *public* and *decentralized* – they also have their own special attributes.

MANAGEMENT IN LOCAL GOVERNMENT

At least four characteristics mark out local authorities from other forms of decentralization.

First, local government has a well-defined structure – that is, a territorial pattern of authorities. Other forms of decentralization also have a structure in this sense but lack the operational importance of local government areas. In Britain the whole of the country is divided up into different types of local government. Each type consists of individual local authorities, each of which is responsible for a prescribed area of land and a prescribed list of services. These responsibilities are in principle unavoidable and exclusive, thus giving rise to what may be called the 'territorial imperative' – the obligation on a local authority to deal with the specified problems of a specified piece of land and no more – with one exception: it can neither expand nor contract the area and sphere of its responsibilities.

Second, local authorities are responsible for a wide range of services. Conventionally this is often expressed in the form 'local authorities are multi-functional', and typically the variety and disparateness of services provided have been reflected in a diverse organizational structure – in particular an elaborate committee and departmental system. Local authorities are what Americans call 'multi-goal organizations'. Of course local authorities are not unique in this respect, but the range and variety of their activities make this a salient feature of local government.

Third, local authorities have a greater degree of decision-making autonomy than bodies in other forms of decentralization. Though they are part of the national system of government and public administration, they enjoy certain independent powers of decision making, including the fixing of the rate at which a local tax is to be levied each year. Though they are limited by the law, the courts, and the actions of the central executive, the same factors also limit the powers of others to influence their decision making. In other words the system guarantees them a degree of autonomy within the legal framework.

Fourth, the local authority is an elected and not an appointed body. The fact that the authority is composed of members who are elected under a system of free and fair elections, and who collectively have the right to make the decisions of that body, means that the problems of control and direction within the organization are determined very differently from the ways they are determined in local appointed bodies. Election confers a legitimacy on the values of the elected person which is a crucial factor in central/local relations and one with which management in local government must come to terms. In fact management thinking must come to terms with all the facts of local democracy – political parties, pressure groups, the uncontrollability of elections, etc.

Thus although the employment of office cleaners and the organization of vehicle repair occur in local government, a discussion of them is not part of the subject *management in local government* unless it can be shown that there are special problems deriving from these or other distinguishing characteristics of local authorities.

With the above as a model, it is easy to see how the subject *management* in other forms of public administration may be developed from their distinguishing characteristics.

Evaluating Public Administration

The discussion of *management* in various types of public body is a useful entry into the problems of evaluation in public administration. The distinguishing characteristics of each type not only serve as the basis for trying to construct a new and more rigorous subject, but are also the objects of valuation. However, a discussion of them does not exhaust the problems of valuation in this context – problems which are central to decision making and choice in the creation of systems of government.

It was remarked that though there are costs involved in providing public services, there are often no receipts and no obvious substitutes for them. This is because demand is not expressed in monetary terms. It might be thought that if the product can be held constant then alternative courses of action can be evaluated by comparing their relative costs. This is logically correct, but it is often the case that by changing the way a service is provided, and thus changing costs, the product itself changes. Irrespective of the relative costs involved, comprehensive education is not the same thing as a tripartite system. Thus, until some way of weighting the different services and comparing different types of provision within a service is discovered, choice in public administration will involve decisions which contain large elements of intuition and guesswork.

But the position is much worse when one comes to consider the evaluation of organizational forms and structures. The values to be promoted by different managerial structures are usually thought to be those of efficiency and effectiveness, democracy, accountability and equality in general terms, and a host of detailed values as well.

Let us take efficiency and effectiveness first. This is a derived value in that judgements about it depend on prior judgements about the nature of public services – of good and bad within the substantive activity itself – and thus all the difficulties are transferred to decision making about organizational forms and structures. Thus, our uncertainty is compounded; there is the uncertainty about measuring the original service, and the uncertainty about the relationship between organizational forms and service performance.

When we come to values such as democracy and accountability, we enter a more nebulous realm. Because of the disputes about the meanings of these words, evaluating different organizational forms and structures often fails to get beyond the level of competing stipulative definitions. It is the same with equality: as this can only receive an operational definition in terms of people's valuations and perceptions, we are constantly confronted with the problems of assigning states of affairs to one category or the other.

The problem of weighting applies to the combination of these general values with those which derive from evaluation of the substantive aspects of service provision. Even if one finds a way of increasing the democratic content of a public body, how does one decide whether this ought to be implemented if it appears to reduce the effectiveness with which the service is provided?

There is one other aspect of the problem of evaluating public administration. This arises because public bodies do not exist by themselves, but as a part of a complicated system of government. It is therefore wrong to evaluate one individual body or type of body in isolation from the rest. To illustrate the point with a concrete case, it is possible to argue that there is a missing dimension in British government – the regional level – and that this ought to be remedied by creating governmental institutions for areas intermediate in size between local and national.[21] It is also possible to argue that another dimension is missing from British government – the community or neighbourhood level – and that this ought also to be created. This sounds fine if each argument is taken separately, but the consequence of the two together would be to create a system of government with at least five and possibly more levels of government. This aspect of the situation is usually ignored by those who are only concentrating on one new level of government.

In fact one of the great difficulties of the British system of government has been that it has never been considered as a system. When royal commissions and committees of enquiry are appointed, their terms of reference invariably limit them to one part of the system. There has been no systematic enquiry into the public service, though at one time two distinct committees were considering parts of it in isolation from each other. Sometimes one meets incredible discontinuities; just as Fulton was arguing that the civil service was too amateur to deal with the problems of the twentieth century, the Redcliffe-Maud Commission was accepting from the civil service unsupported verdicts on complicated matters of social and economic policy. The Royal Commission on the Constitution had to operate at the same time as a series of investigations into aspects of its terms of reference. It was constantly overtaken by events and the decisions of governments to act before receiving its advice – for instance in local government reform, Northern Ireland, and national health service reorganization.

In short the defects we noted in books on public administration in general have been repeated at the official level: there is no wide-ranging investigation of the whole structure of the British system of public administration, looking at the distribution of powers between different types and levels of organization, and the functions of these different bodies in the overall system.

Much of what we have said about the problems of valuation in the study of public administration is essentially negative, but this is necessary. Even if one cannot set out a blueprint for distinguishing good and bad in the system of public administration, one can at least avoid the most naïve mistakes. The fundamentally intuitive judgements which have to be made can be based on a strong sense of the sort of factors that have to be taken into consideration in order to reduce, if not abolish, the arbitrary elements in decision making.

The next step in our discussion of general concerns is again both negative and positive. A proper study of public administration must be founded on a defensible conception of the individual organization – the sort of thing it is perceived to be; and before constructing this it is desirable to look at one of the alternatives which has often implicitly been adopted in the study of public administration – the 'model' of bureaucracy often associated with Max Weber.

Conceptions of the Organization

No study of large-scale organization is complete without a conception of the organization. We are familiar with the sort of problem this entails from traditional social and political theory. For instance, most of the well-known and interesting theories contain a model of man, a picture of society, and a conception of the nature of the state. A conception or model in this sense is a way of looking at phenomena, a set of categories in which to describe them and their behaviour. For instance, economists often look at firms as resource-users and describe the ways they deploy the land, labour, and capital at their disposal. Political scientists sometimes conceive of political parties as coalitions, and sociologists treat tribes as social systems – an expression which in itself contains several distinct meanings.

Each of these conceptions has been applied to formal organizations. The traditional economists' approach to large-scale organization is exemplified by Speight's *Economics of Industrial Efficiency*[22]; Cyert and March treat firms as coalitions in *The Behavioural Theory of the Firm*[23]; the approach associated with the Tavistock Institute sees organizations as open systems interacting with their environment. Examples of these can be found in the study of public administration. For instance the Bains Committee[24] treats local authorities as users of land, money, and manpower and when the Tavistock approach was applied to local government it produced *Local Government and Strategic Choice*, with its emphasis on a dialogue between local authority and local community.[25]

However, one of the most common approaches to public bodies has been to see them as structures of offices arranged in a hierarchy. This, it might be added, is a conception which has lost favour in the study of private organizations. Such a conception may be derived from either of two traditions in administrative thought, both of which conceived of organizations as hierarchies of formal and well-defined positions. The first is that of the classical principles school, associated with H. Fayol and L. F. Urwick and his collaborators. The second is usually referred to as 'bureaucracy', and is regarded as the creation of Max Weber.[26]

Many American students of public administration have seen Weber's work as being especially useful to research and analysis into the functioning of public bodies, the more so as one can produce good arguments that Weber, despite his assertions to the contrary, was mainly thinking of public organizations when he characterized the *ideal-type* bureaucracy. We may take this as an example of a wide range of conceptions of the organization implicit in much writing about public administration, and still naturally seized upon by practical men.

First, Weber did not use the word 'bureaucracy' in its derogatory sense, meaning officiousness, red tape, delays, etc. (in the words of the *Reader in Bureaucracy*, 'the social pathologies of bureaucracy').[27] Occasionally he appears to subscribe to these conventional 'outsider' views of large-scale organization, but for the most part he stresses the efficiency and rationality of bureaucratic organization.

Second, he did not mean by bureaucracy simply large-scale organization. This confusion is one of the most frequent made by academics and results in verbal tributes to his ideas, which are completely ignored in the body of the work. For Weber, not all formal organizations were bureaucracies. On the contrary, some were based on different principles – patriarchalism, patrimonialism, feudalism, charismatic authority, etc. – and bureaucracy was found only 'in the most advanced institutions of capitalism'.

Third, the concept was not intended to be a descriptive one in the sense of providing a set of categories which added up to a generalized picture of a large number of modern organizations. It is an example of an *ideal type* concept, something Weber uses frequently. What, then, is an ideal type?

Again, what it is *not* is important. It is not ideal in the sense of best imaginable or perfect, though some of the things Weber says on occasions may suggest this. Probably the best interpretation is literally 'existing in the realm of ideas' – a concept or essence which stands to material things as chemical concepts stand to chemical substances. The important point about an ideal type is its intellectual function – it is an analytical device or tool whose justification can never lie in terms of descriptive accuracy, but only in terms of its usefulness. As Weber says 'The usefulness of the above classification [referring to a set of ideal types] can only be judged by its results in promoting systematic analysis.'[28]

What, then, were the elements of bureaucratic organization, according to Weber? In two distinct places he gives direct accounts of the separate characteristics which identify bureaucracies (though much of the rest of his work is indirectly relevant). The list is a long one, but it may be simplified by grouping the elements into two sets – those applying to the organization and those applying to the individual public servant.[29]

A bureaucracy is a set of offices ordered in a system of super- and sub-ordination, which creates a hierarchical official authority. An office is a fixed and official jurisdictional area ordered by rules which distribute activities, authority, and duties in a regular, stable and precise manner. The management of the office follows general rules which are abstract, consistent, stable, and exhaustive. Administrative acts, decisions, and rules are formulated and recorded in writing. Bureaucracies create their own special knowledge – the official secret.

The typical person in authority occupies an office and is subject to an impersonal order – strict and systematic discipline and control in the conduct of the office; but obedience is not owed to his superior as a person. Office holding is a vocation. Being an official is a full-time, lifelong occupation, with security of tenure, a pension in old age, and the chance of promotion within the hierarchy. Officials apply general rules to particular cases in a spirit of formalistic impersonality – *sine studio ac ira* (without prejudice or malice). The official does not own the means of administration or his position – he is paid a salary. Thus there is a distinction between bureau and domicile, between official activity and private life, and between business assets and private fortunes. Officials are appointed, not elected, on the basis of free selection of those with technical qualifications, which presuppose thorough and expert training.

Many of the writers who regard Weber highly as a sociologist of organizations find that when they try to make his approach the basis of their own work, they are forced to modify, sometimes out of all recognition, his ideal-type.

For instance, Blau states that the characteristics of bureaucracy should be seen as variables or hypotheses, to be tested or used in research.[30] Others have spoken of dimensions of bureaucratic structure[31]. These are of course defensible research methods, but they bear very little relation to what Weber wrote.

The real difficulty with using Weber's ideas is that he wrote at a time when the methods common to social science today were largely unknown, thus his work does not belong to modern social science approaches to organizations. In fact Weber does not belong to the managerial tradition of thinking about organizations at all. The result is that his ideas are not very useful in trying to construct a conception of the organization which will fit into the overall framework of managerial thought. Weber belongs to traditional social and political theory, in the sense understood by political scientists, rather than to modern social science.

For our purposes, therefore, Weber's approach is defective. It fails to distinguish between formal and informal behaviour, and to accept it is to accept a whole set of surrounding ideas about capitalism, democracy, authority, etc., which can play no part in our study. He picks out for special consideration the superficial and static features of organizations in exactly the same way as does the approach associated with Fayol and Urwick.

If we could pick out one particular defect of the 'structure-of-roles' approach, it is that it says nothing about the relations *between* organizations, and this is obviously a central feature of an approach which stresses the characteristics of the overall system. What we require is a conception of the organization which contains a picture of both internal and external relations of organizations.

The best conception of the organization for the purposes of the study of public administration is to treat it as a decision-making body. This has the advantage that it corresponds to one common picture of the work of the public sector. It also builds into the analysis the idea of reasonable or rational behaviour, which makes it suitable for dealing with the problems raised by the fact there are large normative elements in the study of public administration.

But most important, it is a concept that enables one to relate one organization to another. For the conclusions of one decision-making process can become the beginning of another. Decisions in public administration (and government generally) are *end-on*. Thus a civil service department may decide to recommend the framing of a statutory instrument governing an aspect of a local government service; the local authority associations may decide to oppose it as it stands; when it is implemented each individual local authority has to decide how to deal with it, and when they have decided and acted, the central government has to decide how to react to what has happened. The flow of information arising from decisions is an endless one in a complicated system of public administration, and it ties together the activities of formally disparate bodies.

Some care is needed, however, with the concept of decision making. For it has become widely known in economics and operational research as the name of the study of certain type of rational behaviour, with its own logic and assumptions. For instance, H. A. Simon distinguishes between decision making in conditions of perfect knowledge, risk and uncertainty.[32] A growing literature contributed by economists and psychologists is reviewed by Ward Edwards in *Decision Making*.[33] This literature and the ideas it embodies are very impressive intellectual contributions, but in their present state they are not suitable for use in empirical research on public administration or in thinking about the behaviour of public bodies.

Though it would be be very pleasant to be able to say that we were using these rigorous approaches, in general this is not possible, and thus in this book decision making is a much looser concept than it is in the writings mentioned above. We still retain both of the essential ideas – that decision making is based on information and values (called *premises* by Simon[34]), and that it involves calculations leading to a choice between alternatives. The difference is that neither the premises nor the rules for calculation can be specified rigorously. The rigorous version may be regarded as an ideal towards which the student of public administration ought to work, but that view is not a necessary feature of our approach.

So far we have stressed the importance of looking at the overall pattern of public administration, rather than isolated elements. But it is also necessary to be able to examine individual parts of the system by themselves either as part of the analytic processes needed before a picture of the total structure can be put together (or synthesized), or because a special interest is being taken in one particular type of public body, for good reasons.

The key to this second operation lies in the process of abstraction. All political scientists will be familiar with the way individual political systems are studied, by abstracting them from the international system of which they are a part and concentrating on their internal political operations. Economists abstract the firm from the economy when they consider its internal decision-making behaviour, as do sociologists and social anthropologists when they study social institutions such as a family or a tribe. This approach is the foundation of the modern study of formal organizations and of research into local government.

It is easy to extend the approach used in relation to local authorities and in relation to private organizations to all discrete public bodies, including what can be regarded, if this helps, as *parts* of an organization. To use the approach all that is necessary is to divide the world up into organization and environment, and environment in this context means simply *not-system*. Thus the remainder of the system of public administration, as well as the rest of the political and social systems, become part of the environment of the public corporation, the local authority, the civil service department, or, if the process of abstraction be taken a stage further, the section, the branch office, the committee, etc.

The test for the applicability of this process of abstraction is

never how far it describes the world accurately but always how
far it enables one to understand behaviour within it.

We now turn our attention from these general considerations,
which some would call 'methodological discussion', to the substance of public administration and particularly the British system
of the post-war period. It is important for the reader to understand
how and why we have adopted the particular form of presentation
of the remainder of the book.

First, we have tried to combine the theoretical principles that
should apply to all analyses of systems of public administration
with the practice of British government. The book can be seen
either as an account of the British system based on an application
of these principles or concepts, or as an account of a set of general
concepts illustrated by reference to a particular country.

Second, we begin by setting out the main features of the overall
system of public administration by the application of a set of
theoretically justified distinctions, which themselves are the
subject of further distinctions. The result is rather like a logical
tree, branching out from one central point, or a set of boxes packed
within each other. The major themes of this account are taken
up in later chapters as important subjects in their own right.

Notes

 1 Vile, 1967, p. 276
 2 Brett, 1970
 3 Wheare, 1955
 4 Simmons, 1971; Smith, 1969
 5 Goodnow, 1900
 6 Maud, 1967, p. 39
 7 Laski, 1938; Kingsley, 1944
 8 Smith, 1967; Fesler, 1962
 9 Fayol, 1916, Preface
10 Urwick, 1935; Stewart, 1935
11 Franks, 1947
12 Maud, 1967, vol. 4
13 Brown, 1970; Baker, 1972; Keeling, 1972; Clarke, 1971; Garrett,
   1972
14 Fulton, 1968; Maud, 1967; Seebohm, 1968
15 Fayol, 1917
16 Urwick, 1942
17 Lupton, 1971

18 Warren, 1954
19 Ward, 1964
20 Likert, 1961
21 Kilbrandon, 1973, vol. 2
22 Speight, 1962
23 Cyert and March, 1963
24 Bains, 1972
25 Friend and Jessop, 1969
26 Gerth and Mills, 1948; Weber, 1947
27 Merton, 1954, p. 396ff; Weber, 1947, p. 328
28 Weber, 1947, p. 328
29 Weber, 1947, p. 324–45; Gerth and Mills, 1948, pp. 196–244
30 Blau, 1956, p. 34
31 Udy, 1959, p. 791; Hall and Tittle, 1966–7, p. 267
32 Simon, 1959
33 Edwards and Tversky, 1967
34 Simon, 1945

Chapter 2
The Pattern of
Public Administration in Britain

This chapter is concerned with four different aspects of the system of public administration in Britain: the importance of the system of government in the general fabric of society; the rules which help to create the different types of administrative body found within the system; the relationships between the different parts of the system; and the ways in which individual citizens can influence public decision making, especially when they believe that they have been wrongly treated.

In one sense the importance of government within a society is the basic factor which strongly influences all other features of the system of public administration. It can hardly be doubted that the 'weight' of government in society – measured in any of the quantitative terms (percentage of national income, percentage of the labour force) or in qualitative terms (range and strategic significance of activities) – has greatly increased in the last hundred years in most parts of the world, and that this has been followed by more positive attitudes (not necessarily favourable) on the part of citizens of all types, and the development of more explicit thinking about its nature. The greater elaboration of institutional forms also appears as a reaction to the demands of more and more varied governmental activities, as does the greater need felt by the citizen for redress of grievances.

The Scope of Public Administration

The role of public administration has increased greatly in the last hundred years in both size and scope. There are several reasons for this growth. Underlying it is a pattern of economic development which in the modern economy has led to an increasing proportion of the gross national product being comprised of *tertiary* goods and services (services rather than goods), and public activities tend to belong to this tertiary category. Thus as productivity in agriculture and basic industries rises, income is released for expenditure on leisure activities, on personal services which make life longer and more comfortable, and on services which can now be afforded from the surplus over basic necessities.

The increase in productivity in basic economic activities has created effective demand for other types of goods and services, as well as the ability to provide them ('increasingly sophisticated technique of fashioning external life' according to Weber[1]). There are, however, several factors which influence the role that the state plays in these developments, and therefore the scope of public administration.

First, there are the characteristics of the goods and services themselves, which influence whether or not it is practicable to provide them either through the machinery of government (= by the state) or through some private means (= by the family, a kinship group, private enterprise, etc.). In effect, the nature of the service itself influences the form of its provision.

For instance, there are a large number of services that are now demanded which it is almost impossible to see being provided satisfactorily by any other means than through the machinery of government. These are services in which *externalities* are very great – that is, the costs and benefits of the activities are experienced in large part by people other than the decision makers themselves. This is generally true of the services and goods which are consumed in common rather than personally – public goods in economists' terms. Many of the environmental services fall into this category, as do the regulatory and public order functions of government. At the other end of the dimension there are services which are not normally considered suitable for government to provide, though we must be careful here not to be too dogmatic, as comparative research may show that what we take to be obvious is not obvious to others.

A large number of goods and services, however, are neither clearly public nor clearly private, and the choice of form of provision will be influenced by a second factor – general public attitudes to the role of the state within society. Because of the options left open to a society, the role of public administrative bodies will vary a great deal from one country to another. Not all sections of the general public will be equally important here – obviously leaders of parties, interest groups and the like will be more influential.

One of the key aspects of general public attitudes is the relative values of *needs* and *effective demand* – that is, demand backed by resources in the form of money. If effective demand is regarded as a less important factor than 'need', then it is likely that public administration will have an expanded role in society.

The lack of a clear-cut choice in many services is reflected in some societies in two ways. First, there may exist side by side public and private provision of a service, financed and controlled by different means and often consumed by different sections of the community. Education is an excellent example of this, as are the personal health services, and both show varying patterns from country to country. Second, there has been a growth of public administrative organizations which combine some features of public and some of typically private organization. Public corporations and universities are good examples of these, and in other cases private bodies accept a degree of public influence in return for public support.

The nature of the goods and services and public attitudes to the role of the state do not entirely account for the role of public administration in society. There is a third factor which is of particular importance to the student of public administration – namely the organizational devices and administrative skills available to a society at a given time. It is not sufficient to want to provide a service through public administration; it is also necessary to be able to provide the administrative machinery which will function at a tolerable level of effectiveness.[2]

The late nineteenth and twentieth centuries have seen the growth of administrative forms which have made possible a greater role for the state than was previously regarded as feasible. Two developments seem to be of particular significance: the development of the idea of functional field administration, and the development of forms of organization which are *not* local government or central departments and ministries. The latter are often referred to as 'public corporations' or 'other administrative bodies', but these phrases serve only to disguise the variety of different types of organization and function contained within the category.

Field administration is a long-standing phenomenon of government, but traditionally field officers were generalists – often combining what we would now distinguish as legislative, executive, and judicial functions – and they were often overshadowed by local political 'authorities', sometimes powerful individuals, sometimes local appointed, traditional or elected bodies. It is noticeable that when J. S. Mill wrote *Representative Government* (1861) field officers had virtually no part in his system of government, even though he was quite familiar with the government of British India. For him local administration meant administration by locally elected or appointed bodies, not field officers of the central departments. Field officers existed, of course, in 1861, but they were restricted to customs and excise, the post office, and the peripatetic inspectors.

Britain was of course used to field administration in a different context – that of imperial or colonial government. The British Empire was in fact a gigantic system of field officers organized in an administrative hierarchy, but these were basically all generalists. It is interesting to note, however, that generalist systems have come under pressure from field officers of functional ministries in both developing and western countries, and local authorities are threatened in the same way.[3]

The growth of functional field administration is really a twentieth-century phenomenon in Britain. Apart from brief periods in its history, Britain has had no tradition of generalist field officers since the Middle Ages; in the twentieth century the rise of the Ministry of Agriculture, Fisheries and Food and the forerunners of the Department of Health and Social Security have all posed threats to the traditional system of local administration of public services through local 'authorities' – who may have been elected (as in the case of municipal corporations) or appointed (as in the case of benches of magistrates).

There is no need to spend a long time on accounting for the growth of functional field administration. It is clearly partly a result of demands for expertise in the provision of public services (a function of scientific, technical and professional developments), and partly a result of changes in the nature of communications (the post, telephone, railways, the motor car, etc.) which make responsiveness of dispersed offices to a centre a much more practical matter.

An explanation for the growth of new administrative forms of organization is harder to find. Part of the reason must lie in the fact that the private sector itself has developed a multitude of organizational forms over the years, and these may serve as models for the public sector, especially in relation to those public activities which are debatably public or private. But in many cases the form must be a result of the limited range of possibilities for new organizational systems.

It is harder to document changing attitudes to the role of government, both from country to country and over time, than it is to describe the changing patterns of social activity that are eventually reflected in the activities of the state. Part of the difficulty is that both general public opinion and the opinions of special sections of society have not been measured properly, because either the techniques were not known or, through lack of concern, were not applied.

Nevertheless it may be agreed that both governments themselves and the general public appear to expect that the government will take responsibility for a wide range of matters. The evidence for this is to be found in the public pronouncements of governments and in the pressures that citizens, individually and in groups, apply to them. The reality of these demands is reinforced when a government tries to refuse responsibility for a number of affairs and finds itself later forced to intervene in specific instances contrary to its announced general policy.

But there are differences between countries which can only be ascribed to differences in the general attitudes of society to the role of the state in society. Some of these expectations result from an experience with the inabilities of governments to deal with a wide range of problems, but others are part of the culture of the country.[4]

Related to attitudes towards the general responsibilities of the state are attitudes towards public bodies in general. The respect and trust accruing to public administration differs very much from one society to another, and this may well affect the ease with which public services are provided or public functions carried out. The prestige of public employment is a reflection of this attitude as well as the salaries commanded by public servants. Thus public administration is carried out in an atmosphere, climate or culture comprised of attitudes towards both the role of government in society and the status of public bodies as objects of trust and desired employment.

Types of Public Organization

We begin with a classification and brief description of the various types of public body to be found in Britain. Most other countries seem to have counterparts of all or some of them, though it must be remembered that their role may well differ even when they appear formally to be the same, and also that any given system may have a type unique to itself.

The first distinction that must be made is between those organizations which have a responsibility for the whole of the country and those whose jurisdiction is limited to one part of it. The former we will refer to as part of the central government or central administrative bodies, whilst the latter we will refer to as part of the decentralized administrative system. The situation is complicated by the fact that in practice some bodies operate over only part of the country, but if they can in principle operate over the whole they are counted as part of central administration. A second complication arises because in large hierarchical bodies some sections or parts of the organization may be restricted to one part of the country, in which case they are counted as part of the system of decentralization. Location is not necessarily a decisive factor here – the phenomenon of dispersal of offices which has led to some national institutions being located outside the capital city is not the same as decentralization, and so the Royal Mint, National Insurance Records, and Ministry of Defence Communications are part of central administration. Likewise government research establishments, though often located away from London, are not part of decentralization.

Second, there is a distinction cutting across the above which relates to the type of decision making the body undertakes. Some bodies are advisory and informational, whilst others are executive; amongst the latter are those with a straightforward administrative role and those which are best called 'quasi-judicial'. Administrative bodies differ also in that some of them are in direct contact with citizens whilst others act only on other bodies, some public and some private.

The main part of our catalogue of administrative bodies will concentrate on the central/decentralized distinction and the other distinctions introduced within each category.

Central Administrative Bodies

Within the category of central administration there is a vital distinction – between departments/ministries on the one hand and other bodies on the other. The first group is simple and easy to define, but it will become clear that no one name will serve to identify the remainder because what they have in common is that they are *not* ministries or departments. As we shall see later, the name by which a body is known is not necessarily a good guide to its constitutional status, but very often the other bodies are known as 'boards'.

The *department of state* is the original form of central administrative organization. In the nineteenth and early twentieth centuries the new bodies created tended to be called either boards or ministries, but their constitutional status was virtually the same as that of the traditional departments. In recent years there has been a tendency to use the title of 'department' to indicate a high status and greater importance in the system of government. Departments and ministries are headed by members of Parliament (of either House), and in one sense a ministry or department is simply a collection of powers ascribed to an officer of the Crown.

The rest of the system of central administrative bodies are not headed by politicians but by appointed boards or committees. Formally at least their powers of decision making are to be exercised independently within the legislative framework, subject to clearly defined limitations. In practice, however, they tend to be attached in a loose sense to one of the ministries, and one minister is generally regarded as being morally responsible for each of them.

The above are all executive bodies in the normal meaning of that phrase, but the system of central administration is supplemented by a large number of advisory bodies. It would be wrong to call these administrative bodies in the usual sense of the term but they are equally obviously part of the system of central administration. No account of the decision-making processes of British public administration is now complete without them.

Finally there are the quasi-judicial bodies attached to some of the departments. Many of these, however, are really part of the system of decentralized administration and will be discussed in the next chapter, but in some cases there is a central appeal body which reviews the work of types of administrative tribunal, and there is also the Council on Tribunals.

It will be noted that the ministry is the central organization in the above pattern. It is possible to divide up central administration into broad groups of bodies centred around a particular ministry, with advisory, quasi-judicial, and supplementary bodies arranged round it as clients, satellites, or allies.

DEPARTMENTS OF STATE OR MINISTRIES

Every government when it takes office inherits a set of ministries. When it begins to consider the implementation of its policies it must make a number of decisions about organizational structures. For reasons we discuss later some areas of government activity will be allocated to other public bodies, either central or decentralized, but this leaves the services and functions of government for which the government retains direct responsibility to be allocated to ministers and the organizations they head. An example of the sort of problems encountered and a recent attempt to deal with them were described in the White Paper on *The Reorganization of Central Government*.[5] This gave as one of the aims of a review of government functions and organization that had just been completed, 'to improve the framework within which public policy is formulated by matching the field of responsibility of government departments to coherent fields of policy and administration'. This exercise of matching functions to organizations is something which all governments must consider and has frequently led to major reorganizations of central administration.

In Britain ministries differ from each other in a number of important respects, all of which affect the processes and structure of administration within them and their impact on the rest of the system of government. We shall see that the matching operation mentioned above is by no means a complete account of the way the pattern of departments is constructed.

First, ministries vary in the extent to which they are charged with the direct administration of a policy or the task of formulating policy as a basis for the control of other executive agencies, such as local authorities and public corporations. Second, ministries may be categorized as executive or common service, according to whether they are primarily concerned with the administration of policies authorized by Parliament or with the provision of services for the central administration itself. Third, for historical and political reasons ministries vary in their geographical scope. Not all of them have territorial jurisdictions corresponding to the whole of the United Kingdom. Fourth, ministries differ in the amount to which they operate through decentralized offices. Fifth, ministries vary according to their political and administrative leadership. The main ones are headed by ministers or secretaries of state, although some exceptional titles, such as Chancellor of the Exchequer, remain. Sixth, ministries now vary tremendously in terms of size.

There are many other ways of distinguishing between ministries. One that is becoming of increasing importance is the apparent formalization of the status system that has always existed in the departmental structure. Another is to look at the proportions of different types of civil servant employed within them. The result of all these factors, together with the vast differences in the nature of the powers vested in them (or rather their ministers) by Parliament, is that the structure and administrative processes within departments defy easy generalization as will be seen when we come to consider the internal organization of individual ministries.

NON-DEPARTMENTAL ORGANIZATIONS

Any description of the administrative apparatus of British central administration must devote considerable space to the non-departmental agencies, the number and variety of which almost defy generalization and classification. The complexity of this sector of public administration has meant that there is not even a standard expression with which to label it. These bodies have been referred to as 'ad-hoc agencies', 'statutory, special purpose authorities', 'non-departmental agencies', 'administrative bodies', and 'semi-autonomous authorities', to mention but a few of the terms in general use. One is even tempted simply to speak of 'the rest' after government departments and local authorities have been described,[6] especially since a term which would accurately reflect their difference from both departments and local authorities would have to be something like 'semi-autonomous, non-departmental special purpose central government authorities'.

Under this heading we are therefore considering a wide range of public organizations with statutory powers which do not belong to the two easily recognizable categories above. They need not be national in scope (for instance, the Highlands and Islands Development Board or a regional hospital board), and in law and practice they come under a great deal of ministerial control. But they have this single distinguishing characteristic: they have a degree of independence from Parliament and the local electorate.

The authority's powers are conferred directly on it, and not given to a minister or an elected body.

Numerous attempts have been made, particularly by constitutional lawyers, to create order out of chaos by classification. Most of the classifications have been by function or purpose, such as industrial, commercial, social service or cultural; or by type of administration involved, such as regulatory, managerial, supervisory or licensing. Any classification by function is likely to run the risk of either ignoring important cases for the sake of tidiness or turning categories into a long list of examples. But some sort of grouping by purpose or function is useful, if only to indicate the varying kinds of organization under consideration.

The most obvious and perhaps the most important group consists of the publicly owned industrial enterprises managed by such organizations as the Gas Corporation, the National Coal Board, British Rail, and the Central Electricity Generating Board. In fact non-departmental bodies came to public prominence with the post-war nationalizations of sectors of the economy by the Labour Government, and this still remains the preferred organizational form for further extensions of the industrial and commercial role of the state.

Next there is a range of promotional bodies such as the Science Research Council and the Industrial Training Boards. Some of the promotional bodies deal with cultural matters, for instance the Arts Council. Regulatory and promotional activities over private enterprise are undertaken by such bodies as the agricultural marketing boards, the various licensing authorities, and the Gaming Board.

Since the main feature of such public authorities is the degree of autonomy they enjoy from direct political control (for reasons explained below), the most useful analysis focuses on the variables relevant to this autonomy, namely methods of finance, the membership and tenure of the controlling bodies, the powers of ministers in relation to these, and the ways the organizations are staffed. D. N. Chester has shown the variations that do exist under these headings.[7] They may be financed by their own resources (from the sale of goods and services), from normal Parliamentary appropriations (through estimates), from Parliamentary grants-in-aid, or from levies on their clientele. The members of their controlling bodies are not normally civil servants or active politicians, and they enjoy varying degrees of security of tenure. Ministers' powers also vary considerably, including the extent of the power to issue directions and to approve certain decisions. This is often reflected in the extent to which they are formally responsible to Parliament. On staffing, their employees may or may not be civil servants, an important variable when considering their operational autonomy.

Table 1

THE CONVENTIONAL CLASSIFICATION OF AREA BODIES

THE ADMINISTRATION OF JUSTICE

Local courts, tribunals in the social services, probation committees, prison visiting committees.

AREA OFFICES OF CENTRAL GOVERNMENT DEPARTMENTS

Employment exchanges, tax districts (assessment and collection), Department of Health and Social Security offices, divisional road engineers, Her Majesty's Inspectors of Education, district auditors.

AREA OFFICES OF PUBLIC CORPORATIONS

Post offices, South-Western Electricity Board districts, National Coal Board regional organization, area health authorities, British Broadcasting Corporation regions.

LOCAL GOVERNMENT IN ENGLAND AND WALES

(i) The pre-April 1974 system
County councils, county boroughs, non-county boroughs, urban districts, rural districts, the Greater London Council, Greater London boroughs, the City of London, parish government, water boards, police authorities etc.
(ii) The new (post-April 1974) system
Metropolitan county councils, metropolitan districts, non-metropolitan county councils, non-metropolitan districts, Welsh county councils, Welsh districts, parish government, community government, London as above.

Types of Decentralization

Decentralization occurs when the total territory of a country, part of a country, or a public body is divided into areas for the purposes of government, and a body or authority created with jurisdiction limited to that area. This is the process of decentralizing, and the end product can be any one of a great variety of institutional arrangements.

The conventional classification of area authorities is in terms of the legal status of their parent bodies – that is, the national system of which they are a part. Table 1 lists the four main types within the British system of government, with examples also taken from Britain. The machinery of justice is included partly because of its traditional role in local administration, and partly because it is important in the picture we wish to create of the overall system of government in its social and political context. Judicial and quasi-judicial bodies are of importance in decision-making in decentralized administration. Thus the four main categories are: the administration of justice, including courts and tribunals; area offices of central ministries, such as Department of Employment local offices; the area offices of public corporations and other non-departmental bodies, such as post offices; and local authorities, a type which is just completing a process of considerable change.

Another distinction that has been important in recent years is between the different levels of area. All public services involve the national level of government in some manner, even if only in a minor way, and most require a basic operating area through which the service is provided or activity undertaken. But there are two other possible levels of government – the region and the neighbourhood – which come between centre and locality and locality and the citizen respectively, in terms of geographical scope. Notice, however, that this classification cuts across the previous one; an argument can be made for regional or neighbourhood government *within* each of the legal categories recognized by the national government.

The difficulty with these two classifications is that they look at area organization from the point of view of the central government, not the area itself. Thus when the Post Office was turned into a public corporation the status of its local offices (and regional organization) was changed. From the point of view of the citizen (and presumably the postman) this is scarcely significant. The fundamental central-local relationships remain unchanged.

However, these classifications also fail to draw attention to various important behavioural characteristics which are of great significance in the operation of decentralized administration. For instance, they obscure the fact that both public corporations and extensive local authorities have field officers whose relationship to them is identical to the relationship between a central ministry and its local offices. Similarly in each of the three executive types there are advisory and quasi-judicial bodies whose role is very similar, despite differences in the legal status of the parent body. It is thus necessary to supplement or replace the conventional classification.

Perhaps the most fundamental distinction lies in relationships between the area authority and the centre (*note* that *centre* is a relative concept). The two basic types of area authority are *field* and *lay*. The former is found when a person exercising authority in an area is part of an administrative hierarchy; he is subject to what was earlier called 'bureaucratic' supervision, and his relations with the 'top' of the organization are in principle no different from those of members of sections within headquarters, except for the fact of geographical dispersion. Even this may not occur for officials responsible for the area in which the centre is located.

The form of supervision will of course vary from one organization to another, but the official will normally be pursuing a career within that organization, will have been appointed according to some functional criterion (often through a systematic selection procedure), and may expect to be transferred from area to area as part of promotion processes. He may even expect to spend some time in headquarters. (The two latter points are usually only true of relatively senior staff.)

In systems of lay authority, however, there is typically a discontinuity of personnel and powers, so that the area authority is not subject to general bureaucratic supervision but to a system of specific controls which in Britain are to be found in statutes and their associated regulations. Thus personnel of lay authority will expect to exercise power in one area only – the idea of transfer from one area to another is inappropriate. In some countries it is possible to be well paid in such a role, but in Britain in general only the expenses of the office are reimbursed. The methods of selection and dismissal or relinquishment of office are also quite different. Lay authority is often exercised collectively, but this is not necessary.

The traditional or special status areas are usually extremely good illustrations of the difference between field and lay authority, but within the major subdivisions of a political system the most striking differences are found between local government and the field offices of central government departments. Because of the publicity surrounding local government and the amount of research carried out on it, it provides a very good example of central-local relations in lay authority, and may even serve as a model for the analysis of central-local relations in field authority systems.

TYPES OF FIELD AUTHORITY

No understanding of decentralization, or of public administration generally, is possible without the use of further distinctions within the general categories of field and lay authority.

Field officers may be distinguished on grounds of their status or the nature of their role in the system of government. If each field authority or organization is examined separately it is likely that it will be discovered to be a miniature hierarchy by itself, involving levels of status, pay, discretion, and connection to the rest of the system. Many field officers carry out minor clerical and routine administrative tasks; their degree of personal discretion is usually low because they are subject to immediate administrative supervision by others in the area office. This is not to say that they are necessarily unimportant in the system of government, because collectively their impact can be considerable and they may well be 'locals' in the way that their superiors are not.

Attention is normally focused on those field officers who carry out managerial or controlling roles within the area – partly because these will have a greater degree of personal discretion, and partly because such roles are linking roles, connecting the field authority in its totality to the regional and national offices and to other public bodies in the area. The high status and relatively well-paid officials are therefore managers of employment exchanges, postmasters, regional controllers, prefects and district commissioners, for example. In some administrative systems, field officers are amongst the most important and highest status public officials; for instance, in imperial and colonial administration and in prefectoral systems.

Though status differences are important for the purposes of the general study of decentralization, it is best to use a distinction based on the nature of the activities carried out by types of field authority. The role of field officers in the provision of public services and governmental activities within the state can be seen to vary in terms of a distinction with which we are already familiar – that between specialists and generalists. Some field officers are concerned with one public service only (or a part of one service only), whilst others are concerned with government generally, even though they may also have a range of specialist functions in addition to their general duties.

One kind of specialist is particularly important in our approach. This is the person who specializes not directly in substantive activities of the state but in the machinery of government as such. Thus instead of dealing with citizens directly he deals with other public servants and public bodies, using some special skill such as auditing or a special knowledge of the services carried out by the authority being inspected.

Not all inspectors and specialists of this type are field officers literally, because some of them operate from the centre as peripatetic officials visiting an area when required. However as their role is similar (in fact usually identical), we will not stress the formal distinction between being located in an area and operating from the centre. Amongst the types of person referred to under this heading are district auditors, subject advisers in local education authorities, Her Majesty's Inspectors (of Education, Constabulary, Child Care), and inspectors appointed to hold local enquiries (for instance in planning).

The machinery of government specialists therefore to some extent blurs the distinction between specialists and generalists because they carry out some of the functions of the latter and their powers may be put to uses other than those of the service itself.

TYPES OF LAY AUTHORITY

Within the category of lay authority the most important distinction is between those authorities which are elected and those which are appointed. Elected authorities are referred to as local government authorities or local self-governing units, whilst there is really no collective name for the variety of committees, boards, commissions, etc., which are appointed in systems of decentralization.

Local authorities are always elected bodies in terms of this classification, and the electoral system used is normally the same in most major respects as the system governing national elections. Sometimes however local government has a variety of electoral arrangements and may differ in significant respects from national government. Some local authorities are indirectly elected – that is, their members are chosen by one or more directly elected authorities. Many of the special status areas such as the Channel Islands and the Isle of Man are governed by elected bodies and in this sense they are local government writ large.

There is no best way of creating order out of the chaos of local appointed bodies. Some are appointed by a single minister of the central government, and some by several ministers. Some are jointly appointed by two or more types of local body, and others are mainly central with a right of nomination or recommendation for other local bodies.

However there is another distinction cutting across the types of authority mentioned above which is particularly helpful in understanding the variety of appointed lay bodies. This is a classification made on the basis of types of activity and decisions made by the body – something that applies to field authority as well as lay authority. From the point of view of the citizen, one of the factors that counts most is whether the authority is executive or advisory – in fact, the nature of its activities.

Some area bodies are executive in that they take decisions which directly affect the lives of citizens. They provide services which are consumed by the individual or they regulate his life in some specifiable manner. Some of the decision-making bodies are judicial in impact rather than administrative, the distinction between the two at this level being largely a matter of procedures (judicial ones proceeding in an adversary manner and being regulated by precise procedural safeguards).

Other bodies however have advisory and informational roles. They may be charged with the collection of information or they may gather together and represent opinions and interests to an executive organization. They differ in the focus of their activities

– some advise an area authority whilst others advise a regional or central organization.

Many of the lay-appointed organizations fall clearly into one of these categories. For instance, the bench of magistrates and local tribunals are obviously judicial decision-making authorities, whilst regional hospital boards, area gas boards and hospital management committees were executive. Consultative councils in the nationalized industries are advisory to the area authority, whilst *ad hoc* investigations of decentralization are advisory to the centre. Examples of these can be found within the category of field administration.

It is much easier to classify local authorities into types because local government is a much more clearly differentiated and understood form of organization. Local authorities can best be understood in terms of the type of local government in which they exist.

It is first necessary to distinguish between primary and secondary local government. Some local authorities are directly elected in a system broadly of free and fair elections, and those successful in the elections become members of the governing body as of right. But others are indirectly elected in that their members are nominated by one or more of the directly-elected authorities. Once appointed, and apart from that process, secondary local authorities have the same rights of decision-making and taxing powers as the primary authorities. They are thus authorities in the strict sense of the word. We refer to them as secondary simply because they derive from the basic or primary authorities.

The second distinction is between single-purpose and multi-functional local authorities. Some local authorities are responsible for one or a few public services; they are often referred to as *ad hoc* bodies because they are created for a special purpose. In contrast many local authorities are not tied to a particular service but are regarded as suitable for the provision of a range of public activities. These are known as 'omnibus' authorities and they may expect to have functions added to or taken from them from time to time.

The distinction between single-purpose and multi-functional local authorities cuts across the distinction between primary and secondary local authorities. At present in Britain all the directly elected bodies are multi-functional and all the secondary bodies are single-purpose, but this was not always the case. The mid-nineteenth century saw a great proliferation of special purpose directly-elected authorities, such as poor law guardians, boards of education, highway and sanitary district authorities. The improvement commissions under local Acts of Parliament were rather like general governmental bodies. Secondary general purpose local authorities are found in France in the form of the new *districts urbains*, and in a variety of guises in America.

Primary local government can be divided into two types – simple and complex. A simple system of primary local authorities occurs where there is only a single tier of local government; where only one primary local authority has jurisdiction over any piece of land. In contrast complex systems are those where there are two or more levels of local authority governing the same area. The two or more authorities are said to be co-ordinate, and the analogy with the distinction between unitary and federal states is an extremely useful one for understanding the structural and behavioural differences between types of local government. It is possible to go further and distinguish between two-, three- or more tier local government and between different types of two-tier local government, but this is an unnecessary refinement at this stage.

A system of local government is usually completed by a variety of administrative bodies which are not *authorities*, but which are part of the system of internal decentralization within the individual local authority. These include joint committees, area administration, and institutions such as schools and police stations. These occur irrespective of the distinctions made above.

We have now created a picture of the great variety of organizations or distinct public bodies which exist in one system of public administration only. For convenience of reference we have presented the distinctions we have employed in the section on decentralization in a series of figures (nos 1–3). It should be remembered that the distinctions are useful guides to the complexity of the elements of a system of public administration, but they should not be used as a set of rigid categories. In fact public bodies often prove to be obdurate in relation to any simple system of classification, refusing to fit neatly in only one category or even into any category.

The next stage is to describe the main features of the relationships between these disparate elements in our system of government.

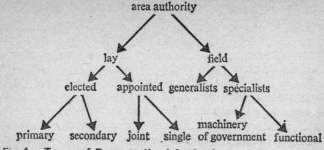

Fig. 1. Types of Decentralized Authority

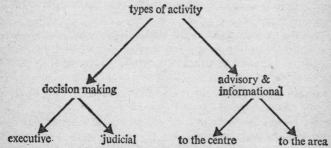

Fig. 2. Types of Activity and Decisions Made

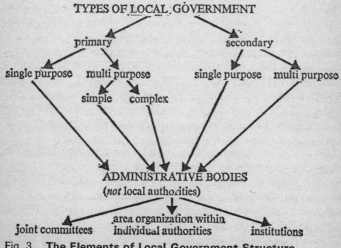

Fig. 3. The Elements of Local Government Structure

Allocation of Functions Between Types of Body

The major characteristics of the overall pattern of public administration are determined by two sets of decisions or two processes of allocating governmental activities (services or functions) between public bodies. Let it be stressed that each set of decisions constitutes a process, and this process may be repeated several times over. How far the processes will be taken and what sort of end product they will create will depend on the nature of public services and on various factors (historical, cultural, political, etc.), some of which may look rather irrelevant to rational decision making.

We have already established that the role and importance of public administration in a given society will depend on the role given to government or the state generally. This will itself depend on a number of factors, including the availability of administrative forms deemed suitable for different activities. These factors will produce a long list of activities which are expected to be performed by one or more public bodies, and groups of which are called services or functions.

It is sometimes thought that public activities fall naturally into groups having obvious names with which to label them. A service or function is therefore a group of activities which are organically related to each other and distinct from the rest. Services in practical terms, however, are the creation of law in many systems of government; a statute groups together separate activities and gives them a name. In fact it is easy to forget how contingent and arbitrary is the specification of each service or function. The concept of a service or function of government can only be understood by reference to the perceptions of people in a society of the way social reality is divided up, and by reference to the purposes of governments. In other words a service is a relative and normative concept, not a descriptive one.

This point can best be understood by considering the intricacies of service provision in different countries. Britain, for instance, operates with a concept of health services which distinguishes between public health and personal health. The provision of fresh water is usually grouped with sewerage and sewage disposal, refuse collection and clean air as an environmental service, whereas it can of course be regarded as a trading service (and some vestiges of this conception still remain in the British system). The situation in relation to the provision of homes is more complicated – we draw a distinction between providing homes through houses and homes through residential accommodation. Some aspects of dwellings are dealt with as part of the environmental health services, others as part of the consumer protection service (even if not recognized as such). Houses are provided for a variety of motives and their location is controlled as part of a policy towards the physical environment.

The encouragement of economic development in agriculture is in Britain regarded as something separate from economic development of industry and commerce. We seem to swing between regarding libraries as part of the educational system and as part of recreational services. In the field of services for those suffering from some identifiable illness, handicap, or personal difficulty, a large number of distinctions have been tried. At present we are using the difference between those activities which rely on a primary skill which is social and those which rely on a primarily medical skill. This does at least have the advantage of grouping a score or more previously separately defined services into two categories, but as it draws clear organizational lines between them it may be thought to have its own defects.

The important point to grasp is that services are not natural but social phenomena, created by societies and the people who comprise them. The consequence for the pattern of public administration is that its main features will be strongly influenced by social perceptions of what counts as a separate service as well as what counts as a proper activity for the state to undertake.

The process of allocating functions therefore starts from what are regarded as separate services or functions. But each of these soon comes to be seen as an internally differentiated group of activities, differentiated in at least two ways – vertically in respect of the type of decisions taken and horizontally in terms of distinctions *within* the group of activities regarded as a separate service.

If a service involves contact with the citizen either individually or in recognizable groups, then there are only three ways in which it may be administered: through a central office to which citizens come (or approach by post or telephone), by peripatetic officers of the centre, or through decentralized machinery. A choice between these three methods is usually made partly on grounds of the nature of the activity itself, partly on historical and political grounds, and partly on administrative grounds, in terms of the relative viability of alternative systems of organization.

In traditional discussions of public administration it used to be held that it was possible to distinguish between national and local services, and theories of local government from John Stuart Mill onwards have had this or a similar distinction as part of their basis. The distinction has proved to be a particularly elusive one, especially as what appears to belong to one category at one time may belong to the other at the next. Today the distinction usually appears in the form of isolating national as opposed to local elements and interests in a service. The growth of vertical differentiation within each public activity provides the basis for one way of allocating responsibilities between the geographical levels of government.

It should be noted that by defining decentralization as a process we have made the concept of a centre a relative one – in fact relative to this process. Private bodies undertake the same operation, for instance, when they establish branches throughout the country and create the position of regional manager to deal with these local offices. Thus in public administration decentralization is not limited to the creation of the major subdivisions of the unitary state. It obviously occurs within each of the major territorial divisions of the state, within the states of a federal system, within many public corporations and other non-departmental bodies, and within extensive local authorities.

The phenomenon of multiple decentralization is repeated in essence with the second of the major processes – that of allocating functions between types of body once the geographical level of provision has been determined. We first consider allocation of functions at the centre and then the choice between different types of decentralization.

MINISTRIES OR OTHER BODIES?

It is a reasonable judgement that in the political systems that we have been considering the normal way of administering functions at the centre is to make them the responsibility of a member of the executive, either by adding them to the powers of an existing office or by creating a new executive office. The pattern of the Labour Government's post-war legislation shows a considerable use of the latter, as Acts of Parliament expanded the role of the state or reorganized existing public functions.

As the use of ministries is in some sense normal, the problem of the allocation of functions at the centre becomes one of deciding when it is more appropriate to use a non-departmental body. As these vary so much for the reasons given above their use tends not to be capable of easy explanation. Why has this special type of organization been created at all? This became a topical issue when the concept of 'hiving off' was recommended by the Fulton Committee. It has led to extensive enquiries within central government into the likely benefits of further delegation of powers to semi-independent agencies. This is an interest in the possibility and desirability of reorganizing the provision of existing functions rather than of designing structures for new ones. But the political and administrative factors relevant to both problems are the same.

The motives for allocating statutory powers and responsibilities to non-ministerial agencies can be grouped under two broad headings. One aim has been to depoliticize administration by freeing the organization from ministerial and Parliamentary control. The political elements in such a motive range from a fear of partisan control through patronage at one extreme, to a concern that legislative involvement in detail might undermine commercial incentives or professional expertise at the other.

Fear of partisan patronage undermining the impartiality of administration has by now largely disappeared. It is worth recalling, however, that the Civil Service Commission owed its special organization and independence to the need to ensure that all appointments to the civil service were made strictly on merit. Even now the pressures for an integrated approach to personnel management, which have brought it within the Civil Service Department, have left its independence protected by formal arrangements governing the appointment of the Commissioners and their relations with the rest of the Department.

A more important reason for establishing special statutory authorities has been to protect management from legislative interference. Classic cases are found in the origins of the nationalized industries. Despite disagreement on how far publicly-owned industrial enterprises should be regarded as purely commercial concerns, and despite varying degrees of ministerial control and involvement, there is a broad consensus that public accountability must be combined with methods of business management to ensure commercial efficiency. Financial and managerial efficiency for commercial enterprises required that 'the boards of the industries would be answerable to their customers, their employees and their creditors rather than to the House of Commons.'[8] A recent example of this principle in operation was the decision to turn the Post Office into a public corporation.

The way in which this managerial autonomy and reduction in public accountability is achieved and the particular reasons for it in some examples will be shown later.

CHOOSING BETWEEN TYPES OF DECENTRALIZATION

The second type of allocation decision involves a choice between different types of decentralized administrative organization. It can be argued that the structure of the overall pattern of decentralization within a country is one of the best guides to its general social and governmental systems. Different forms of area administration score very differently on the characteristics or dimensions mentioned earlier. Werlin has argued that the nature of society and government determine the elasticity of control which a central government can tolerate or achieve.[9]

The broad distinction is between field administration and local government. Field administration tends to score highly on technical efficiency, equality, security of the state and protection of national unity. Local government tends to promote the recognition and protection of local identities, adaptability and area accountability (rather than national responsiveness), democracy and participation; in each case the system tends to score badly on the other factors.

Thus the choice of types of decentralization will depend on the values and perceptions of the central government, which in turn will be related to the level of economic, social and political development of the society in which the government is located. If a society stresses equality, and has relatively poor methods of influencing autonomous bodies, then it will be driven to rely on field administration; but if it stresses adaptability and the promotion of separate identities it will prefer local government.

The latter can be regarded as an expensive form of administration in terms of its call on human resources, and on motives and behaviour patterns which are necessary if it is not to cause great difficulties in the system of public administration. This point is often ignored in discussions of the 'theory' of local government – a theory which tends to try to prove that local government is always a superior form of decentralization.[10]

There is a difference between a system of decentralization and the various types of administrative arrangement we have distinguished. A system of decentralization is characterized by the relative weights of the different types compared with each other, the relations between them and the degree of autonomy from the centre that each achieves.

ALLOCATION OF FUNCTIONS BETWEEN DEPARTMENTS

The process of allocating functions to distinct organizational entities does not end with the determination of the role of ministries and non-ministries at the centre and of the role of each of the forms of decentralization in the country at large. We turn now to the problem of the structure or pattern of central government departments. It should be noted that the problem of allocation between non-departmental bodies is of a different order and has already been considered to a large extent.

When we look at the scope and complexity of British central government, two things are particularly clear. First, while some activities must be separately organized, others offer great scope for grouping and regrouping under different ministers. Defence could not be merged with health, and health probably has to be kept distinct from education. But should health be linked organizationally with social security, and should a children's service be placed in the Home Office rather than with health or education? Why was regional policy with the Department of Trade and Industry and not with regional planning in the Department of the Environment?

The machinery of central government, and particularly its departmental aspect, is constantly changing. New ministries are created and existing ones abolished or merged as successive governments attempt to produce a grouping of diverse activities which cohere with their policy objectives. This has been referred to as 'a continuous process of creation, fission, fusion and transfer . . .'[11] The reasons for one change can be quite different from the next; they vary from the narrowly political, through the public relations operation, to the genuine attempt to improve the decision-making structure of central administration.

Nevertheless attempts have been made on occasions to apply the principles of administration developed in the study of management and organization generally to the process of classifying governmental activities in such a way that the best allocation of functions between individual ministries can be discovered. Implicit in such attempts is an effort to enforce some kind of administrative logic on the erratic process by which the structure of central government has been determined.

From time to time guidance has been sought in the classical principles of administration or organization. These were developed in the 1920s and 30s, and claimed to constitute a new 'science of administration', applicable not only to large-scale industry (with which its creators were most familiar) but to all formal organizations. The founder of this tradition in administrative thinking is often held to be a Frenchman, Henri Fayol, whose book *General and Industrial Administration*[12] contains a list of fourteen principles of organization and sixteen managerial duties of the organization. But the most coherent statements of this approach are to be found in writings of L. F. Urwick[13] in Britain and J. D. Mooney[14] in America, both of whom attempted a synthesis of a large variety of writings on management and a large amount of practical experience.

This approach is often confused with scientific management, but its intentions and its methods of discovery and proof were quite distinct. Briefly, what people working in this tradition sought to do was to find and formulate principles of organization and management which would apply to all organizations at all times, and which would constitute rules on which leaders could draw in a relatively straightforward manner in order to solve the sort of problems that arise from time to time in all such bodies. They were largely agreed amongst themselves as to the list of principles that were to be included in this new science, and those who are familiar with old-fashioned textbooks on management and with management education in the 1940s and 50s will recognize many of these – span of control, unity of command, line and staff, hierarchy, etc.

One of the most important of these principles (Fayol made it number one) was the principle of specialization, which stated that administrative efficiency is increased by grouping members of organizations according to *purpose*, *process*, *place* or *clientele*. *Purpose* here means the objective of administration, such as public health, defence, or the maintenance of law and order. *Process* refers to the professional knowledge or technical skills required for a particular activity, such as civil engineering or medicine. *Clientele* means the recipients of public activities, such as war pensioners, farmers, or the unemployed. *Place* refers to organization according to some territorial requirement.

The reader will immediately recognize this approach as highly relevant to a rational attack on the problem posed earlier – of allocating functions between ministries. It suggests a way of determining the number and scope of central ministries by the application of principles of organization which derive from experience outside public administration. But relevance is not enough. The principles must be justified in their own terms – that is, shown to be good guides to organizational behaviour of certain types.

This is where the main difficulties arise. First, the logic of the whole approach has been given a detailed scrutiny by H. A. Simon, who has pointed out that the so-called principles are like proverbs – they occur in pairs and contradict each other. Not only that, many of them are internally vague or ambiguous, so that it is often difficult to be sure exactly what they mean. Others have focused on the empirical claims implicit in the principles and have discovered, as did Joan Woodward, that there is little or no relation between organizing according to these principles and organizational effectiveness and success.[15]

We are fortunate that the principle of specialization has been especially picked out for critical scrutiny by Simon and studied in well-known empirical research by Woodward and Burns and Stalker.[16] Simon showed how two of the bases of specialization cannot be meaningfully described in their own terms and how all four conflict in that it is not usually possible to follow all of them at the same time. Burns and Stalker and Joan Woodward independently found evidence suggesting that in some circumstances an emphasis on the division of labour, which is what specialization essentially is, is not only unhelpful but positively a formula for failure.

The problem facing the organization planner is how to choose a basis for specialization. A simple classification in itself offers no guidance on how to organize work as there are an infinite number of possible ways of classifying government activities. In a report to the Ministry of Reconstruction in 1918, the only thorough examination of the subject in Britain, the Haldane Committee recommended defining the responsibilities of each department according to the service it renders to the community (that is, by function rather than by clientele). In this way functions or services such as health, education, finance and foreign affairs 'would each be under separate administration'.

We have already remarked on the arbitrary nature of *service* and *function* in public administration; they are defined by government, and do not exist prior to it. This point also applies to attempts by others, such as E. N. Gladden,[17] to provide a logical scheme for general reference. Gladden himself suggested ten categories of Direction and Finance, Economic Affairs, Employment, Social Security, Culture and Research, Home Affairs, Justice, National Security (Defence), External Affairs, and Common Services. Such headings give an idea of the scope of modern government, but are of course by themselves no indication of the kind of activity in which ministers and their ministries are engaged – for example, under social security. It is evident that a classification cannot serve as a principle by itself – it requires a justification in terms of advantages that can be expected to accrue.

More recently[18] the government justified reorganization by 'the application of the functional principle' to the allocation of responsibilities – 'government departments should be organized by reference to the task to be done or the objective to be obtained, and this should be the basis of the division of work between departments rather than, for example, dividing responsibility between departments so that each one deals with a client group'. Departures from this principle might be justified if there are 'strong reasons', as in the case of grouping functions according to the area to be served in the Scottish and Welsh Offices. But in the great majority of cases administration should be by task or policy rather than client or area.

As we shall show later, however, it is easier to announce an adherence to a principle than to carry it out rigorously. When we examine the present distribution of services and functions, we find all sorts of oddities and apparent divergencies from the government's policy, as well as debatable decisions.

NON-DEPARTMENTAL BODIES

It might be expected that the same problem of allocation would arise between different types of non-departmental bodies, but a consideration of their nature will soon show that this is not the case. For as each is created to perform a specified function, the problem is answered (for that body) by the decision to create it in the first place. Thus, the National Coal Board has its defined responsibilities; it would have been amazed if anyone had even considered allocating to it the functions of the Post Office when it was decided to remove this from the ministerial sector of public administration. With gas and electricity the situation is less straightforward, but again in a sense the issue has been predetermined by the decisions in the 1940s to create separate organizational systems to deal with the two power industries – on the basis of the commodity produced and supplied.

LOCAL AUTHORITIES

The same problem does, however, arise in an acute form in local government. Primary local authorities are multi-functional bodies, and when each as an individual comes to determine its own internal organization for the disposal of its obligations and exercise of its rights, it has to decide how to group activities in order to create its committee system and its departmental structure.

The traditional method by which local authorities organized themselves was by use of a simple principle, thus:

1 service→1 committee→1 chief officer→1 department.

As local authorities became aware of the existence of what they call 'horizontal functions', they added another principle of the same form, thus:

1 horizontal function→1 committee→1 chief officer→1 department.

The principle may be adapted to apply to the internal organization of the units created by the first application of it, thus:

1 part of service/function→1 subcommittee→1 section head→ 1 section.

What was counted as a separate service or function depended on two factors. The first was the decisions of the centre as embodied in statutes and in the activities of central ministries. Thus, a long series of Acts of Parliament laid an obligation on local authorities to provide a 'service' which is specified by the Act; sometimes the legislative provision goes further and requires a particular organizational form – the widely separated *Education Act, 1944*, and *Local Authority Social Services Act, 1970* both prescribe a similar administrative pattern on each local authority charged with responsibility for the services. Thus local authorities were strongly influenced by the ideas of the centre as to the distinctions between one public service and another.

Secondly, the values and perceptions of the individual local authority modified to some extent the national legislative provisions, by giving greater or less weight to a particular governmental activity than did the centre. This in turn was influenced by the circumstances of the local authority – in particular its size and the extent of demand for the service in the locality. Thus what were recognized as separate services or functions in some areas were treated as parts of a service or function in another.

The general consequence of the operation of the principle and its variants was that local authorities tended to have very elaborate internal organizational structures, with large numbers of committees and departments and intricate divisions between public activities which required special co-ordinative arrangements.[19]

The problems of the allocation of functions do not cease when decisions have been made about their distribution between different types of public body and between different individual bodies within each type. A public corporation such as the Post Office is responsible for distinct activities, and though the difficulties are not as acute as they are for a primary local authority, nevertheless those who have to create the organizational pattern of the corporation must make decisions about its internal allocation of duties and responsibilities. Similarly each local authority department will be divided into sections and subsections for the discharge of smaller and smaller parts of its obligations. In fact there is no logical reason why the functional allocation of responsibilities for government activities should stop until the individual public servant is reached. The same is true of decentralization – one can always find a smaller area than the one being used at a particular time. Conversely, the processes of functional and territorial *aggregation* can be repeated until the whole world is regarded as one unit.

Relations Between Different Types of Body

The nature of the relations between different public bodies within the system of public administration of a country is another good guide to the nature of the constitutional and political system of that country. The linkages between the different parts of the governmental system are a vital part of the operational state and account for the actual behaviour of individual parts to a large extent.

British government and politics are executive dominated. That is, the executive plays the major role in the structure of decision making and controls, co-ordinates or influences actions and behaviour in all or most parts of the system. Political processes inevitably seem to centre on the creation, composition and behaviour of members of the executive, so much so that one can be pardoned for thinking that the British state consists of the government and little else.

This is of course not true of other countries. The role of the legislature is such in the United States that some commentators have preferred 'government by whirlpool' as the best description of American government. The whirlpool brings together the congressional committee, the executive agency, bureau or division, and the pressure groups concerned with a particular topic in such a way as to exclude the participation of many 'outsiders' in decision making relating to the specified area of public activity.

Government in the Third and Fourth Republics of France might almost have been described as 'administration dominated'; the unstable nature of the executive and the patterns of French legislative policies gave an independence of action to public servants which may account for the growth of elaborate internal control mechanisms – originally the devices of an autocratic regime – in a democratic context. The Fifth Republic has obviously strengthened the executive and this may well have affected the processes of administration.

None of these short phrases is an adequate description of the nature of government in the countries mentioned, but taken with modifications they provide a guide to the environment in which individual public bodies operate. Obviously the executive has increased in importance in the United States; equally obviously there are trends within British government which may either strengthen or weaken the judiciary, the legislature and the general public. French government has always been too complicated to encapsule in a single phrase. Nevertheless, with this proviso, the expressions are a good starting point for the study of public administration in each of the countries. Our concern is mainly with Britain, but it is worth remembering that in other systems of government a different starting point would be chosen.

In one sense, however, the system of inter-organizational relationships within the system of public administration is comprised of a vast number of *ad hoc* interactions, conflicts and adjustments. Decision making, as we have said, is mainly an end-on process in that one public body often takes over when another has completed its own decision making. The conclusions of one are the premises of the other. It is not that the interactions defy classification, but rather that they occur as and when circumstances dictate them; as circumstances themselves contain large random elements there will be large random elements in the occurrence of the different types of relationship between public bodies.

Many examples of the end-on nature of modern public administration can be given. For instance, if a council changes its rents policy this may pose problems for the Supplementary Benefits Commission. Public corporations may come into contact with local authorities when they seek to expand or contract their activities. None of these relationships in Britain are provided for formally in the structure of public administration; some of them work themselves out through mutual adjustment and compromise.

In France there is a system of administrative courts, part of whose function is to deal with disputes between different types of public body as well as between public bodies and private citizens. In America some of the interactions will be the subject of judicial review. But nothing similar is found in the United Kingdom, and where *ad hoc* adjustment does not suffice it is necessary for the executive to intervene.

In the United Kingdom the executive has inherited the royal prerogative powers which enable it to provide a degree of integration of government activities within the British Isles outside the Republic of Ireland. The other main support for the position of the executive is its power to control Parliament and therefore, ultimately, legislation. This is not to say that the government of the day never gets deflected from its chosen path or thwarted by other parts of the political system. On the contrary, we shall argue that within the structure of public administration itself there are a number of factors at work affecting the ability of the centre to extend its influence throughout the system. But the starting point must always be the power and role of the executive.

First, there are the direct interactions between one public body and another, as for instance when a local council protests to the Post Office about the closure of a sub-post office or a change in service provision. But secondly there is the deliberate intervention of the central government to deal with problems created by the complexity of the system.

The realization that many of the interactions between public bodies resulted in *ad hoc* adjustments of varying degrees of satisfaction has led to the growth of machinery for co-ordinating the work of administrative bodies, both in parts of the system and throughout it. The stress on co-ordination within the central government departmental system is only one aspect of this development. The same phenomenon can be seen at the local government level and within the sphere of economic management. This subject is treated more fully in a later chapter.

The Public Administration Year

So far we have been commenting on the lateral flow of business between bodies at more or less the same point in time. But time is also an important aspect or dimension of the flow of business; indeed it is not too much to say that temporal constraints impose a form on the activities of public servants which gives them characteristic shapes. To speak of the public administration year is not entirely accurate, as different twelve-month periods are used for different purposes, and public administration operates in some respects over both longer and shorter periods. Yet any twelve months will include a cycle of basic activities which are of great importance to public bodies.

First, the activities of public bodies are geared to the Parliamentary year, particularly if the organization is concerned with the promotion of legislation in any form. This applies with special force to central ministries, but is equally important to other bodies when they wish to promote private acts or are likely to be affected by public legislation. If it is not the year of a General Election, which disturbs the normal pattern, then the Parliamentary year runs from October/November round to the summer recess. This is important to public bodies because legislation of any substance needs to be ready, or almost ready, for mention in the Queen's Speech and introduction as a bill at the beginning of the session, to maximize its chances of passing through all the Parliamentary stages safely.

Part of the Parliamentary year is taken up with financial procedures relating to the estimates which form the working basis of the operations of many public bodies in the year to come. In some cases this process affects the finances of the body directly, sometimes indirectly, and occasionally hardly at all. These estimates need to be prepared, collated, co-ordinated, defended, published, and defended again, until they are finally approved.

When they have been finally approved the funds appropriated must be spent, and generally in an allotted time, and according to a process which is both controlled at the time and *ex post facto* through auditing and accountancy procedures. Again, the exact form this takes varies from body to body but it is always present in some manner – a reminder that public administration involves public accountability in this sphere as well as others.

The Parliamentary estimates procedure is fundamental to the British system because it determines the amount of money that is to be transferred from central government funds to the funds of other public bodies. (Money rarely seems to move in the other direction.) Thus it determines some of the parameters of the local government and other budgetary processes.

The importance of the Parliamentary estimates for the non-departmental bodies varies with the extent to which they are self-financing (through receipts, etc.) and the extent to which they incur deficits in a given year.

Over the years a substantial body of opinion has grown up which argues that a single year is too short a period to plan and administer complex activities in modern government. This has led to the use of longer periods for certain purposes and to rolling programmes which in effect deny the desirability of thinking in finite time periods. These new developments must, however, be seen as additions or modifications to the traditional system rather than as replacements.

Another weakness of the traditional system was that it was an unintegrated one – each public body operating in part isolation from all the others so that the total effect of all decision was only partly predictable and controllable. As public expenditure is such a large part of the national income and governments wish to control and manipulate the national economy, the unintegrated system was obviously a source of danger to economic policy. A second development has therefore been the growth of devices which introduce a degree of overall control into the system. Some of these operate through controls on capital expenditure and others through control of wage and salary settlement procedures. We have chosen to illustrate the growth of overall planning and integrative measures from the local government field, which has seen the most striking changes in recent years.

British local authorities have always had a legally autonomous budgetary procedure, compared with countries such as France, in that they have had complete freedom to fix the details and level of the estimates and of the local tax (called the rates), subject only to *a posteriori* control through auditing and court actions. Between 1945 and 1958, when the local government financial system was dominated by specific grants, all that the central government did was announce the rates at which the various specific grants would be paid to claiming authorities, and the rules for distributing a small equalization grant to some authorities, and leave the overall level of local expenditure to be determined by the outcome of 1400 separate decision-making processes. To control local expenditure it was necessary to intervene suddenly and crudely through capital expenditure controls.

A new system has gradually been built up since 1958 which provides for some degree of overall control of the local government current expenditure and which brings together local and central decision making so that a degree of harmony can be achieved between the two sets of plans. The system as it was at the beginning of the new financial year, 1973–4, is shown in figure 4 with amounts for the national government and for one particular authority – Exeter County Borough Council.

The important things to notice in this diagram are, first, how the decisions at the two levels are related to each other throughout the process of estimating and spending public funds; and second, how the central government puts the onus on local authorities to decide whether or not to exceed proposed local government expenditure by their control of the rate levy. In ways outside the scope of this section, this overall control has enabled detailed control in other spheres to be relaxed, so long as this does not touch on vital governmental policies.

The Flow of Funds from Citizen to Citizen

For one set of public bodies the year takes on a different pattern. These are the bodies charged with collecting the various taxes at both national and local level. We are not concerned specifically with tax administration but it draws attention to another flow within the system of public administration – not so much a flow of business or decisions but a flow of money. This is literally a flow from one citizen to another, but the student of government has been especially concerned with certain general features of the flow – particularly that between types of people, usually referred to as social classes. Another flow which has been ignored to a great extent and which is also of great importance is the flow between territorial parts of the whole country.

The logic of a consolidated fund system is quite simple; as the receipts from all taxes are paid into the same account, and their origins lost in the process, it breaks the connection between paying taxes and receiving or benefiting from public services which the proceeds of these taxes finance. It thus enables taxation to be used for other social and political purposes and makes a redistribution of income in any direction theoretically possible.

The central-local financial system as it has developed under the *Local Government Act, 1966*, illustrates many of these processes in a particular context. It shows the interaction of information and 'decisions' at two separate levels in the system of government; it is patterned on the public administration year as it occurs in central government and in a particular local authority; it involves special machinery for the co-ordination of the two separate elements; it is based on the values and perceptions of two distinct sets of actors; it structures very complicated patterns of flow of funds from citizen to citizen; and it is end-on to other processes within each level – for instance, the sequence of central financial planning, which is described later.

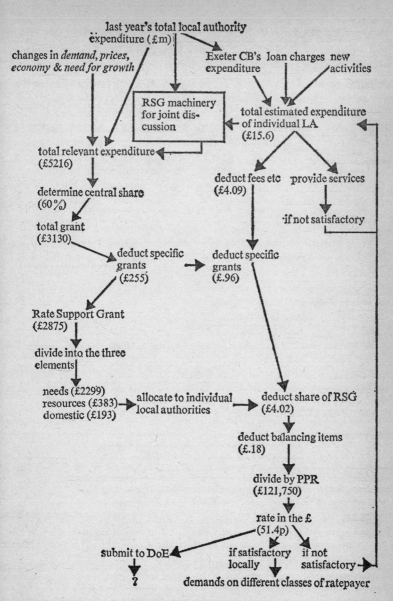

last year's total local authority expenditure (£m)

changes in *demand, prices, economy & need for growth*

Exeter CB's expenditure   loan charges   new activities

RSG machinery for joint discussion

total estimated expenditure of individual LA (£15.6)

total relevant expenditure (£5216)

determine central share (60%)

deduct fees etc (£4.09)   provide services

total grant (£3130)

if not satisfactory

deduct specific grants (£255)   deduct specific grants (£.96)

Rate Support Grant (£2875)

divide into the three elements

needs (£2299)
resources (£383)
domestic (£193)   allocate to individual local authorities   deduct share of RSG (£4.02)

deduct balancing items (£.18)

divide by PPR (£121,750)

rate in the £ (51.4p)

submit to DoE   if satisfactory locally   if not satisfactory

?   demands on different classes of ratepayer

Fig. 4.   **The Present Central-Local Financial System**

Public Administration and the Citizen

The massive growth in the activities of government during the last hundred years – both in number and variety – has multiplied the number of individual contacts between public officials and citizens enormously. Governments commonly see themselves as responsible for the achievement of economic objectives, for controlling the physical environment and ensuring the health and welfare of citizens, in addition to the traditional functions of public authority. The new functions of government also intrude into aspects of the citizen's life that were previously regarded as sacrosanct.

So far in this book we have been concerned with the effects of this growth on the system of public administration itself – on the machinery governments devise and operate to suit their purposes. But the purposes of individuals are also affected and we now look at the government-citizen interface from the point of view of the individual.

The relations between state and the citizen in the type of governmental systems we are considering are dominated by the principles of accountability and equality, as mentioned earlier. That is, public officials and public bodies (i.e. all public authorities) are expected to give an account of their decisions and actions in terms of other people's values and to treat all individuals in the same condition alike. These are of course moral rather than legal principles but if they are violated the individual may feel that he has suffered an injustice.

Not all the grievances of the individual are injustices; he may suffer hardship from a decision of a public authority which that authority thinks right and he may be harmed by a decision which he believes to be bad, imprudent or foolish, but which is legally correct. From the point of view of the individual what matters is whether he feels that he has a grievance, whether this is investigated, and if found to be justified, whether it is redressed.

The effects of the system of public administration on the citizen are fairly obvious; but what of the effects of the individual citizen on governmental actions and decisions? This subject will be discussed under two headings: the nature of grievances and the methods of influence.

GRIEVANCES

From the point of view of the outside observer the grievances that an individual may feel can be classified in a number of ways. We mentioned above the difference between 'hardship' which is caused by injustice and the other types. But it must be realized that citizens do not always, or even often, draw distinctions between different types of grievance. Nor do they always accept the categories that are dictated by the government itself. In fact, when we come to consider the methods by which citizens may attempt to have their grievances redressed, it will quickly be realized that these may also be used to produce 'favours' as well as the elimination of hardship.

The most obvious case of grievance that the system of government will recognize is the *injustice*. This occurs whenever it can be shown that an individual has been treated in a manner different from that prescribed by the rules, and that he regards this difference as bad or harmful to him. The practical test of this is often that of comparison with the treatment of others; as the rules by which public officials operate can never be prescribed in such a way as to remove all discretion from them, it is easier to test the fairness of a decision by comparing it with other decisions than against some abstract standard. Thus, if one considers something similar to the notional rent by which the valuation officer is supposed to determine the rateable value of a property for local taxation purposes, it is easy to see how it is impossible to show what this 'rent' ought to be but simple to show that similar properties have or have not been given comparable values.

This is not always the case, however, and when we consider the sort of grievances that are encountered in practice by the various agencies of redress – for instance the Parliamentary Commissioner and the Supplementary Benefits Commission appeals procedure – it can be seen that public officials, in the exercise of their authority, are as liable to human error as the private citizen – malice, sloth, bias, carelessness, etc.

There are cases, however, when no fault on the part of a public servant can be alleged – sometimes the very opposite is true – yet the individual is harmed in some way. Over the years the position of the individual who is indirectly affected by government actions has been increasingly given recognition. A good example is the recent change in the compensation to be paid to those whose homes and land will be affected by road development, even if they do not lose either.

The difficulty, however, arises when there is a conflict between the values that the state recognizes and those that an individual actually has. Again we may refer to the instance of valuation for rating, which illustrates the difference between price and value. If a new school is built near to a house this may reduce the subjective value to the retired owners of the property whilst increasing its desirability for rent to families with small children. Thus though the present owners will argue that their rateable value ought to be decreased because it is less valuable to them, in fact on present law it ought to be increased.

Nor do citizens always distinguish between their grievances against individual decisions and their dislike of the policy adopted by the public authority, usually with direct sanction of law. If however the use of the methods of examining individual grievances brings to light harmful effects of a policy on certain types of people or conditions then this may set in motion the processes for legal change. This is another example of the interrelationships which create the overall pattern of government within a country.

METHODS OF INFLUENCE ON PUBLIC AUTHORITIES

The classical way by which grievances are redressed in Britain is through the legislature. The responsibility of all governmental bodies to the elected representatives of the people is regarded as an essential feature of democratic government. This responsibility is not only a matter of being responsive to public opinion but also requires executive actions to be accounted for, if required, to the legislature as the organ of the governmental system which confers legitimacy on public bodies. These are the means, expressed in terms of constitutional or quasi-constitutional rules and operated through organizational and procedural devices, by which Parliament seeks to scrutinize and control the administrative apparatus of government.

It has become clear however that many of these traditional methods have defects which can only be remedied by a different type of institution or procedure. The result has been the growth in specialized institutions which deal with specific types of grievance.

Notes

1 Weber, Gerth and Mills, 1948, p. 212
2 Hunter, 1967; Steer, 1964
3 Blondel, 1959; Smith, 1967
4 Almond and Verba, 1963
5 Cmnd. 4506, 1970
6 Chester, 1953
7 Chester, 1953
8 Coombes, 1966
9 Werlin, 1970
10 Whalen, 1960; Mackenzie, 1961; Sharpe, 1970
11 Hanson and Walles, 1970, p. 119
12 Fayol, 1916
13 Urwick, 1942
14 Mooney, 1947
15 Simon, 1945; Woodward, 1958
16 Burns and Stalker, 1961
17 Gladden, 1961
18 Cmnd. 4506
19 Maud, 1967

Chapter 3
Decentralization

Most general textbooks on individual countries ignore the subject matter of this chapter, except possibly for local government, which may be given a separate section of its own. Even when this occurs, local government is likely to be the topic whose treatment is least satisfactory. Books devoted to public administration or to the administrative process in an individual country seem to be equally deficient, even though decentralization provides the machinery of the 'operational' state and has an immediacy for the individual that central institutions lack.

The reason why general textbooks ignore decentralization, apart from local government, is that very little research and writing has been devoted to it, as a survey of the specialized journals will reveal. Articles on field administration, the local courts and the working of the public corporations in Britain are rare; it is only in recent years that Northern Ireland, Wales and Scotland have attracted attention, and the Channel Islands and the Isle of Man are still *terrae incognitae*. Until the appointment of the Crowther (now Kilbrandon) Commission[1] official enquiries were conspicuously lacking, and even those, for instance into the civil service,[2] which might reasonably have been expected to deal with aspects of decentralization did not do so.

Yet decentralization comes as near as possible to being a universal process of modern government and a universal part of the structure of the modern state. Only the very smallest states do not find it necessary to adopt extensive decentralized machinery of government; many of the territorial and functional parts of larger systems also find it desirable, if not necessary, to create their own internal decentralization.

It will be noted that we have conceived of decentralization as a process rather than as a particular state of affairs. Its study has been marked by considerable terminological confusion, as different writers have proposed different meanings for 'devolution', 'deconcentration', 'regionalism', etc., and sometimes modified them with adjectives such as 'administrative' or 'political'.

To avoid the confusions of traditional terms we have stipulated that decentralization is a process whereby the total territory of state, public body or recognizable part of state is divided into two or more parts for its purposes, and for each smaller part an institution or organization is created with jurisdiction over that part only and with a prescribed range of functional authority.

There are two major consequences of this definition. First, the notion of the centre is a relative one – relative to a process of decentralizing – and secondly, the process is not limited to the creation of the major subdivisions of the unitary state. It is found *within* each of the major territorial subdivisions of a country; *within* each state in a federal system; *within* extensive local government units; *within* central government departments; *within* many public corporations. In principle there is no reason why the process should end until the individual is reached, just as the process of aggregation may continue until all the world is included.

This phenomenon we will call 'multiple decentralization'; double decentralization occurs when a territorial part of a larger whole is further divided; if the process is repeated then triple decentralization occurs, and so on. The student of public administration must be vitally concerned with this phenomenon and with all the different forms that it may take.

Studying Decentralization

In an earlier chapter a brief description was given of different ways of classifying decentralized administrative bodies, and a list of types with examples used to indicate to the reader what sort of things were intended to be included under this heading. Now it is time to change to a different approach – one which uses the three key characteristics of all decentralized systems as variables. The great advantage of the 'variable' approach is that it enables one to see the similarities of administrative structure irrespective of the level of government in which they occur. It applies to the machinery of the unitary state, to the administrative organization within provinces of regions of a federal state, to extensive local authorities and to the decentralized arrangements of public corporations.

Areas

To avoid confusion an *area* is defined as any distinct part of a country's territory which is recognized in the system of government and which has a governmental institution responsible for it alone. It may also be conceived in cartographic terms; that is, as a map whose lines represent the boundaries of territorial jurisdictions. No distinction is here drawn between types of area such as regions and neighbourhoods.

There are two approaches to the study of the division of a territory into separate parts. The first is the *causal* approach which seeks to account for any existing system of areas and boundaries in terms of the operation of social, economic and political forces in the past (the historical approach) or in terms of the forces of human geography (the spatial or locational approach). In each case (the two may in fact be used together) the areas are regarded as 'natural' phenomena, to be accounted for by whatever means are thought to be appropriate or defensible.

The second is the *principles* approach whereby areas are thought of as the artefacts of man, to be created and recreated according to the operation of a set of principles of rational decision-making behaviour by those responsible for the pattern itself. There is no reason why the decision maker should not take into account the same forces as does the person explaining the pattern, but he will treat them as something to be adapted and manipulated in the pursuit of stated values.

A distinction must be drawn between two types of area – the traditional territorial divisions of the state, which we have called the 'special status areas' and the areas into which the country is divided in a regular and systematic manner. The first are created and sustained because their separate identity is recognized by their citizens and by others within the country as meriting special treatment. Most large countries have parts whose special characteristics have been and are recognized as justifying a special place in the constitutional structure of the state.

It will be discovered that there is a connection between the type of area and the approach to its study that seems most appropriate. The *causal* approach may be seen in relation to Northern Ireland (political forces), Scotland and Wales (historical and cultural development), offshore islands (locational factors) and new state movements in federations (many factors). In discussions of the identity and boundaries of these areas little or no reference is made to technical considerations in the provision of public services, either from the point of view of the citizen as recipient or the centre as provider. The area is accepted as a fact of the governmental structure, and only extreme radicals will challenge its existence.

Other areas of public administration, however, tend to be discussed in terms of their reasonableness as bases for the provision of public services, and they are created and recreated by the application of 'principles' of area delimitation. Central departments and public corporations revise their systems of local and regional areas fairly frequently; local government structure however displays an interesting tension between rational and traditional considerations. Few would doubt that local authority areas and boundaries ought to be closely related to the services for which they are responsible, yet many local government units have had a long history and possess great salience for their inhabitants.

SPECIAL STATUS AREAS

Many states, whether they be federal or unitary in constitutional theory, have attached to or associated with them territories which are not ordinary parts of the political system. In federal states this means that they are not provinces, regions or states; in unitary systems they are not governed through the conventional machinery of decentralization – field administration, local government etc. – yet in both cases they are not in international law or international practice independent states.

The condition of being a special status area is not a simple phenomenon; on the contrary the phrase merely indicates a location on a continuum which ranges from complete assimilation as part of a state to complete independence recognized in the international system. This continuum may be represented for heuristic purposes in the manner of figure 5. Logically of course all of the special statuses are alternatives both to integration and to independence, but it is helpful to see some of them as one rather than the other.

There has been virtually no research or analysis of these conditions and their implications for our understanding of the pro-

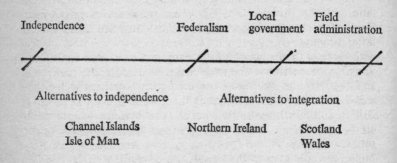

Fig. 5.　**The Independence – Dependence Continuum**

cesses of modern government. It is of course legitimate to abstract
a special status area from the political system of which it is a
part, just as local authorities and federal provinces, when they
are studied as individual entities, are abstracted from the state of
which they are parts, and the state itself is abstracted from the
international system when its government and politics are the
objects of interest. But this has rarely been done in the case of the
special status areas. Nor has the other aspect of their governance
– their relations with the larger unit – been given much attention,
even though from the point of view of the ardent devolutionist
these are the most significant cases or experiments.

It is a consequence of their *special* status that they cannot be
grouped into a few simple categories; each one tends to have a
unique constitutional position, though of course there are broad
similarities between some of them. Equally there can be no simple
test for inclusion or exclusion from this set.

The British Isles – a set of islands off the north-west coast of
the Eurasian land mass – exhibit a more complicated pattern of
territorial differentiation than is commonly assumed. Most people
are aware that the southern part of the second largest of the islands
is an independent state in international law, even though its

economic, social and political systems are entwined with those of the rest, but the remainder of the geographical structure is little understood.

The core area is England with almost four-fifths of the population of the British Isles. For most purposes of government England is closely integrated with Wales and Scotland, but the latter have their own general institutions of government which deal with some of the functions of the state within the Principality and Kingdom respectively. The three together are correctly referred to as Great Britain. The latter is united with Northern Ireland for some purposes of government as the United Kingdom of Great Britain and Northern Ireland, but the province created out of the six north-eastern counties of Ireland has its own political institutions, responsible for a wide range of governmental activities. Ninety-five per cent of the population of the British Isles live in the United Kingdom.

Most of the small offshore islands are parts of England (the Scilly Isles, the Isle of Wight), Wales (Bardsey, Anglesey), or Scotland (Orkney, Shetland, the Hebrides) but there are two groups which are not part of the United Kingdom in any form. The Isle of Man is a crown possession with its own distinctive government, whilst the Channel Islands constitute a geographical expression – the name of a group of crown possessions. The islands are organized into two bailiwicks, Jersey and Guernsey, and the latter has its own dependencies in Alderney and Sark, each with its own governmental institutions.

Figure 6 presents the structure of the British Isles in terms of the distinct traditional areas within them. Population figures are given to indicate relative sizes, as this is an important factor in understanding their government.

The governmental systems of Wales and Scotland are very clearly alternatives to integration as they are not treated in the same way as an English region, say East Anglia, in a number of specific ways, and have institutions which are concerned in limited ways with their territories only. In contrast the Channel Islands and the Isle of Man enjoy considerably more autonomy than do provinces in a federal system, the former more so than the latter. They are obviously alternatives to independence.

The best known case is that of Northern Ireland which will have known at least three distinct systems of government within the space of a few years – the traditional system established by the *Government of Ireland Act, 1920*, direct rule, and the system created by the *Northern Ireland Constitution Act, 1973*. All three systems have one thing in common – they are alternatives to both of two forms of integration – with the Republic to the south and with the mainland to the east. Both direct rule and the 1973 system provide for greater integration than did the Stormont system, but some of its citizens still prefer integration not with Great Britain but with the rest of the island. At the time of writing it appears that a fourth system may be emerging.

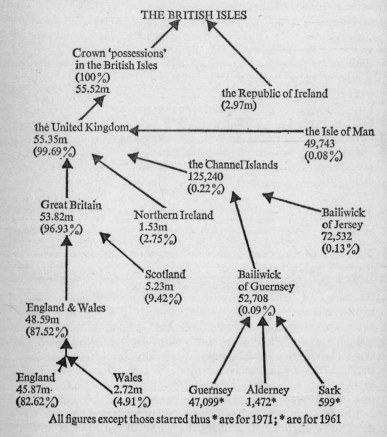

THE BRITISH ISLES

Crown 'possessions'
in the British Isles
(100%)
55.52m

the Republic of Ireland
(2.97m)

the United Kingdom
55.35m
(99.69%)

the Isle of Man
49,743
(0.08%)

the Channel Islands
125,240
(0.22%)

Great Britain
53.82m
(96.93%)

Northern Ireland
1.53m
(2.75%)

Bailiwick
of Jersey
72,532
(0.13%)

Scotland
5.23m
(9.42%)

Bailiwick
of Guernsey
52,708
(0.09%)

England & Wales
48.59m
(87.52%)

England
45.87m·
(82.62%)

Wales
2.72m
(4.91%)

Guernsey
47,099*

Alderney
1,472*

Sark
599*

All figures except those starred thus * are for 1971; * are for 1961

Fig. 6. **The Territorial Divisions of the British Isles**

'RATIONAL' AREAS OF GOVERNMENT

We now turn to a different sort of area and a different sort of study – the approach through principles of area delimitation. The process of subdivision (and re-subdivision) according to the convenience of the centre is found not only in England (the metropolitan or core area) but also in each of the special status areas itself. Thus, whilst the English local government system was being reformed the same process was occurring in relation to Wales, Scotland and Northern Ireland, in each case separately from the others (though the English and Welsh parts were intertwined).

The best way of studying the creation of territorial patterns of areas is through the concept of *principles*, because those responsible for the drawing of the boundaries of areas themselves think in such terms. But as *principle* is a word with a number of distinct meanings in political science it is important to characterize it carefully. In this context a principle is a rule of decision-making behaviour of some generality which offers a guarantee that if it is followed the actor will be better off in some specifiable way.

In the following discussion we are going to illustrate the problems of creating a pattern of areas from the local government system, partly because of the greater knowledge of local government reform and partly because the dilemmas of decentralization are better illustrated in this sphere than in any other.

There are basically two types of principle of area delimitation in public administration. The first consists of those that help to determine the characteristics of the overall pattern; the second of the principles of differentiation, those that help to determine the division of the total area into its separate parts. It will be seen that the arguments over the principles of the overall pattern are now mainly of historic interest, but the principles of differentiation are still highly controversial.

The first requirement is that the pattern should be *complete* in that it should apply to the whole of the (relevant) territory; that is, there should be, in the language of the nineteenth century, no extra-parochial places – places which are outside the jurisdiction of any authority of a given type. For those public activities, such as coal mining, national parks and port health, which do not occur in all parts of the country, it is first necessary to specify the relevant territory. As a complement to this no point of land should be within the jurisdiction of more than one authority of a given type, though of course an area may be used by several different public bodies without there being any clash of authority.

These two criteria may be summarized thus: no point of land should be in less than or more than one area of the same type.

It is also generally accepted that each area should be continuous in the sense that no part of it should be spatially detached from the rest. This was the problem of the *outliers* in nineteenth-century local government. An extension of this line of reasoning is to be found in the requirement of *compactness*, for an irregular area may have the same effects as a discontinuous one.

In local government the battle for these three criteria was largely won in the nineteenth century; the adverse effects for citizens and administrators can easily be appreciated in each case, but many good illustrations are given in the early pages of V. D. Lipman.[3]

Another requirement is that the pattern of areas should be clear both to the official and the citizen; that is, the boundary as a line on the ground should be easily known and marked. This is largely a matter of relating the line to other factors such as physical features (rivers, mountains, etc.), features of social geography such as social watersheds, and the settlement pattern. These may be conflicting bases for the identification of boundaries as lines. Again it can easily be seen that following this principle will promote certain typical citizen and official values.

Sometimes it is felt that the *number* of areas is important as this relates to span of control in the centre and to the average size of areas in terms of workload. It is also felt that areas should be equal in size in order to equalize the work to be done by each authority. Neither of these is today a very popular principle, probably because it is hard to relate them to any material advantage to citizen or official. In fact one might well argue that unequal sizes of area provide better career prospects for staff, more flexibility in promotion and retirement policy and greater possibility of adapting to the dictates of the principles of differentiation.

It might be thought that a country should be divided up into a system of areas for *all* purposes of government; that public services should be decentralized to a set of areas common to all of them. This indeed was the system used in earlier times; it was the foundation of imperial administration and of the autocratic regimes of continental Europe and is still associated with developing countries, military regimes and states threatened with internal and external disruption.

But everywhere the use of general systems of areas is in decline as the increasingly professional and technical nature of modern governmental activities leads to demands for areas and boundaries adapted to the special needs of each service. Some countries do not have a system of general areas at all, other than local government ones; others have such a system in formal terms but use it as the basis for departures from the common pattern or struggle to maintain it against the pressures of specialization. In Britain the structure of local government provides the only general focus of the overall pattern of decentralization, and other areas, both public and private, are adapted to it.

The arguments for and against general as opposed to special purpose areas cannot be dealt with in a simple manner. The choice is one which depends partly on the political and social circumstances of the regime in which the decentralization is taking place and partly on the outcome of the discussion of the principles of differentiation.

Principles of differentiation are those which are used to determine where the lines that mark boundaries should be drawn; they are principles of division. In public administration two types of principle of differentiation have been of general importance. The first relates the pattern of areas to the spatial distribution of communities and living patterns, on the grounds that a system which coheres with people's daily lives is more easily understood and more convenient to them. The second relates the areas to the technical characteristics of individual public services, on the grounds that certain areas are more efficient or effective for the provision of one service than are other areas. The characteristics of the areas are held to determine or influence the ease with which a service can be properly provided.

The first is reflected in discussions of the location of public office buildings and in such statements as 'the city region ought to be the basis of local government reorganization', whilst the second is reflected in arguments about the boundaries of metropolitan areas for planning purposes and such statements as 'Rutland was too small to be an administrative county'. Both types of principle are much more controversial than most of those previously discussed but unfortunately they still belong to a sphere of public administration in which intuition and prejudice dominate dis-

A.B.   D

cussion. We therefore intend to discuss the logic of the common arguments in some detail, since this is an especially important consideration where rational behaviour is being considered.

The concept of *community* is a difficult one to use properly in the social sciences and the difficulty is also encountered in public administration. It may be defined in a number of ways and the problem then is to adhere to the chosen definition without slipping unnoticed into another meaning. In fact it is impossible to divorce the meaning of the word from the methods used to identify empirically distinct examples of it.

In its sociological sense it implies a reference to a pattern of interactions between people, but patterns may be described in many different ways and may be approximated with strong or weak justification. There are at least four ways of identifying communities in practice.

First, they may be equated with *distinct settlement patterns*. This method has the advantage of easy intelligibility and simple use. For instance, a person flying over England soon becomes aware of a social landscape showing varied visual patterns. In some places there are only scattered dwellings; in others small or large nodes of buildings, usually called 'villages' or 'hamlets'. Then there are the larger groupings, towns and cities and finally the massive conglomerations called 'conurbations'. These patterns may be mapped or shown by aerial photography.

Secondly, they may be equated with *homogeneous* areas, distinguished on grounds of some social characteristic such as economic activity, race or religion. This method is widely used in geography and leads to the series of maps at the end of large atlases, showing vegetation and climatic regions identified by dominant features.

The above two methods are relatively easily used but they are only justified if they are reasonable approximations of the pattern of social life.

Thirdly, they may be identified by an examination of the spatial patterns of social life. A spatially distributed community (as opposed to an organizational or occupational one) has the points within it related to each other behaviourally in a regular fashion. The relations may be in terms of economic transactions, but more commonly personal mobility is used as the basis for delimiting communities (economic transactions often involve personal mobility). Amongst the aspects of mobility usually chosen are the diurnal ones of commuting, shopping and recreation, and the long-term one of residential change.

Any of these aspects of social life may be made the basis of a map, by calculating the score of each point in relation to a chosen central point, and then drawing lines joining points with equal scores. The result will look like the familiar contour maps of physical geography.

Though this obviously is the most appropriate meaning of *community*, it is also the most difficult to use in practice. There are parts of the country where social geography is simple but in many parts the situation is extremely complicated for several reasons. There are problems of discontinuities in behaviour, over-lapping communities, non-coincidental maps of different aspects, and the weighting of different aspects of life. If the patterns are approximated by settlements or by some other easily observable feature of social life then the problems are more soluble.

The fourth method of identifying *community* is by asking people which they belong to, and mapping the answers. The only system-atic way of doing this is by questionnaire and interview methods. Unfortunately such research methods are difficult to employ properly and it seems that the few studies that there are have fallen foul of the usual pitfalls, including the self-answering question and problems of validity and reliability. Surveys of this sort also meet the problem of what to do if people's responses and behaviour diverge.

It is easy to show how a system of areas which is related closely to the pattern of daily life is likely to be both more convenient and intelligible to citizens and thus to promote values that many citizens actually have. If administrative areas coincide with social areas then it is simple for the citizen to integrate his public and private activities.

A service principle is one which relates the performance of a public function or the provision of a public service to some definite characteristic of the areas themselves, and shows how, by creating areas having this characteristic, citizens will be in some clear sense better off. Any feature of the area as area may be used, provided only that it is systematically connected with some value or values, but in practice only two types of charac-teristic have attracted much attention in the past. One type of factor is comprised of geographical characteristics and the other is simply scale of operation.

Areas have precise geographical characteristics, both physical and human. It is fairly easy to see how these factors influence the way certain public services are provided and have significant consequences for the citizen as consumer.

Many of the factors studied in physical geography can be shown to be closely related to proper provision of certain services. Climate, for instance, influences air pollution measures and water supply, flood control and drainage. These services are also affected by topographical factors, for instance the pattern of catchment areas, and by sub-surface features of the terrain.

Geographical factors seem to be important in the traditional services as mentioned above; newer services tend to be influenced by the factors of human geography. Planning, economic development and housing are strongly influenced by the composition and distribution of the population. Public transport and highways both influence and are influenced by the distribution of the population. The relationships between the organization of the police and the spatial patterns of society provide a good example of the influence of changing social geographical factors.

There are two aspects of the population of an area – its size and its composition. But in practice the latter is mainly important in as much as it serves to modify the effect of size measured in crude terms. Size of population has long been thought to be of crucial importance in determining the efficiency with which certain services are provided, particularly as in public services it often is a proxy for *scale of operation*. At different times however it has been argued that there are minimum, maximum or optimum sizes.

Originally this belief was an intuitive one, often thought not to need rigorous proof. But as the intuitions of different people pointed in different directions, it was found necessary to try to replace commonsense with more systematic analysis. Two sorts of attempt may be made to discover what the relationships are between scale of operation and measures of performance by a public body in individual services.

The first way is to try to use the methods of econometricians which aim to determine the supply and demand functions of industrial firms in particular industries. There are obvious differences between the two types of situation; in particular the products of public services are not normally bought and sold so that it is necessary to obtain some non-monetary measure of performance, or simply to equate monetary costs with the product. The problem is to find out what the empirical relationship is for a set of local authorities (or other public bodies) between this measure of 'value' and scale of operation.

Let it be assumed that y is the measure of performance and x the size of population served by a local authority (standing as a proxy for scale of operation). Both of these are variables, usually continuous ones, with the sort of mathematical properties that permit the use of powerful statistical techniques. The next step is therefore to advance some hypothesis about their relationship: in conventional mathematical language to assert

$$y = f(x).$$

This is the simplest possible hypothesis; it states only that the two variables are related in some definite but unspecified way. The next step is therefore to try to specify the form of the relationship. If there is a relationship it may take any one of an infinite number of forms, but it is usual to examine the simplest first; for instance, that it was a simple linear relationship (one which is a straight line when drawn as a graph):

$$y = a + bx.$$

If this form of relationship does not appear to hold for a set of public bodies when the appropriate statistical method is used (this means that the correlation of the two variables is too weak to be statistically significant) then other forms may be tried.

If none of the forms involving only two variables are satisfactory then the original hypothesis may be modified thus:

$$y = f(x_1, x_2, x_3, \ldots)$$

x_2, x_3 etc. are the names of the other variables which are believed to be influential, such as wealth or density of population of the area.

Again it is necessary to examine some of the possible forms that the relationship between several variables may take, thus:

$$y = a + b_1x_1 + b_2x_2 + b_3x_3$$

If this is not satisfactory then the process of search may be repeated.

There have been a number of studies of this type on the performance by local authorities of some of the services for which they are responsible, but their conclusions have provided little support for the traditional intuitions that size of population served is the important factor. On the contrary there is clear evidence that there is no strong or definite relationship between size and performance in local government services.

There are two difficulties with all of these econometric type studies; they all require *a priori* stipulations of *good* performance and they all rely on evidence from the existing system of public bodies, which consists of a very biased sample of the range of possible bodies.

The logic of thinking about the relationships between size of population and the efficiency or effectiveness with which services are provided can be examined more fruitfully with the aid of a theoretical model which exposes the assumptions of the traditional discussion and throws light on the inconclusiveness of the statistical research. The model does not have any positive functions; it simply draws attention to a number of basic points that tend to be ignored in the conventional analyses of local government structure.

Certain conditions must be fulfilled before this model can be profitably used; these are:

(a) the service being investigated must be a labour intensive one.
(b) it must be provided for individuals by individuals.
(c) demand for it must be statutorily determined rather than by the forces of market demand.
(d) those who provide the service must work in groups or aggregate units.

Those who provide the service will be called 'workers' and those who receive it 'cases', though neither of these is a good idiomatic expression in relation to many individual services. Many public services, however, do fit the assumptions reasonably well; a high proportion of their total cost is wages and salaries, a right to benefit is statutorily determined, individuals 'consume' the service by dealing with public employees, and these work in offices, institutions or groups. Good examples include education, the social services and medical services, whilst by simple extensions, police and consumer protection activities also fit the model.

First, the definition of *case* must be provided by law and public policy, which will state who is entitled to receive the service. Then the *case-load* of the individual worker must be specified by reference to service standards, which again are determined by public policy. Finally, the minimum size of the aggregate unit or working group must be specified by reference to considerations of specialization and operational factors.

The combination of case-load and size of aggregate unit combine to determine a minimum number of cases below which either one of the service standards must suffer, or cost will be greater than necessary. The definition of case adopted above permits the assumption that the number of cases is a proportionate function of a homogeneous population.

Population size and service provision units may be brought together either by algebraic or graphical means and a minimum population determined below which either costs will be high or service standards violated.

Thus if public policy determines that the teacher-pupil ratio should be $1:15$, and that a school should contain at least fifteen teachers, then

$$c_1 = 15 \times 15 = 225$$

If school children are $\frac{1}{10}$ of a homogeneous population then

$$c_2 = p \div 10$$

If $c_1 = c_2$, then

$$225 = p \div 10$$

Therefore

$$p = 2250.$$

Alternatively the same analysis may be presented graphically.

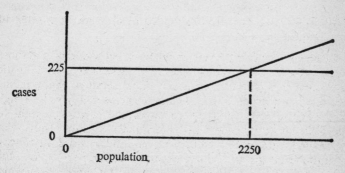

Fig. 7.   **The Size – Performance Relationship**

This model may be used in either of two ways: it may simply help to determine existing minimum sizes of population given existing standards of service provision, or it may be used to investigate the consequences of changing the assumptions in a number of ways – for instance, the service provision standards may be raised or lowered, the definition of case changed or a heterogeneous population considered.

There is not sufficient space here to elaborate on the second way but the results of such an analysis throw light on some of the problems encountered in the econometric approach, as well as the general problems of the logic of rational areas.

First, the minimum size of population for a given service or part of a service cannot be determined without prior decisions being taken about standards of service provision. If these are changed so is the conclusion of the analysis.

Secondly, the minimum size of population depends on the latter's composition in relevant respects.

Thirdly, the logic of the model dictates that the sizes established by its use, with certain other minor assumptions, are minima, not maxima or optima.

Fourthly, the confidence attaching to the conclusions is directly related to the confidence with which it is felt that service standards have been correctly specified. If these are uncertain then so are the conclusions about sizes of population.

There are also some obvious limitations on the usefulness of the analysis. In particular it does not apply to capital intensive services – which require a different form of model. Nor does it examine the position of small areas in a system of small areas only, in contrast to their position in a system also containing large areas.

A systematic application of this model to the list of relevant services would almost certainly reveal that in many cases the major activities constituting the service require relatively small populations and only the marginal ones will require very large populations. In these considerations lie the answers to the questions of the failure of statistical investigations and the unhelpfulness of traditional intuitions.

There are doubtless many other features of particular services with relevance to the determination of administrative areas, but to deal with these it is necessary to have a detailed knowledge of the services themselves – a point that frequently occurs in the study of public administration. There are also some general problems related to the factors discussed above which arise because governments are necessarily responsible for a variety of public activities.

First, the technical requirements of individual services often appear to point to different shapes and sizes of areas. There is no reason why the demands of the primarily geographical services should coincide with the demands of the population-determined services. Many of the services which depend on population are in practice hierarchies of activities, each with its own special requirements. Again these may not coincide. The consequence is that any practical system of areas is likely to involve either the weighting of the conflicting claims of different services or the creation of many special purpose areas for services or parts of a service.

Secondly, the areas suggested by the technical requirements of individual services may not coincide with the spatial distributions of communities. This is particularly likely to occur with the geographically influenced activities. The factors of physical geography will have influenced the development of the territorial pattern of living but not necessarily in a straightforward way.

Thirdly, any system proposed on the basis of 'rational' considerations (community and service principles) may conflict with demands that an area be treated as a 'traditional' or 'special status' area. This can be seen quite clearly by looking at the most stable of British boundaries – those between England and Wales and England and Scotland. Neither of these make much sense in terms of any of the rational considerations adduced above, but any attempt to change them would be extremely contentious and probably impossible.

Local government boundaries are of special interest to the student of areas of government. They do not obviously enjoy the status of provinces in a federal system of long standing, but neither do they have the impermanence of internal administrative boundaries in central government departments. Thus both types cf argument are deployed in discussions of local government reform. Local authorities are for the most part multi-functional; the pressure for the creation of special purpose areas for some local authority services is an example of the problem mentioned earlier. But equally the opposition to *ad hoc* bodies shows an awareness of the problems of overlapping jurisdictions and the co-ordination of authority.

Authority and Personnel

Within every area – whether it be a general or a special purpose one, or a neighbourhood, locality or region – there will be an *authority*; that is, some person or body with power to take decisions within the territorial and jurisdictional limitations centrally determined as part of the system of government, subject only to prescribed controls within those limits. This person or body will be referred to as the *area authority* and the definition adopted here clearly implies that the concept is a relative one – relative to the area as a jurisdiction.

Different types of area administration of public services are distinguished from each other by the number and type of *decisions taken* by the area authority, the nature and extent of *external supervision* of area decision making, the *form* the authority takes and the sort of people holding office or offices, and, as a sort of summary of the above points, the *degree of autonomy* in decision making the area achieves.

The importance of specifically recognizing the nature of area authority is well illustrated by the neglect of field administration in studies of modern government. Because of legal fictions it is often thought that there is no allocation of discretion to a field agent of a central body, but this is to misconstrue both the nature of government and the way governmental rules are framed. The abstract rules of public decision making can never be framed in such a way that no discretion is left to those that apply them. At the very least there is the problem of *recognition*, but most rules also involve *interpretation*, and in decentralized administration of all types there is a third feature – *adaptation* to varying area circumstances. This is a particularly Anglo-American mistake, because in those countries where generalist field officers are of great importance and high status (colonial, military and some continental regimes) students are much less likely to miss the discretionary elements in their behaviour.

The above characterization of *authority* concentrates on formal powers and legal limitations, but no account of *authority* is complete without a consideration of the effects (or functions) of the powers and the ways they are used or related to each other. The part that an area authority plays in the system of government may be quite different from that implied by a reading of the list of formal duties and powers. This role may or may not be recognized by the centre or the area itself.

The authority may take one of several forms. It may be lodged in a single person or in a collectivity, such as a council, board or committee. It may be personified to the outside world (including the citizens of the area) as a building or an institution. Though insiders may well have an understanding of the structure of power within the walls of an office block, outsiders may have to treat the building as an undifferentiated institution. The study of power relations within a decentralized authority, however, raises problems which cannot be treated here.

Authority requires an *authority-holder* or *holders*. The contrast, following Weber, is between the office as an enduring formal social role and the temporary occupant of it. The impersonal characteristics of the office help to account for the behaviour of office-holder, but do not completely determine it. It is also necessary to look at the latter as individuals.

In an earlier chapter we presented a list of types of decentralized administration, distinguished by virtue of their decision-making roles. By concentrating on decision making we relate our discussion of decentralization to our general conception of public bodies, and also provide some guidelines for understanding different types in practical operation.

For instance, the nature of the decision-making powers of the area authority partly determines the potentiality of the system for exploitation in the pursuit of values and perceptions other than those of the centre, and thus to affect local *adaptability* and *responsiveness* to varying conditions, the nature and extent of area *accountability*, *inequalities* between areas, the degree of technical *expertise* involved in decision making, and the *integrity* of the state.

The same points may be made about personnel. Different types of person are more or less likely to try to exploit the potentialities of the system in the pursuit of non-central values. Public office holders may be examined under two headings: first, their characteristics, which derive from the administrative system itself – those determined by the formal rules governing the occupancy of the office – selection, training, tenure, career patterns, qualifications, dismissal, remuneration etc.; secondly, empirical characteristics deriving from their membership of the rest of society – occupation, religion, partisanship, birthplace etc. Differential participation is as important at the local and regional levels as it is at the national.

Each type of authority determines the special formal features that will characterize its holders, and these will relate directly or indirectly to their behaviour as public officials. Some of these have been implied in our earlier discussion, but we must pick out three of special importance in field administration, and three further ones for lay authority.

First, the status of a field officer within the organization itself is of great importance, particularly in comparison with headquarters staff. This is partly a matter of salary grading within the hierarchy and partly a matter of how people are selected – their qualifications – both of which will be reflected in the prestige that area employment enjoys in the parent body. It is sometimes said that the local government world is very sensitive to the status of regional and local civil servants with whom it deals, and knows how far a particular individual is authoritative.

Secondly, field officers may follow any one of several career patterns. They move from area to area, or rise higher in the ranks of their own area. They may move between area and headquarters and back again. They may be recruited locally or nationally.

Thirdly, field officers will have varying status within the area itself. These may be presumed to be a function of their status within the organization, the openness with which their duties are performed and their impact on the life of the area. Some are completely unknown outside a limited circle whilst others are significant figures in their community.

These three characteristics are important in the study of decentralization generally because they affect the way local values and perceptions enter into decision making, the power of the locality against the centre, the standing of one public body against another, and generally, the local 'face' of the state.

As we have seen, the major differences between lay and field authority lie in career patterns, including selection and transferability, and in relations with the parent body.

Lay personnel may be appointed or elected. Obviously, the processes of election give a person greater potential for autonomy, since dismissal is not usually in the hands of the centre. Some appointed persons are chosen in the area, but many are appointed by the centre and subject to periodic renewal. Some appointment processes give the centre more power than others.

Whatever the process of selection the person holding lay authority will almost invariably be a local person and not subject to the transferability rules that govern field officers. Thus, potentially the connections between the area and the holder of public office are stronger in lay authority than field authority.

A further aspect of the relations between public officials and the area lies in their membership of other organizations in the area. Lay office-holders are likely to belong to a number of area organizations, including pressure groups and political parties, which will give them a perspective and position which the field officer is likely to lack. They are also sources of power in relations with the centre.

As election processes are externally uncontrollable, that is, in the pursuit of externally specified values, whilst appointment processes are not, at least in principle, the degree of relevant expertise of office-holders in this category will vary tremendously, and will in fact be an entirely fortuitous matter. The same point arises if appointment is on representative rather than technical grounds.

The combination of these differences may be thought to give lay personnel in general greater freedom in relation to the centre than have field officers, and this must command support as a generalization. But it is only a potentiality unless it is exploited. Lay authority may be restricted by lack of expertise and by specific detailed controls.

A common assumption in discussions of political systems, both by participants and academic observers, is that the sort of people who achieve public office is an important factor in understanding the decision-making behaviour of public authorities. This is made frequently in studies of national government – hence research into the social characteristics of members of legislatures, cabinets and the higher civil service. Little has been done systematically on area personnel generally but it is possible to create a realistic picture from a variety of sources, some rigorously constructed and others more impressionistic.

We have chosen to consider four major characteristics of individuals which are usually thought to be important in such a context – *sex*, *age*, the *occupation/social class/education* complex, and *partisanship*. It will be found that not all these have the same meaning in each type of decentralization.

Social Trends no. 3[4] reported that 51·3 per cent of the population of Britain was female, yet only in the lower levels of the civil service did they approach this proportion. There are few women in leadership positions in either lay or field authority. For instance, an examination of the *Municipal Year Book* reveals that only a negligible number of chief officer posts are held by women even though women form a substantial part of the local government service. Women were completely or virtually completely absent (less than 1 per cent) from the headship of departments in the protective services (fire, police, inspectorates), the environmental services (engineering, architecture, planning, surveying) and from the strategic posts of clerk and treasurer. Surprisingly, education and personal health are also of this order – 2·8 per cent of all medical officers were female. Even in the more favourable departments such as social services, libraries, museums, and housing, the proportion rarely rises above 20 per cent.

It will be rightly pointed out that much of this is intelligible in a very simple way. The professions which provide many of the top local government officers are themselves overwhelmingly male, and were perhaps more so when the present cohort of chief officers was educated. In some of the services this simple explanation will not suffice but unfortunately this is not the place to explore the mechanisms of selection to public office.

In dealing with the age factor we must distinguish between lay and field authority. The latter are usually governed by retirement rules prescribing 65 or 60 years as the terminal age. Given career patterns it is not surprising that many senior field officers are in the last decade of their employment. The influence of age is seen most clearly in lay authority where very high proportions of boards, councils and committees are over 60. In some spheres the problem of old age is so marked that there have been demands for the introduction of retirement ages for membership of these also.

Social class also requires a distinction between lay and field authority. Members of boards, committees etc., have been shown on many occasions to be overwhelmingly middle class as compared with the population from which they are drawn. But as the field officers with which we are concerned are necessarily middle class, and usually highly educated, we have to use parental status as the relevant measure of social class. Again we find an over-representation of the middle class, this time in terms of origin.

The above descriptions might be summarized as follows: the British state in its operational aspects is a male bourgeois gerontocracy.

Partisanship is a much more difficult factor to investigate but also a theoretically more important one. The best place to look at party affiliations of public office holders is in local government, and the consequences of opposed party control of different levels of government can be examined in some detail. But the partisanship, if any, of field officers is completely unstudied in Britain, though not in other countries, even if it is possible to make educated guesses.

It is worth remembering that in the above discussion we have been concerned only with the most prominent of area office holders. But the field office itself will contain a variety of people of differing structural and operational significances. It will be a miniature hierarchy, containing counter clerks and front line operatives, as well as heads of the agency – postmasters, regional directors etc. Lay authority itself may also have a large number of employees organized into an administrative hierarchy. In both cases we know virtually nothing about their characteristics.

The four factors mentioned above do not exhaust the list of those that may be important. In some countries, language, religion or race may be the characteristics which are significant in the study of area personnel. There is however one other factor which is of general significance in decentralization – *localism*, the degree of attachment the person has to the area. This is obviously conceived as an attitude, but it is often measured indirectly by behavioural factors such as birth and childhood, length of residence, commuting, shopping, recreation. This factor is itself influenced by the characteristics of area public office and itself influences the working of the system.

Local Government

In public administration much greater attention is given to local government than to any other form of decentralization. This reflects its greater general salience in the system of government. In Britain about 10 per cent of the labour force is employed by local authorities, and they spend over 11 per cent (an increasing proportion) of the national income. Though J. S. Mill had different circumstances in mind when he wrote 'it is but a small portion of the public business of a country that can be well done, or safely attempted, by the central authorities', his belief has been repeated frequently since that time.[5] It is reflected in the debate on *local self-government* in developing and, to a lesser extent, developed countries today. In fact the spatial distribution of power and the role of subordinate territorial entities has been a topic of some importance in traditional political thought, though often ignored by the historians of political ideas.

In addition the relative openness of its activities has led to greater academic knowledge of it and systematic research into the problems of decentralization as illustrated by it. Many of the formal processes are open to inspection; council meetings and some committees may be attended by press and public; there is often a local newspaper which gives prominence to its work, the council has to publish many of the details of its operations and decisions, and in many areas political parties make it a primary focus of their conflict. Local government boundaries have greater operational significance and force citizens to become aware that their rights and duties, including the amount of taxes they pay, depend on what their local authority does.

The third reason for the stress on local government is that its distinctive characteristics create very marked contrasts with other forms of decentralization. Thus, it is regarded as having a greater potential for illuminating the general problems of decentralization than have many other forms.

CHARACTERISTICS OF LOCAL GOVERNMENT

No satisfactory *definition* of local government has ever been devised, partly because the significance of different attributes changes with time and place. It is however possible to specify four characteristics of modern *primary* local government which serve some of the functions of a definition – they delimit the field of interest and point to the major features of academic concern.

First, local government has a well-defined *structure*; that is, a territorial pattern of local authorities, each with a jurisdiction limited in respect of area and services. All forms of decentralization have a structure in this sense but in local government it is a fact of great salience and operational significance, about which sentiments and vested interests develop, giving it a permanence. Many other systems of areas are based on local government boundaries.

Secondly, primary local authorities are *elected* not appointed. This fact creates the whole machinery of local democracy and is the reason why the analytic device of treating local bodies as miniature political and administrative systems developed first in local government studies.

Thirdly, local authorities have a degree of *autonomy*, arising from independent powers of taxation and decision making, but are also subject to a number of specific controls and influences which restrict or modify their freedom. The formal autonomy and the specific restrictions create an obvious subject – central-local relations – which will serve as a model for our understanding of other types of decentralization.

Fourthly, local authorities are *multi-functional*. The individual local authority is responsible for a range of services in its area, though the range varies from one type to another. They are thus often described as 'omnibus' rather than '*ad hoc*'. This fact is one of the causes of the traditional pattern of internal organization by which local authorities exercise their rights and dispose of their duties.

Most countries have a system of primary local government even if only in principle – the system may have been suspended temporarily because of corruption, inefficiency, threats to internal security etc., but it is hoped eventually to restore it– but many will also have other types of local government body playing some part, sometimes a significant one, in the system of decentralization. These may be referred to as 'secondary' because they derive by indirect election, or nomination, from the primary authorities. In the typical example, say an English water board, the body was responsible for a single service in the territory of several primary authorities, and each of these had the duty of choosing a pre-determined number of members of the ruling body and of paying any precept asked of it towards the expenses of the board. It thus had the power of taxation. As its boundaries were those of primary authorities it had a well defined and permanent structure.

Secondary authorities could have a wide range of functions but usually in the twentieth century they are confined to a single service or a closely related group of activities. In Britain examples include port health authorities and joint burial boards; in America 'special districts' substantially meet the above criteria – they include districts for soil conservation, drainage, fire protection, urban water supply, cemeteries and above all education. In France the *district urbain* is a secondary authority with more extensive powers than any in Britain.

We remarked that the proliferation of appointed bodies at the national level produced a situation which made it very difficult to classify according to any simple scheme. The same is true at the local level where in recent years there has been the development of appointed bodies that are derived in part from local government, yet contain other elements. The new arrangements for the national health service and for water administration, as well as the older combined police authorities, illustrate this tendency.

The bodies mentioned above are all authorities in their own right but primary local government also generates a variety of institutional arrangements which are not literally separate authorities but which are administrative organizations which may achieve a considerable prominence and operational significance. Many of these are produced by the process of multiple decentralization mentioned earlier. The main examples are found in extensive local authorities, and include the authority's own field administration and equivalent to lay authority - appointed committees and executives. This phenomenon is likely to increase with the increase in size of local authorities in the new system. There are also joint arrangements between separate authorities which are usually called 'joint committees'.

PRIMARY LOCAL GOVERNMENT

We have already distinguished between simple and complex local government on the grounds of the number of levels a particular type contained. Prior to April 1974, English and Welsh local government consisted of three basic types of local government – two complex and one simple. From that date onwards it will consist of four distinct types, all of them complex. The traditional textbooks usually present these patterns in the form of an organization chart, showing the relations *within* a complex system as hierarchical. This is misleading as the relations between levels in multi-tier systems is rarely hierarchical, and a different sort of diagram is required to show the true natures of complex systems. (See figures 8 and 9.)

Though London government was (and still is) entirely two-tier, in the rest of England and Wales some large and medium-sized towns had single-tier local government whilst the rest of the country was a mixture of two- and three-tier systems. The single-tier or simple system contained only one primary authority – the county borough council – and this was responsible for all local government services other than those allocated in that part of the country to a secondary authority.

As a type of local government the administrative county contained basically two levels of authority, with a third found in some parts only. Each county had a county council responsible for certain local government services throughout the whole of the county. Its territory was divided into districts, each with its council responsible for some local government services within its area. There were three different legal types of district – two intended to be found in small and medium-sized towns, and the other in rural areas. The first two were the non-county borough

ADMINISTRATIVE COUNTIES (53%)**			GREATER LONDON (16%)**	COUNTY BOROUGHS (31%)**
level		authority		
first tier	CC (58)		GLC (1)	CBC (83)
second tier	NCBC (259)	UDC (522) · RDC (470)	GLBC* (33)	none
third tier	none	none · parish government (c. 11,000)	none	none

*including the City of London
**approximate proportions of the 1971 population of England & Wales
CC=county council
GLC=Greater London Council
CBC=county borough council
NCBC=non-county borough council
UDC=urban district council
RDC=rural district council
GLBC=Greater London borough council
parish government=rural borough council, parish meeting & parish council, parish meeting only, joint parish council, joint parish meeting.

Fig. 8. **The Traditional Primary System of Local Government**

and the urban district, the distinction between which was so largely a historical and ceremonial difference that they may be put together as town districts. The other type was the rural district which was itself further divided into parishes, each of which was supposed to have its own authority responsible for its territory only. Thus the rural district was a complex system within a complex system.

When the traditional pattern came under severe criticism, as it did from the 1930s onwards, most of the arguments advanced were in effect that the original principles had not been properly put into effect. It was alleged that the system had failed to adapt to changing social geography so that boundaries bore little relation to the facts of daily life. The conurbation, an urban form which was coming to be recognized as distinct from the large town, was not provided for, except in London (especially after 1963), and in many parts of the country the structure of local government divided areas of common interest or which made some sort of organic unity.

The changing technical characteristics of public services were another source of difficulty. As services became more and more internally differentiated those responsible for them demanded larger and larger areas of administration and greater population catchment areas. Though British local authorities tend to be very large by international standards, within each legal category there were many very small, sometimes minute, authorities, and their existence influenced governmental attitudes to all. The result of this was a constant pressure towards large units of administration – something with which we are familiar in other spheres – either through reform of local government or through the removal of services from local government control.

The third major criticism of the traditional pattern was that it created friction within the local government world, but this is something that cannot be accepted as it stands, for it is based on a misunderstanding of complex systems of local government. Multi-tier local government is a response to the existence of different levels of society, different levels of community and different technical requirements of individual public services; the interests that conflict in complex systems of local government are created by extra-governmental factors. As we shall see, this criticism has been explicitly rejected in the new local government system which is *entirely* multi-tier.

It should be realized, however, that the pattern of local authorities prior to 1974 withstood the tests of the principles of overall structure mentioned earlier in this chapter. There were only a few outliers left; extraparochial places had been eliminated and generally the boundaries were clearly marked even if they did not correspond in many places to socially significant lines on the ground.

Thus when reform came it was a matter of increasing the size of local authorities and remedying the obvious incompatibilities of areas and social geography. The creation of the new system was in the end a relatively simple operation.

First it was decided to leave Greater London unchanged. It had been reformed radically as recently as 1965 and in the opinion of many the reform was at least a qualified success. The argument against disturbing the members, officers and citizens of the metropolis was regarded as overwhelming.

Secondly, the distinction between England and Wales, introduced because of the demise of the Local Government Commission for Wales in 1963, was maintained into the new system. The structure of Welsh local government is set out in its own parts of the Act, even though in practice the system created looks very like one of the English variants – the non-metropolitan county.

Thirdly, it was decided that the whole system should be based on multi-tier local government. This meant the end of the county-borough as a legal form, though most individual authorities have survived as recognizable areas – as metropolitan or non-metropolitan districts.

Then it was decided that some parts of the country needed more radical treatment than others. These were the ones picked out for reform rather than reorganization, in the old terminology. The six major conurbations outside Greater London were chosen for metropolitan status – a complex system somewhat like the Greater London system in that the lower tier authorities were to be very large, and the whole structure was to be 'bottom heavy'. These were therefore taken out of the existing system of counties and county-boroughs. In addition geographically new areas were created around Bristol (Avon), the Lake District (Cumbria), the Humber estuary (Humberside) and Teesside (Cleveland). The latter four were to be non-metropolitan counties, 'top-heavy' structures with generally smaller lower-tier authorities.

The creation of these ten new areas left much of the country unchanged and some of it as 'rumps'. The new system in these parts was derived from the old by the operation of a few very simple rules. First, each old county or rump was merged with any county boroughs within its boundaries. This rule accounts for sixteen of the thirty-five remaining new areas. A further eleven are accounted for by this rule and a slight adjustment of boundary lines. Another five involve the above rules with the addition of neighbouring small administrative counties. This leaves only three and these are all ones which have been very seriously affected by the creation of the new areas. North Yorkshire is the residue after the creation of five of these areas; Lancashire had territory given to three new areas, two of which united to cut off part of the former county from the rest. This detached part was added to Cheshire, the third county to suffer badly, this time from the creation of two of the new areas. The only other area where noticeable changes have taken place is in the Oxon/Berks/Bucks region, where boundary adjustments have given markedly different shapes to Oxfordshire and Berkshire.

A similar analysis may be made of the changes in Welsh local government. Glamorgan was given a radical treatment, being divided into three new counties, each based on a former county borough, but the rest result from the simple rules mentioned above. Three new counties are mergers of three existing administrative counties, one a merger of two, and one a merger of a county and a county borough; in four of the five cases there were also minor boundary adjustments at the same time.

In the metropolitan areas and in Wales the district structure of each county was settled in the Act itself, perhaps a reflection of the work that had been undertaken previously on their problems. Most of the metropolitan districts are recognizably the same as the county boroughs they replace in terms of geographical area – they have a former county borough as their core, and adjacent small town districts have been added. Most of the Welsh districts have been created by simple mergers of rural and town districts to produce areas of at least an acceptable minimum size.

In the rest of England the process was entrusted to a boundary commission whose task it was in the first instance to produce a scheme in a very short time for the district structure of each of the non-metropolitan counties. This again turned out to be a simple operation (the time factor made it impossible to do anything else); most county boroughs and large town districts maintained their geographical identity as lower-tier authorities. For the rest the Boundary Commission simply merged groups of small town districts with neighbouring rural districts, to produce minimum-sized areas, balancing population against density.

In Wales existing parishes and town districts maintained their identities as communities, the new name for parish government, the third-tier throughout the greatest part of Welsh local government. Parishes were retained in England and some small town districts were also given this status, so that non-metropolitan local government is a mixture of two- and three-tier systems.

	ENGLAND NON-METROPOLITAN AREAS (54·5%)†	ENGLAND METROPOLITAN AREAS (24·0%)†	WALES (5·5%)†
level	authority		
first tier	NMCC (39)	MCC (6)	CC (8)
second tier	NMCDC (296)	MCDC (36)	CDC (37)
third tier	parish government‡	virtually none	community§

*the structure of local government in Greater London is left unchanged
†estimated proportions of the population of England and Wales
‡parishes to remain where they now exist and some new creations to be made
§communities=former parishes, ncbs and uds, with a few exceptions (Wales only)
NMCC=non-metropolitan county council
MCC=metropolitan county council
CC=county council (Wales only)
NMCDC=non-metropolitan county district council
MCDC=metropolitan county district council
CDC=county district council (Wales only)

Fig. 9. The New (1974) Structure of Local Government in England & Wales Outside Greater London*

To complete this picture of the new local government system it is necessary only to remark on the allocation of services within each structure. Though all are multi-tier they differ very much in that Greater London and metropolitan England have bottom-heavy systems whilst Wales and non-metropolitan England have top-heavy systems, the 'weight' of the structure being measured in terms of the services provided by each tier.

Local Authorities

MINIATURE POLITICAL AND ADMINISTRATIVE SYSTEMS

Just as when the government and politics of a particular state are studied, that state is abstracted from the international political system of which it is a part, so for analytical purposes the government and politics of a locality may be abstracted from the national system of which they are a part.

A local authority (analytically though not legally) is composed of two types of person – council members (sometimes called elected representatives) and employees (officials, paid staff etc.). Each type has its own characteristic form of aggregate organization – the first a committee system and the second a department structure – and a major structural aspect of decision making in a local authority lies in the transactions between official and member organization.

Membership of a local council is restricted to those with some definite connection to the area, at present defined by law as one of the following: the franchise, residence, property occupation or ownership, and principal place of work. There are also the usual disqualifications for felony, lunacy and foreign nationality. Members have traditionally been unpaid in Britain (unlike the United States) but they may claim various expenses and allowances related to the performance of their role.

All members (except the presiding officer) are legally equal in decision-making powers, that is, they each have one vote in collective decisions, but they may be very unequal in real power and status.

Local councils employ a great variety of staff. Some of these are specialists in a particular service (education, health, police etc.). Others are generalists – administrative and clerical staff of the sort found in all large organizations. There is also a great variety of 'outdoor' staff – the local government manual workers.

To some extent council members have traditionally carried out their duties and exercised their rights in the council meeting itself, but in most authorities there is an elaborate system of *committees* and *subcommittees* which provide the major focus for the elected representatives. The complexity of this system reflects both the *multifunctionality* mentioned above and the pressure on *elected* holders of authority to determine a large number of matters personally.

Committee systems must be described in terms of a large number of variables – size, number, pecking order, terms of reference, frequency of meeting, time of meeting, duration, functional role etc. The committee meeting is in itself an important part of the operational structure of the whole local authority, because it brings employees and members together.

In addition there are joint committees and area committees of extensive local authorities (an aspect likely to become more important in the future); the combination of all the different types of committee has produced a situation where the role of council member demands a considerable amount of time.

The key to understanding *employee organization* is to distinguish between the four major organizational locations – the institution, the area office, the depot, and the headquarters (which is internally differentiated into sections).

Many local authority employees are located in institutions such as schools, police stations and old people's homes. Often these regard themselves as separate from the local government service proper and have their own trade unions or professional associations. In extensive authorities the area or divisional office is an important feature; this is the authority's own field administration system. Outdoor staff are normally located in a building or site geographically separate from headquarters; and the generic name for this is 'depot'. (This is often a form of dispersal of offices.)

In the past most attention has been focused on headquarters itself because the central staff provide the basic structure of employee organization and the rest are attached to it. A group of 'locations' is a department. These vary in size, internal differentiation, status in the overall structure, composition etc. but they nearly all have one thing in common – in Etzioni's terminology they are *professional organizations*. The position of specialists in relation to generalists is exactly the opposite of that found in the civil service. The tensions and frustrations experienced by specialists in central government are felt by generalists in local government.

Central-Local Relations

If each local authority is an individual political and administrative system then the central government and the remainder of the governmental and political system are parts of its environment, both remote and proximate. For instance, the central government's economic and financial policies will affect a whole range of factors which will eventually become demands on the local authority; at the same time the centre will be making specific demands and requests of the authority to which it must respond directly.

The relationship between local authorities and the central government has been widely misunderstood. Local authorities have been treated as simple transmitters of impulses from the centre, or as 'will-less' agents of the government. The view that local government has been destroyed by an increasing central control has been stated frequently and has become part of the conventional wisdom of the subject. Research on a number of levels in the last five years (most of it taking its inspiration from the sort of considerations discussed above) has shown this position is untenable and that the accounts of local government in general textbooks are defective on this point.

A part of the variations in behaviour between local authorities can be accounted for in terms of the actions of the central government but this still leaves much unexplained. The local environment appears to account for another part of this variation but there remains a substantial amount which may be attributed to the fact that each local authority has its own internal structure of decision making and interacts with its environment in its own characteristic ways. Its behaviour cannot be seen simply as a function of the behaviour of the government of the day.

The system of central-local relations where the area authority is a local government unit must first be analysed in terms of the factors giving local authorities a greater degree of autonomy than those in most other forms of decentralization and secondly in terms of the factors pressing towards central intervention.

THE AUTONOMY OF LOCAL AUTHORITIES

The relative degree of autonomy of local authorities compared with field administration and appointed lay authority derives from several factors:

First, the *statutes allocating services* to authorities. Though in one sense these limit the powers of the locality they also provide a protection by prescribing the formal powers of the centre so that there are things that the centre can*not* do, sometimes except by a special procedure. Thus the discretion of the area authority is guaranteed to some extent by the limitations placed on central government and other public bodies.

Second, the fact of *popular election*. In western countries generally the fact that a person has been elected rather than appointed to a public office confers a certain legitimacy on his values and perceptions and is a source of confidence in dealings with other people in positions of authority. It enables an authority to exploit its formal powers more effectively in the pursuit of its own ends.

Third, the *independent powers of taxation*. The amount of money that an authority has at its disposal each year is not a fixed sum but is variable at the discretion of the locality. It is thus possible for local authorities to vary the range and intensity of their activities in a way that is not financially possible for other forms of local administration.

Fourth, the *territorial responsibility* of the authority. The fact that an authority deals with the specific problems of a defined area of land means that the questions it faces are in a sense substantially unique. 'Services' are abstractions created by the central legislature to suit central purposes and the concrete problems of areas and citizens do not necessarily fall into the formal categories so constructed. The solutions to the problems therefore also may not fall into neat categories.

The reality of the discretion that these factors help to create can be seen from an examination of the variability in service provision between areas that exists in the British local government system.

DEMANDS FOR CENTRAL CONTROL AND INFLUENCE

Perhaps because of the discretion described above there are strong pressures towards central intervention in local government affairs. In fact it might be argued that without considerable central influence and control over local authorities local government would be an unacceptable form of decentralization in many Western countries today.

The major demands for central intervention are:

First, the demand for *efficient and honest government*. As local authorities spend a large amount of public money and are an important part of the operational state there is a general demand, by centre and citizens alike, that they meet the usual standards of behaviour required of public authorities.

Second, the demand for *equality* by the centre. In western terms governments are generally concerned about differences between areas; thus the centre often wishes to promote equality of service provision or the achievement of minimum standards throughout the whole country.

Third, increasing *geographical mobility* of the population. The effect of diurnal and residential mobility is to lessen localism, promote knowledge of differences between areas and to reduce their acceptability. This growing impatience with a real variation in public services is probably also a result of the growth of the mass media.

Fourth, *regional and national elements* in public services. As the technical nature of local government services has changed towards increasing vertical differentiation (within the service itself) local government areas have become inappropriate. There are increasingly national and regional aspects of service provision which only the centre can properly tackle.

In these circumstances the demand for an unfettered discretion for local authorities (as some of the extremists in the local government world seem to want) is unrealistic and unreasonable. The problem is one of balance and interaction between levels of government.

THE BASIC PATTERN OF CENTRAL-LOCAL RELATIONS

The pattern of central-local relations can only be understood if certain assumptions are made. First, it must be assumed that each local authority and each separate part of the central government organization is an individual decision maker with its own set of values and perceptions which may or may not coincide with those of another.

Second, each individual authority has a series of moves open to it, to be used in the pursuit of its own aims and beliefs. These moves differ in severity of impact and frequency of use and can only be understood in connection with the moves made by other individuals.

Third, control and influence operate in both directions in the system of central-local relations. Not only does the centre exercise controls over local authorities but also they, individually and collectively, influence the centre.

Fourth, the pattern is structured by the central-local financial system which relates taxation and expenditure decisions at one level to those at the other. Thus both operate within the same overall framework – the national financial year.

The whole pattern can be analysed from the point of view of the centre and from the point of view of the locality. It is very important to undertake both analyses and to integrate the results in a general framework.

THE CENTRE

It is often forgotten that the centre is itself internally differentiated and that the separate parts may well act differently. In Britain the centre is generally oriented towards individual services as separate entities and thus collectively the centre views local authorities as collections of services defined by statute and departmental policy. This produces a fragmentation of the central-local control system, which is almost as likely to produce conflict within the centre as between centre and locality.

Traditionally the powers of the centre are conceived of as methods of control, but this is a mistake if it is regarded as being the whole story. It is important to distinguish control from influence and also the different forms each may take. In addition each plays a different part in the structure of moves open to the centre.

First, local authorities are subject to legislative and judicial control of their actions. Like other bodies and persons they are controlled by law and the courts, but this control tends to be more obvious in the case of local government because of the *'ultra vires'* doctrine which states in general that local authorities can only do those things which they are specifically empowered to do. Control of legality is mainly achieved through district audit, though there are also a variety of specific remedies against authorities through the ordinary courts.

It should be remembered that the central government is also bound by the law and the courts in its dealings with local authorities; the crucial difference is that it is in a much better position to change an inconvenient or ineffective statute.

Second, local authorities are controlled and influenced by government ministers and (in practical terms) by central departments themselves. The relations between ministers and local authorities are of a different character than those between Parliament and the courts and local government. The relations are characterized first by day-to-day activity and concern with routine matters; secondly by a great number of specific interactions repeated frequently; and thirdly by ministerial discretion which makes the relationship more flexible but also more uncertain from the point of view of the locality.

The difference between methods of control and methods of influence lies in a distinction between situations where it is envisaged that there is a conflict of wills between centre and locality and those where there is agreement. Methods of control are those which provide formally for the resolution of conflict in favour of the will of the centre, whilst those of influence are directed at removing the conflict by affecting the disposition of the locality.

Figure 10 presents a picture of these 'powers' as a pattern of moves available to the centre, the moves being used in accordance with the judgements of the centre as to the satisfactoriness of the situation or otherwise. When the centre (or a part of it) is satisfied with what is happening it will stop exploring the possibilities open to it. It may of course never be satisfied or may accept something as the best that can be achieved.

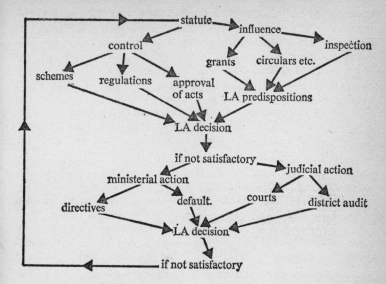

Fig. 10.   **The Centre's Moves**

THE LOCAL AUTHORITY

Local authorities have no direct statutory controls over the centre but often individually and collectively they appear to exert an influence over the decisions of central government departments and ministers. The basis of their influence is not clear but its reality can hardly be denied.

Individual local authorities exercise influence on departments through local political parties and the local MPs. Most of this sort of action focuses on the minister and on Parliament, though often only by implication, and is of an essentially private nature. But if an authority is dissatisfied by the results of the usual channels it may organize more public occasions such as petitions, deputations, hostile questions in Parliament, etc.

Collectively local authorities are organized in a series of pressure groups or associations which attempt to promote the interests of their members in general and in particular cases. Most of the local government professions are organized so that they can act as pressure groups on occasion. There is considerable prior discussion of legislation and statutory instruments by committees of the main associations and often ministers and departments like to obtain prior approval of the local government world for their proposed courses of action. Local government opinion is also well represented on royal commissions and committees of enquiry.

A considerable number of MPs (in both Houses) have had local government experience and there appears to be a general opinion in Parliament favourable to local government, thus enabling local authorities to obtain a sympathetic hearing and practical help in their conflicts with the central departments.

Figure 11 presents these means of influence as a pattern of moves open to local authorities in attempt to bring about a situation that is satisfactory to them. The search for such a situation continues until the local authority is satisfied or decides that something is the best it can achieve.

THE PATTERN OF CENTRAL-LOCAL RELATIONS

To construct a picture of the pattern of central-local relations it is necessary to bring together figures 10 and 11. Traditional discussions of this subject have been dominated by 'central control' and 'freedom' of local authorities. This is a wrong emphasis. It is more realistic to see it as a complex subject which starts from the possibility of a conflict of wills, values and interests between centre and localities and ends with a sort of reconciliation and adjustment of differences that previously existed. Local authorities are autonomous but not sovereign; the centre is powerful but not omnipotent.

There is perhaps a typical political process by which local and national interests and claims are balanced and reconciled.

If the central government *chooses* to make a service administered by local authorities a matter of national importance then it frames legislation in consultation with interested parties and sometimes (perhaps often) modifies it at their request. This legislation will lay duties on local authorities, give the central government the right to issue regulations and directives, also framed in consultation with interested parties and require some specific acts of local authorities to be approved by a minister.

The granting of approval is the occasion of discussion, perhaps even bargaining. The minister finds out about local authorities through inspection and requests for advice, as well as through the

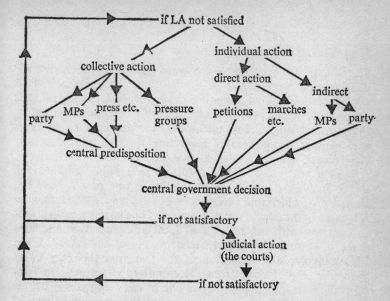

Fig. 11. **The Local Authority's Moves**

collection of statistical information. He embodies any superior technical knowledge he may have in speeches and circulars and makes his advice more palatable by giving specific grants, which are another type of occasion for discussion and negotiation.

Thus the balancing takes place through discussion and negotiation during periods of 'normalcy' but when one or both levels are dissatisfied then the tone of relations will be transformed. Local authorities may turn to opposition and strong public pressure; the centre may be forced to resort to one of the coercive measures such as default or even to legislation if it finds that the present system restricts it too much. As an extreme measure it could remove responsibility for a service from local government altogether. The change from 'normalcy' to 'crisis' appears to take place in Britain less frequently than in many other countries and thus the harsher aspects of central-local relations are less in evidence.

Field Administration

Though the French reserve the word 'deconcentration' for the phenomenon we consider in this section, the expression 'field administration' seems preferable, as it involves placing officials 'in the field'. It is usually contrasted with devolution, including local government, because the authority in any area is seen as an extension of the powers of the centre through a bureaucratic subordinate geographically separate from the rest.

Thus a field officer is a subordinate in a public authority or public body who carries out his duties in one part only of the territory for which that authority or body is responsible, and who is located in the area in which he works. Thus he has some features in common with other forms of local administration and also some in common with peripatetic officers of the centre. Some offices involve a combination of the two, and this may be of particular importance in some decentralized structures. His relationship with the parent body is one of *employment* and his relationships with every other member of that body are those of *hierarchy* (superordination, subordination, equality). He is thus typically, though not necessarily, a full-time, career member of a larger organization, appointed, promoted, remunerated, supervised, disciplined and retired by the usual bureaucratic means, differing from members of headquarters staff only in that he is spatially remote from the centre.

Most of these characteristics distinguish field officers from other personnel of decentralized administration, for instance, council members and the leaders of special status areas. In particular control of field officers is of the sort often referred to as 'bureaucratic', being generalized (as opposed to specific), continuous (as opposed to sporadic) and formless (as opposed to prescribed in detail). The significance of this can be seen if one contrasts the relationships between the centre within each type of local administration or special status area and its own field officers, and its relationships with the national government.

TYPES OF FIELD OFFICER

We have already drawn the major distinctions between the different types of field officer in Chapter Three.

Generalists tend to be found in systems where the emphasis is on the elemental activities of government – public order, public morals, external security, collection of taxes, protection of property – where societies are culturally unsophisticated and where the demand for public services is itself generalized. These conditions are still found today in imperial systems, under-developed countries and military regimes. The only recent development in the role of generalists has come from an increasing stress in some countries on the spatial integration of public activities *within* each area. Even here, however, the generalist is only an alternative to a system of local government.

The role of specialists can be illustrated by an examination of the organization of the large field office departments such as agriculture, employment or social security. The growing elaboration of the professional and scientific knowledge that is deployed within the services is reflected in the increasingly detailed specialization within the department. The pressure for expertness is generated both internally and externally and different systems try to come to terms with it in different ways.

FIELD ADMINISTRATION SYSTEMS

In any individual country a variety of kinds of field agency are likely to be found existing side by side; these, their relationships with each other and their relationships with other forms of decentralization constitute the *system* of field administration of that country.

We may distinguish two basic types of system, one based on the primacy of specialists and the other on the primacy of generalists. A *functional* system is dominated by the field officers of individual substantive services, each subject to the supervision of hierarchic superiors at regional or national levels, and related to each other at the area level only by *ad hoc* or informal arrangements. A *prefectoral* system is one in which structure of area administration is dominated by a generalist field officer who in some sense controls and supervises all other public officials in his area.

It is fairly easy to see how prefectoral systems are likely to be preferred in certain social and political conditions and by certain types of regime because they reflect an emphasis on the elemental activities of government – those necessary to the survival of the state – whilst functional systems reflect the pressures for technical expertise in the operations of the government as service provider. This latter tends to a result of the increasing 'sophistication' of society.

In a fully developed prefectoral system there is a high official of the state in the area who controls and supervises all other public officials and public bodies in his territorial jurisdiction and who may be personally in charge of certain functions of government, either continuously or sporadically (in emergencies etc.). He thus has a general concern with the working of the machinery of government and with the spatial impact of all the public services together. He will be responsible for the protection of both the citizen and the state, and for the maintenance of national unity.

Generalists usually stand in a special relationship to the centre – one of greater confidentiality and trust – and they are therefore expected to play a political role, not so much explicitly in the partisan sense (though this does also occur) but in the way they make use of formal powers. The power to provide public services can be used to promote other ends than those of the narrow sense of service provision to citizens.

Not all countries with an important generalist in the main areas of government give him all the powers and the role outlined above. First, there has been a tendency for specialists to encroach on his position as a result of the increasing professionalization of the public service. Secondly, there has been a decline in the relative (and in many cases the absolute) stress on the elemental functions of government as a result of expanded aims of central governments and the greater stability of many states in the face of forces of separatism. Thirdly, other forms of decentralized administration have shown an increasing ability to exert political power on their own behalf and thus to escape from generalist type supervision. Fourthly, there has been a decline (at least in Western countries) in the partisan roles of public servants generally.

Thus today generalists find it hard to maintain their former position and often the result is what is called 'an unintegrated prefectoral system'. But in military, totalitarian and one-party regimes the generalist has tended to remain in his former role.

In modern systems of government specialist field officers constitute the primary field administration and even if there is a generalist in the area he often appears to be an uneasy graft or addition to the fundamental organization of specialist officers.

It should be remembered that there is a constant drive towards further specialization arising from the expansion and greater differentiation of knowledge. Public services do not 'exist'; they are creations of the legislative activities of central governments and the latter have tended to respond in organization terms of the demands of 'disciplines' for recognition in the machinery of government. Thus many departments with large field office organizations are really collections of related specialisms.

Notes

1 Kilbrandon, 1973
2 Fulton, 1968
3 Lipman, 1949
4 HMSO, 1972
5 Mill, 1861

Chapter 4
Public Organization

In this chapter we continue the themes of Chapter Two. In contrast to the processes described in the previous chapter we will now examine the principles by which public functions are allocated to different types of public body, and the ways in which those bodies are internally organized.

Though every government inherits a system of departments of state, some of which, such as the Home Office and the Foreign Office, have maintained a distinct identity for a long period, it must take a series of decisions about organizational structure in planning the implementation of its policies. Likewise, though to a lesser extent, local authorities when a new council is elected, and public corporations when a new board is appointed, have to make similar decisions. The first of these is how to allocate the numerous and varied functions for which they are responsible among the members of their 'executive' – in the case of central government, ministers and secretaries of state, and in the case of local government, committees.

Another set of organizational problems is created by the need to group individual public servants into work units. Decisions have to be taken as to whether these individuals should be related mechanistically in strict hierarchy, or organically in more flexible, team-like, groups. If the units are hierarchically structured, decisions have to be taken about the right size of unit, number and type of supervisors, the relationships between administrative and professional staff, and the extent of delegation of authority to lower level personnel. As we will show, administrative agencies in Britain, particularly government departments, have come in for a good deal of criticism in recent years for the way in which they have handled these problems. It is perhaps surprising that so little attempt has been made to examine the problem systematically in the light of organization theories which have had some measure of success in explaining variations in organizational design, and the effects on the administrative processes of internal social structure and external environment, in private bodies.

The System of Departments

The executive branch of government extends beyond the departments and ministries of state to include non-ministerial agencies, the significance of which is discussed in a later section. However, in British central administration, the main organizational unit is the department or ministry. These vary in a number of important respects, all of which affect the process and structure of administration within them.

In the first place departments vary in the extent to which they are charged with the direct administration of a policy or with formulating policy as a basis for the control of other executive agencies, such as local authorities, public corporations and other public bodies. With the creation of large departments by the amalgamation of smaller units, few departments have no responsibilities for subordinate organizations. But it is still possible to compare departments, and even divisions or sections within a department, by the use of this factor.

For instance, the Department of Trade and Industry was created in 1970, basically by the merger of the Ministry of Technology and the Board of Trade. It was responsible for the direct administration of the Secretary of State's powers supporting and controlling British industry and commerce. These included policies on tariffs, company law, monopolies, mergers, export promotion services, export credits, advisory services for small and medium-sized firms and regional industrial development, including investment grants. However, the Department also administered the Government's relations with a number of public industrial corporations and research establishments, thus introducing an element of indirect administration into the organization. It is interesting to note that the process of 'fission' affected this department after only four years, and it was broken up into the four new departments of Industry, Trade, Energy and Prices and Consumer Protection.

By contrast, the Department of the Environment, which was also created in 1970, was a fusion of three departments all concerned in some way with the physical environment. The largest was the Ministry of Public Building and Works with 24,000 non-industrial staff mainly engaged in executive activities connected with the provision of offices and other buildings for the civil service and armed forces. The Ministry of Housing and Local Government, however, was the smallest department involved in the merger (4,800 non-industrial staff) and was wholly concerned with the control of local authorities. Finally, the Ministry of Transport, with 10,000 staff, combined both executive and supervisory functions in its highways programme and its relations with local highways authorities and the nationalized transport industries.

Second, departments may be categorized as executive or common service, according to whether they are primarily concerned with the administration of policies authorized by Parliament, or with the provision of services for the administration itself, ranging from manpower planning to the supply of office space and equipment. Again the picture is complicated by, first, the absorption recently of the largest common service department, the Ministry of Public Buildings and Works, into a 'functional' department, the Department of the Environment. And secondly, all departments have sections concerned with supporting the organization itself rather than with directly executing its field of policy. Examples of such supporting activities are personnel management and accounting. Nevertheless, it is important to remember the significance of organizations which service the administration rather than the community. In Britain these range from Her Majesty's Stationery Office (HMSO), for the supply of office materials and government publications, to the Office of Parliamentary Counsel for the drafting of Government Bills and Parliamentary motions.

It is possible to include within the category of common service departments the main co-ordinating and controlling departments, the Treasury and the Civil Service Department. While these organizations obviously play much more than a servicing role they are involved to some extent in providing support to the central administration in general, as in the case of Civil Service Department training. However, both the Treasury and the Civil Service Department are more important as parts of the planning and co-ordinating process at Cabinet level and must therefore be considered in that context. An additional factor is the Treasury's responsibility for developing a strategy for the management of the country's economy, and for monetary and fiscal policy, which obviously puts it in the group of policy departments.

This distinction between executive and common service functions is identical with the distinction in local government between vertical and horizontal functions. Thus, a local authority typically will have some committees and some departments which deal with all aspects of one service – such as education, personal social services, police and fire – and some which deal with one aspect of all services – finance, establishment and perhaps contracts. A local authority treasurer's department, like the Treasury, may combine financial house-keeping duties with substantive activities such as house loans.

Third, for historical and political reasons, departments vary in their geographical coverage. The territorial jurisdictions of the departments of state do not all correspond to the territory of the United Kingdom. The Foreign and Commonwealth Office controls and administers the whole of the United Kingdom's policies towards overseas governments. Similarly, the Board of Customs and Excise collects and administers customs and excise duties throughout the United Kingdom. However, the Department of Employment's responsibilities relating to the efficient use of manpower do not extend to Northern Ireland. The Department of Education and Science is responsible for the development of further and higher education in England and Wales, and the Department of the Environment is responsible for the Government's involvement in housing, water supply, town planning and the supervision of local authorities in England alone. A further complication is added by the fact that the Secretary of State for Wales shares responsibility for agriculture with the Minister of Agriculture, Fisheries and Food. And in Scotland the Secretary of State discharges his statutory functions through four Scottish departments responsible for matters which in England are organized in a different departmental system. Thus departments can be ranged along a continuum representing geographical scope with their position on it having serious implications for the administrative process within them.

A fourth variable is the extent to which departments decentralize their administrative operations and the forms which such decentralization takes. This subject is analysed in Chapter Three above. But it is related to a factor which must be referred to here, namely the extent to which the staff of departments come into direct contact with members of the public rather than with the leaders of representative bodies or the officials of other public agencies, both central and local. The Department of Employment, the

Inland Revenue and the Social Security side of the Department of Health and Social Security are examples of organizations in close and frequent contact with the public and therefore requiring considerable geographical decentralization.

Fifth, departments vary according to their political and administrative leadership. The main departments are headed by ministers or secretaries of state, although some titular exceptions remain, such as Chancellor of the Exchequer and President of the Board of Trade. Such heads of departments are usually assisted by one or more junior ministers (Parliamentary secretaries or Parliamentary under-secretaries of state). Large departments have ministers of state to take charge of major blocks of work, while statutory authority remains vested in the minister or secretary of state in charge overall. In the Department of the Environment under the 1970 reorganization, for example, the Secretary of State was supported by a Minister for Local Government and Development, a Minister for Housing and Construction and a Minister for Transport Industries, each having charge of a functional wing of the Department, while the Secretary of State retained final responsibility and statutory powers. These ministers of state were given the rank of non-Cabinet ministers. Whether or not the head of the department is a member of the Cabinet is a further distinguishing feature and determines to some extent the priority given in the Government strategy to the department's policies.

Some ministers are responsible for departments which are otherwise under the control of permanent officials. The Central Office of Information, for example, is headed by a Director-General and HMSO by a Controller who is a civil servant of deputy secretary rank. Both departments are responsible to Treasury ministers. The Board of Customs and Excise is composed of a permanent secretary who is its chairman, a deputy secretary who is deputy chairman, and eight under-secretaries as commissioners. The Board of Inland Revenue is similarly constituted. Both departments are the responsibility ultimately of the Chancellor of the Exchequer, and advise him on policy.

Sixth, with the emergence of the 'giant' departments, such as Health and Social Security and Environment, size is an important variable. The Ministry of Defence with nearly 113,000 non-industrial and 143,000 industrial staff may be contrasted with the Department of Education and Science with just over 3,000 non-industrial staff. Many of the internal managerial problems faced in these two Departments vary greatly.

Finally, departments vary according to the nature of the powers vested in their ministers by Act of Parliament. Government policy embodied in such statutory form takes a variety of different guises. We have already noted the distinction between supervisory and executive departments. Within these very broad categories the powers vested in ministers are of almost unlimited variety. Consequently the administrative process in departments defies easy generalization, as we shall see when we come to look at the structures of departmental organizations and the processes of administration within them. These powers are now so extensive that they directly affect the whole of society in more ways than ever before. Government has extended beyond its traditional regulatory functions to embrace economic aims, such as full employment, and physical planning, research and development and comprehensive social services.

The Allocation of Functions

The machinery of government, and particularly the departmental sector, is continually changing. New departments are created and existing ones abolished or merged as successive Governments attempt to produce a grouping of diverse functions which accord with their policy objectives or meet other conditions that they think important.

From time to time guidance is sought from the classic principles of organization in the allocation of functions. One such principle states that administrative efficiency is increased by grouping workers in organizations according to *purpose*, *process*, *clientele* or *place*. *Purpose* here means the objective of administration, such as public health, defence or the maintenance of law and order. *Process* refers to the professional knowledge or technical skills required for a particular administrative activity, such as civil engineering or medicine. *Clientele* refers to the recipients of public policy, such as war pensioners, farmers or the unemployed. *Place* refers to administrative organizations in which functions are grouped according to some territorial requirement.

The problem which faces the organizational planner is how to choose between the four types. Obviously a classification in itself offers no guidance on how best to organize work. In a report to the Ministry of Reconstruction in 1918, the only thorough examination of the subject in Britain, the Haldane Committee recommended defining the responsibilities of each department according to the service it renders to the community (i.e. by function rather than clientele). In this way functions or services such as health, education, finance and foreign affairs 'would each be under separate administration'. More recently, the Government justified reorganization by 'the application of the functional principle' to the allocation of responsibilities: 'government departments should be organized by reference to the task to be done or the objective to be attained, and this should be the basis of the division of work between departments rather than, for example, dividing responsibility between departments so that each one deals with a client group'.[1] Departures from this principle might be justified if there are 'strong reasons', as in the case of grouping functions according to the area to be served in the Scottish and Welsh Offices. But in the great majority of cases administration should be by task or policy, rather than client or area.

These principles give rise to three main problems. First, organization according to clientele without regard to function would create the 'Lilliputian administration' rejected by Haldane, whereby every service for a limited class of people is provided by a single organization. Secondly, a distinction between function and clientele as bases for specialized organizations offers no solution to the problem of whether, say, school health should be the responsibility of a department of health or education. Thirdly, single purposes or processes cannot be defined and isolated in an organization as complex as modern government. If drug addiction was made the responsibility of a law and order body rather than a health department it would involve different processes and purposes.

It is easy to show that there are many practical problems of allocation of functions to which the classical principles have no answer. For instance, as we have seen, though some services are quite distinct and no one would think of organizing them together, there are many others that have alternative homes, and these are the ones which are most frequently re-allocated. Secondly, the purposes of government are too many and varied for each to be organized separately, even if the boundaries of functions could be demarcated. There must be groupings and the reasons for any existing pattern have little to do with the principles of administration. We now turn to the factors which lie behind the distribution of functions between government departments in practice.

In the first and most obvious place the location of a governmental service or activity depends on the policy of the government within a particular functional field. Any policy area can be used to illustrate this. Take the history of defence procurement over the last few years. In 1967 the research, development and procurement (including defence) functions of the Ministry of Aviation passed to the Ministry of Technology. It had been decided that military procurements could not be separated from the government's overall interests in engineering, electronics and aeronautics. These considerations outweighed the Ministry of Defence claim to defence procurement functions.

However, in 1970 a new government chose to emphasize the defence element in the aerospace industry, rather than its technological content. Even the civil aerospace industry overlapped with defence interests. The 'major part' of the responsibilities of the Ministry of Technology for aerospace research, development and procurement concerned the procurement of aircraft and similar equipment for defence purposes. Thus the Aviation Group of the Ministry of Technology was temporarily made a Ministry of Aviation Supply together with the civil and military aerospace functions of MinTech.

Thus function alone tells us nothing about the basic pattern of administration or how it should be organized. The process of creation, fusion and fission, involving the creation of new departments, the winding up of existing ones and the transfer of functions, now almost an annual ritual, reflects the changing priorities and programmes of different governments within an ever-widening sphere of public policy. Professor Mackenzie has written that 'the great changes in administration have come about through causes partly fortuitous, partly political, but on the whole outside the range of administrative planning'.[2] If 'administrative planning' here means a more permanent structuring of administrative organization according to universal abstract principles, then there is no alternative to the situation he describes. Governments plan the use of resources, including organizational structures, to achieve ends which are determined by their political objectives. As these change, so the organization of work will change.

Organizational problems are bound up with changes in public policy. This will obviously be so when organizational change is seen as a necessary condition of the attainment of new objectives. What often appears to administrators as unnecessary tinkering with the structure of government usually reflects a major policy innovation by the Executive. The creation of the Department of Economic Affairs in 1964 signified a belief that the traditional methods of managing the economy through fiscal controls and monetary devices at the disposal of the Treasury needed to be supplemented by more positive expansionist planning concerned with the structure of the economy as a whole.

The political significance of organizational change is even more pronounced in the United States where administrative bureaux and regulatory agencies are often formed as a response to interest group pressures and operate as sponsors of sectional interests. The organization of the Forest Service is a classic example of political conflict between interests opposed to forest conservation seeking to keep forestry within the Department of the Interior (known to operate a policy of land exploitation) and conservationists attempting to have it transferred to the Department of Agriculture (known to favour forest conservation).

A second group of factors relevant to the changing allocation of functions is an organizational one. It concerns the hitherto accepted maxim that governmental activities should be grouped so as to provide a normal departmental hierarchy with enough work to keep it fully occupied. Related to this is the need to have a single minister at the department's head to preserve the principle that for every governmental power an individual minister should be responsible to Parliament. But even this can be overruled by the power of policy. Ministers can be given deputies if the Government's policy demands a grouping of programmes that would overwhelm a single individual as political head of the organization.

A government may well be encouraged to engage in this type of reorganization by the need to reduce the size of the Cabinet in the interest of centralized control and co-ordination of effective policy initiatives. Since it now seems possible to spread an otherwise excessive administrative burden over a number of ministers in a single department, the amalgamation of functions enables a Prime Minister to reduce the number of senior ministers and thus the size of his Cabinet.

The need to keep the Cabinet and government to a manageable

size has obviously affected administrative developments in the past. The number of ministers has not increased in proportion to the growth in government functions, public expenditure and the number of civil servants. There is clearly a presumption in favour of adding new programmes to existing ministries and departments or of 'hiving-off'. Recent trends towards the 'super-ministry' to facilitate strategic planning at Cabinet level have made it easier to contain the number of ministers with departmental responsibilities.

Finally, there is the importance of political personalities involved in the reshuffling of functions. Undoubtedly the political leaders available at any given moment will be one of the factors to be taken into account when reorganization is planned. But this must not be allowed to obscure the point that it is the Prime Minister who controls the machinery of government, as he chooses the men and women to hold office within it. Recent experience does not suggest that large-scale reorganization is solely dependent on the availability of suitable political leaders.

The problem of grouping functions within departmental structures is equally important in local government. As a multifunctional body, each local authority has to provide its community with a range of services – education, land-use planning, social services, highways and so on. As we showed in Chapter Two, since each service tends to be based on a separate profession, professional interests and rivalries have, in the past, tended to create separate departments for each service. In some cases, such as the children's service, the law prescribed that there should be a separate committee, chief officer and department. These factors have combined to produce in each authority a large number of independent departments, an arrangement which was often found to impede co-ordination in both management and policy formation. Each local authority department tends to look to one committee, not to an individual politician, and committees have also tended to proliferate. The result often, according to the Maud Committee, produces 'a loose confederation of disparate activities, disperses responsibility and scatters the taking of decisions'.

The internal reorganization of local authorities which has taken place on such a large scale recently has been set in motion by factors very similar to those influencing the reorganization of central government. Departments have been grouped to improve co-ordination in the planning and administration of inter-related functions. Increasingly, as in central government, 'programme areas' have been defined, with a group of departments administering related services integrated in 'directorates', for example, a Directorate of Education incorporating education, arts, museums and libraries. However, there are in local government strong forces pulling towards departmentalism, such as the powerful professional bases of local services, the traditional links between elected members and chief officers heading single-profession departments, and the problem of merging formerly equal and independent departments.

Nevertheless, the corporate approach in local government, paralleling the strategic planning approach in central government, has led some local authorities to group their committees and departments by programme areas which correspond to the objectives established for the authority's different spheres of activity. A comparison of the 1970 White Paper on *The Reorganization of Central Government* with the 1972 Report of the Study Group on Local Authority Management Structures[3] reveals the influence in both levels of government of the same approach to the grouping of functions. In the present climate of opinion, then, rationalization for strategic planning is the dominant motive. But at other times, in local as in central government, other factors may be more influential. The Bains Report itself, for example, shows a greater awareness of the problems involved in grouping committees and departments than did the Maud Committee Report in 1967.

Elements of Departmental Organization

We now turn to the internal organization of government departments. A full understanding of the administrative process requires a knowledge of how the organizations of central government are structured to carry out the tasks laid upon their ministers by Parliament.

The organization of government departments to some extent reflects both the different objectives of each and the existence of general principles. The fact that effectiveness and efficiency in the performance of a particular function has to be combined with (or even measured by) accountability to Parliament, overall control by the Treasury, and compatibility with civil service rules and procedures is often overlooked by critics of public administration who assess it by the standards of private business, without either recognizing or rejecting the standards of public administration.

The central government departments have a number of organizational features in common. A generalized picture of these is presented in figure 12. The first is that they are *headed* by ministers or secretaries of state who are members of the Government and who are responsible to Parliament for the decisions taken by themselves and their staff. The political fact of ministerial responsibility has significance for the organization of a department. Considerable pressures are placed on the organization from the scrutiny which is given it by parliamentary committees, MPs and the public. This means that great care has to be taken to ensure that decisions conform strictly to the minister's statutory powers. Organizational structures and procedures reflect the constitutional principle that ultimately the minister is answerable for everything which is done by the staff of his department.

The second common feature of departmental organization is the concentration of official authority for all aspects of administration, particularly financial control, in the hands of the *permanent secretary*. This is the highest rank in the civil service and the most senior permanent office in the departmental hierarchy. The permanent secretary has the special designation of accounting officer of his department and as such is responsible for ensuring that expenditure is strictly in accordance with the appropriations voted by Parliament after the proper submission of estimates. In this capacity he is answerable to the Public Accounts Committee for any irregularities in departmental expenditure revealed by the Comptroller and Auditor-General. Even in 'giant' departments of state where it has proved necessary to appoint more than one official of permanent secretary rank, one will be designated the senior permanent secretary and accounting officer. The office of permanent secretary reflects the concern within a government department for financial propriety and accountability, as well as centralization of authority. These militate against the delegation of financial authority and lead to the close control of subordinates by line managers in the departmental hierarchy.

A third feature of the typical department is the minister's *private office*. This is the personal secretariat of the minister and is generally headed by a civil servant of principal rank. The private secretary's job is to organize the work which from day-to-day has to be dealt with by the minister himself, such as obtaining

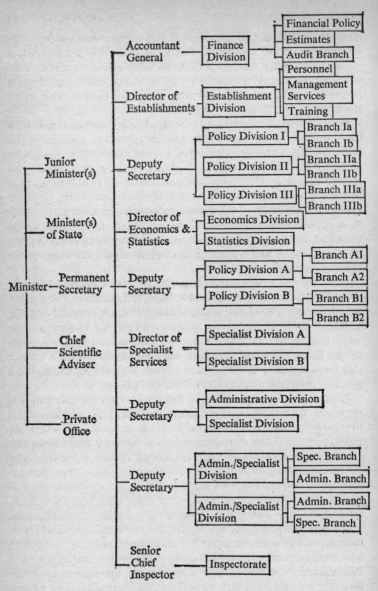

Fig. 12. The Internal Organization of a Department

answers to Parliamentary questions and correspondence from the relevant branch or division in the department. He has a political counterpart in the minister's Parliamentary private secretary who is a back-bench MP in the government party and who acts as a link between the minister and his political world in Parliament and the party.

Fourth, most departments are divided into *divisions* responsible for the major functions created by the statutory powers of the department's minister. Each division is headed by an under-secretary and further divided into branches, normally headed by an assistant secretary. Branches are then usually divided into sections under the control of an officer at principal level. Two or three divisions are likely to be grouped under a deputy secretary, which thus completes the hierarchy between permanent secretary and principal. Below principal level, work involving different degrees of responsibility will be delegated to officers with the appropriate grade and status.

The fact that a department is staffed by civil servants has direct effect on organizational structure. The levels in the organization tend to reflect grades in the civil service. There will usually be, for example, an assistant secretary level between a principal and an under-secretary. The pressures to create large numbers of levels in the hierarchy come from the requirement within the service that promotion will be achieved only by moving through all grades in the individual officer's class or group.

It must be emphasized that to talk of a 'typical' organizational structure in a government department can be misleading. It obscures the immense variety of forms which is found within the machinery of central government, even when the extra-depart-mental statutory boards are excluded. However, within any department there are usually fairly clear distinctions between ad-ministrative, executive and specialist divisions or branches. Ad-ministrative divisions tend to be formed for policy formation and implementation with a high political content. They are concerned with financial planning, the control of 'subordinate' authorities (such as local authorities and public corporations), preparing legislation and with the day-to-day political work of the minister – Parliamentary questions, letters from MPs, speeches and so on. Such groupings within the department tend to have very narrow spans of control, with tall hierarchies of single officials at all levels between deputy secretary and principal. The tasks of these divisions can be grouped into four main categories: financial planning and control; policy development; casework; and personnel and line management. It will be noticed that these four broad headings were not ones that appeared in our discussion of the classical principles of service allocation between departments. Within departments administrative activities can more easily be grouped into coherent units on the basis of the nature of the tasks performed.

Executive branches, dealing with work where the policy content is less and the routine greater have broader-based hierarchies of executive and clerical officers concerned with the management of contracts, purchasing arrangements, social security case work, stores and accounting units. Very often such units constitute the lower levels of a hierarchy the top of which consists of administrative grade personnel.

Specialist grades are organized in structures according to the nature of the work – accounting, economic analysis, urban planning, research, engineering, surveying and so on. One of the distinguishing features of specialist structures has been the way in which they have been kept organizationally distinct from the administrative and executive units (see below).

No two departments are exactly alike structurally. Spans of control vary and thus so does the shape of the department's organization. More important, the flexibility of the 'typical' system should be noted. Work organized on the basis of the relatively small specialized group with narrowly defined areas of responsibiiity can be regrouped in response to changes in departmental policy, minister or government. Also, it is easy to graft new structures on when departments increase in size as they have tended to do in recent years.

To complete the picture of the 'typical' departmental structure we must include the groups of *professional staff* which most departments employ. The expansion of government activities into the scientific, technological and industrial fields has led to an increasing demand for staff with relevant professional qualifications, such as scientists, engineers, economists and medical officers. The growth of administration generally has increased the demand for the specialist support groups found in all large-scale business organizations, such as accountants, lawyers, and statisticians. There are now more professional, scientific and technical civil servants than administrative and executive officers.

In the past specialists have, with some important exceptions discussed in the next chapter, been organized in one of two ways. Some are organized in the traditional way of 'staff' advisers to 'line' managers (i.e. administrators). Most have been organized in structures peculiar to the civil service and producing varying degrees of co-operation between specialists and generalists. The two structures have been designated as 'parallel' and 'joint' hierarchies. Parallel hierarchies occur when the administrative and technical aspects of the same work are carried out by separate units within the department. Joint hierarchies have an administrator and a specialist as joint heads of a branch (e.g. an assistant secretary and an assistant chief engineer) but with parallel hierarchies of generalists and specialists under them. The Fulton Committee's management consultants found an example of this in the construction of motorways. The Ministry's engineers discuss projected routes with the local authority concerned, check recommended lines, advise on the preparation of schemes and give technical supervision to the construction work. Administrators are responsible for preparing the relevant land-use schemes, setting up inquiries, deciding the line to be followed, considering objections and relating technical and financial facts to political considerations. When construction starts administrators are also responsible for co-ordinating the engineering, financial and legal aspects of the scheme

The specialist's role has been predominantly an advisory one. Professional accountants advise on financial matters, but administrators carry out financial estimating and control, routine accounting work, and the negotiation of contracts. Where there is an administrative element in the work of professionals, as in the organization and control of work in a scientific research establishment or in the management of groups of professional and technical staff on architectural, engineering and planning schemes, it tends to be managerial in the strict sense; that is, concerned with directing staff, planning work, measuring results and reviewing procedures, rather than with forecasting and controlling expenditure, recommending new policy and legislation, negotiating with outside bodies or dealing with ministers' parliamentary and political work. This distinction arises from the special role of higher civil servants in the British system.

The final common elements of departmental organization to be noted are the establishments and finance divisions. Every department has an *establishments* (or personnel) division under an officer of under-secretary or, in the 'giant' department, deputy secretary level. In many respects establishment divisions correspond roughly to the personnel departments of any large business. They are responsible for staff deployment, training, welfare, discipline, promotions and organizational matters. They are concerned with increasing efficiency through the application of management techniques such as Organization and Methods (O & M), automatic data processing and staff inspection. In recent years traditional O & M studies of the relationships between routine tasks, processes and organizations have been significantly augmented by the application of operational research and behavioural science to organizational problems. Increasingly, too, the management services side of establishments work has been concerned with the utilization of computers in the planning, control and review of departmental activities.

To support the permanent secretary in his role of accounting officer each department has a *finance* division to supervise financial policy, revenue and expenditure. The titles of such divisions vary (Finance and Economic Appraisal Division in the Department of Trade and Industry; Finance Division in the Department of Employment) and some departments have more than one (the Department of Health and Social Security has two, and the Department of the Environment three, each corresponding to one of the department's 'wings' or blocks of functions). The chief officer, generally an under-secretary, is usually designated 'accountant general' a title which perhaps reveals the full extent of his division's responsibilities. It is not only charged with the payment of bills and the preparation of annual accounts for the Comptroller and Auditor General, but also with preparing the annual estimates for submission to Parliament. A good deal of the work in a finance division arises from inquiries by the Exchequer and Audit Department and from the need to support the accounting officer in any appearance which he may have to make before the House of Commons Public Accounts Committee. On the budgeting side there is a need for continuous negotiation with the Treasury on the preparation of expenditure plans to be submitted in the form of estimates.

Unfortunately limitations of space prevent us from setting out in detail the internal structure of local authority departments and public corporations, but a similar analysis and description could be undertaken in relation to these and other public bodies. This would reveal much common ground as well as distinctive features arising from their special legal position.

Non-Departmental Organizations

We now return to the subject of non-departmental bodies, a complex category of 'semi-autonomous, non-departmental, special purpose central government authorities'. These are the statutory organizations which are not part of the local government system or the system of central departments. As was pointed out in Chapter Two, the main characteristic of such authorities is the degree of autonomy from political control that they enjoy.

These bodies are responsible for a great variety of governmental activities in the industrial, promotional, cultural and regulatory fields. It is important to understand why non-departmental organizations are preferred for such activities. Of course, as each one can be regarded as a special case, part of the explanation will be in terms of the particular characteristics of the individual body, but there are two broad headings under which the motives for this choice can be grouped. The first is to remove the activity from too close an involvement in day-to-day political conflict; the second, to exempt them from the traditional procedures of civil service departments, for instance, Treasury control.

The examples of 'de-politicized' administration most commonly given are the Civil Service Commission and the British Broadcasting Corporation. However, it is important to understand that activities are not only 'hived-off' from central government or organized under *ad hoc* bodies, as an alternative to departmental administration, but may be also alternatives to local government administration. Though it is clear that postal services, coal mining, electricity generation and steel production are cases where the only possible alternative to *ad hoc* bodies is a central department, electricity supply, road passenger transport and water supply are organized as alternatives to local government rather than central.

The case of the gas industry is particularly interesting because when it was first nationalized this was an alternative to local government – local authorities had owned about a third of the undertakings – but with a change in technology, its organization was changed so that it was in effect an alternative to a central department. Even its statutory area organization has disappeared and been replaced by decentralized management within a national corporation.

Other examples of 'hiving-off' from the local government sphere can be cited to illustrate how motives may combine to determine the required administrative structure. In the case of local government additional factors may be important, such as the inadequate size of many local authorities for the efficient administration of a particular service or the multiplicity of bodies responsible for a group of closely related services. An example is the provision of water, sewage and related services. These have been reorganized on the basis of ten Regional Water Authorities responsible for local authority water and sewage disposal functions and the functions of river authorities. The majority of members of the Regional Water Authorities are local authority nominees.

The national health service is another case of public administration being organized to avoid close legislative control, at the level of local government. Before the National Health Service Act of 1946 the personal health services in the public sector had been administered by some form of local government organization. Although the decision to provide a comprehensive health service included leaving many personal services with local authorities, pressure from the various professional bodies, hostile to local government, was a major factor leading to the establishment of a tripartite system. The structure of local government was also found to be defective because local authorities lacked the population and resources to organize an adequate and efficient service; and because demarcations between town and country, represented by the county and county borough system, cut right across the appropriate areas for the planning and administration of hospital services.[4] Under the 1946 Act hospitals were managed by boards acting as the agents of the minister. General practitioners worked under contract with executive councils. Both the regional hospital boards and executive councils were outside any system of democratic legislative control by local authorities, although decentralization in the national health service was obviously necessary.

The tripartite system has now been found in need of overhaul. A new structure has been devised which reduces the role of local government in the national health service even further, despite the reorganization of the local government system. Neither the Labour nor the Conservative Governments of the last ten years have seriously considered reorganizing the health services within local government. Professional fears about clinical freedom led the Government to reject such a policy in 1970, even though it admitted that democratic control would be more effective under local government and that a close relationship between the health services could best be organized in that way. Again the financial consequence to local authorities of transferring the hospitals to them was an important consideration.

The new health service organization thus unifies the three parts of the old system under area authorities with boundaries corresponding to the new counties or, in the conurbations, the metropolitan districts. The area authorities are responsible for planning, organizing and administering comprehensive health services to meet the needs of their areas. In each of fifteen regions a regional health authority has responsibility for general planning, allocating resources to the areas, and co-ordinating and monitoring area authority activities. The chairmen and members of the regional authorities are appointed by the minister. In the area authorities the chairmen are again appointed by the minister, but some members are appointed by the corresponding local authority, one by the medical university in the region, and the rest by the regional authority after consultation with the health professions. Contracts with family practitioners are administered by committees of the area authority composed like the old executive councils. The minister has power to determine national objectives, priorities and standards and allocate resources to the regions. Thus the national health service has been thoroughly 'depoliticized', mainly as a result of pressure from the professional organizations such as the British Medical Association, until it has virtually become what one observer has called 'a closed syndicalist corporation' (Klein, 1971).

The alternative general objective of delegation or 'hiving-off' to statutory bodies is to free decision makers from the restraints on personnel and financial management which organization within a government department is said to impose. The current concern with this in fact reflects both motives but at present the dominant one is to free the organization from departmental management constraints. One also has to consider the effects of 'hiving-off' on the parent department, for instance, its effects on policy planning. The need for such delegation arises when those aspects of departmental organization which militate against accountable management cannot be suitably modified from within. Conflict between traditional methods of departmental administration and modern management techniques increases as we move into the activities of government which are of a commercial or quasi-commercial kind.

The first is in *management accounting*. When the activity is financed under the department's votes (money paid to the department from the Consolidated Fund after the formal presentation of estimates and authorization by Parliamentary legislation) the accounts are expressed in terms of types of expenditure and not objectives. So while it is possible to know how much is being spent on salaries, materials, transport, accommodation and so on by the department, it is very difficult to assess the cost of a particular activity and compare costs over time and between functions and thus provide a measure of operational efficiency. In place of vote accounting methods, and Parliamentary supply procedures in budgeting, the quasi-commercial activities of government increasingly require functional costing and management accounting so that objectives can be clarified, costed and compared.

Related to accounting methods is the second problem, that of *management structures* in government departments. As we will see, the administrative structures within departments are sometimes regarded as obstacles to the creation of accountable units of management. For instance, the centralization within the Post Office was said to be caused by Parliamentary control.

Third, *personnel procedures* in organizations staffed by civil servants are said to militate against the flexible deployment of staff required by accountable management. The line manager in the civil service does not have the freedom necessary to deploy staff efficiently.

Fourth, there is the constraint which *Treasury control* places on accountable management. This control arises from the role of the Treasury as 'custodian of the Exchequer' which makes it necessary for departments to obtain Treasury approval for future expenditure (the estimates), for increases in current expenditure over the previous year's estimates (supplementary estimates) and for any legislation requiring expenditure (financial resolutions).

Finally there is the aspect of departmental organization which brings us back to the 'depoliticization' argument. Allocating a function to a minister to be carried out by his department means *answerability to Parliament*. A semi-independent statutory authority, like the public corporations, can claim some immunity from Parliamentary scrutiny, thus leaving management free to take decisions on the basis of commercial rather than political criteria.

This point brings us to the arguments against 'hiving-off' departmental functions to semi-independent boards or corporations. For in the first place no such authority can escape Parliamentary scrutiny and control completely. Indeed, it may be considered particularly appropriate that close Parliamentary scrutiny should be allowed to exist through direct ministerial responsibility.

Even when industrial and commercial freedom are considered of vital importance, the interests of the public as represented through Parliament cannot be entirely overlooked. In the case of the Post Office, for example, senior officials were forced to admit to the Select Committee on Nationalized Industries,[5] that 'the fact that any individual action can be challenged and raised at the highest level certainly is a safeguard against slipshod work or careless work or laxity in applying procedures and rules. It is a safeguard against any local manager kicking over the traces in the way he handles his customers or his staff.'

It is extremely difficult to draw the line between the public's interest in the nationalized industries, as represented by Parliament, and the consumer's interest, as represented by the free operation of market forces. In the case of the nationalized industries ministerial control of investment programmes, pricing policies, staffing and wages questions, has generally increased in recognition of the political implications of decisions affecting the financial and social obligations of the industries. Since ministers are liable to account to Parliament for the actual and possible exercise of their statutory or informal powers, Parliamentary control has increased accordingly. Whatever obstacles to Parliamentary control exist now seem to be related more to the general problems which Parliament faces *vis-à-vis* the Executive than to the special status of the nationalized industries. The fact that in the very case where freedom from legislative scrutiny was thought to be of greatest importance, Parliamentary control is running at about the same level as control of other executive activities, should constitute a warning against unrealistic promises of 'depoliticization' through 'hiving-off'. In fact, it may be useful to the executive who lose no real control but gain an exemption from criticism. The second set of factors militating against 'hiving-off' is related to the special relationships existing between the quasi-commercial activities of some departments and the rest of the government. It is not easy to free part of a department from overall ministerial control when most or all of its product is purchased by the Government itself. The services provided by the Works Division of the Department of the Environment in equipping government establishments with furniture, fuel, building materials and other supplies come into this category.

Again, where the government is the main or sole customer there is no market mechanism to determine prices. The supply of stationery, office machinery, automatic data processing equipment and printing facilities by HMSO to central departments is a case in point. As a supplier, it is in a monopolistic position in relation to the Government. Also the work of some organizations may be dependent on a heavy government subsidy to support production. The work of the Forestry Commission and the Ordinance Survey comes into this category. In the former case, for example, the Commission produces about 1·5 million tons of timber annually and earns about £7·5 millions from sales, rentals and other sources. But it is also charged with promoting forestry interests and the development of afforestation through grants to woodland owners, research, the implementation of legislation concerning plant health and the licensing of felling; and with providing facilities for public recreation, wildlife conservation and plantation landscaping. Its expenditure each year thus amounts to roughly twice its earned receipts. As a consequence the Commission is funded by Parliamentary vote and comes under the direction of the Minister of Agriculture, Fisheries and Food.

Co-ordination in Government

So far in this chapter we have tried to stress the ways in which the public administration system has been divided up into separate bodies, each of which may be further subdivided into departments, divisions, branches, sections, etc. We pointed out in Chapter Two that each identifiable organizational unit can be treated as an individual in its own right, with its own distinctive behaviour patterns and its own 'culture'. This is something which becomes very clear if research is undertaken into recruitment and social-ization in, say, a local authority department, or a division of a ministry in Whitehall. One can find local government officers who will describe themselves as working for the education or health department, rather than the city council.

But as a result of the lack of definite distinctions between government activities, especially at the level of their impact of the individual citizen and the individual piece of land, there is a need to put them together again; to ensure that the decisions of separate agencies are coherent rather than contradictory.

Some of the mechanisms by which this is achieved are described in other chapters, for instance in the discussion of aspects of decentralization, but recent years have seen a growing stress on mechanisms within the central government whose role is to co-ordinate the activities of central departments and non-departmental organizations. In a system of government patterned on British lines, to do this is also to provide a degree of co-ordination throughout the structure of public bodies.

Co-ordination is the controlling of activities and decisions of individuals or agencies so that they are harmonized in the pursuit of some stated common goal or objectives. As this is the essence of organizational decision making and permeates the whole administrative process, it may be regarded almost as synonymous with management.

For instance, H. A. Simon says 'group behaviour requires not only the adoption of correct decisions, but also the adoption by all members of the group of the same decision'[6] and defines organizational authority as a 'relation that serves by subordinating the decisions of the individual to the communicated decisions of others'.[7] At a more practical level the line manager's role is often defined in terms of co-ordination.

The co-ordinating function of the line manager is only one device for integrating interdependent activities and processes. When these activities are performed by the often very large organizations which together constitute the machinery of government of a modern state, special devices are needed which correspond to the types of activity or decision to be controlled. This section surveys these devices and the different kinds of co-ordination they are designed to achieve.

The reasons why these mechanisms are required in government will become obvious as they are examined in detail, but as a preliminary it can be seen that these needs in general arise from a number of common factors: the complexity of government and the immense variety of its objectives; the size of the organization (if reference to the government as *an* organization can be excused in the present context), measured in manpower and expenditure terms; the political consequences of agency activities and their impact on public opinion and support for the governing party; the demands and constraints of financial accountability through the Parliamentary system.

The most common method of achieving co-ordination within an organization is through a central decision maker who has the authority to control and influence the actions of his subordinates. The line manager is the classic case of this. This concept of co-ordination is reflected in central government in the role of a department's permanent secretary and its heads of divisions and branches. In local government the head of each department – the director of education and the medical officer of health, for instance – were the main line managers, and the traditional co-ordinating role of the town clerk had to be carried out by other means. But some schemes for reorganizing the internal structure of local authorities envisage the creation of the role of chief executive who would have line authority over all other departmental heads.

At the level of interdepartmental co-ordination, however, such figures are relatively few; the processes of line management are not generally used. Instead there are co-ordinating individuals such as the Prime Minister, some special members of his Cabinet, such as ministers without portfolio and the secretaries of state for Scotland and Wales, the head of the civil service, the secretary of the Cabinet and the secretaries of state for the 'giant' multi-functional departments. The role of the traditional town clerk has already been mentioned, but in local government the authority's treasurer has also played such a role, and new co-ordinating officers have been recently appointed in many areas, particularly in the specialized administrative techniques field.

Central co-ordination and direction in British government are also achieved through special organizations such as interdepartmental committees and the common service or 'horizontal' departments mentioned earlier, depending on the type of co-ordination required.

There are two basic types of co-ordination. The first is the supervision and control of decisions of agencies to ensure that they function harmoniously in meeting agreed objectives. The essence of this type of co-ordination is control. It follows the establishment of policies whereas, as we shall see, the second type precedes policy making.

CONTROL OF POLICY EXECUTION

The objectives of the first type of co-ordination may be expressed either in terms of a set of procedures and methods governing administrative action (for example, accounting or staff recruitment procedures) or in terms of the achievement of the policy goals of the government (for example, a certain level and pattern of public expenditure). The two kinds of objective correspond to Simon's distinction between procedural and substantive co-ordination: 'by procedural is meant the specification of the organization itself – that is, the generalized description of the behaviours and relationships of members of the organization. Procedural co-ordination establishes the lines of authority and outlines the spheres of activity of each organization member, while substantive co-ordination specifies the content of his work'.[8]

Co-ordinating individuals rarely act alone; they are supported by special staffs whose function it is to deal with day-to-day relationships with other agencies. Perhaps the best example of this is the Executive Office of the President of the United States and there has been some discussion recently in Britain of the need for a Prime Minister's Department. In local government the co-ordinating role of a supplies officer will be carried out largely by specialists within his department.

We must now consider the co-ordinating functions of such central agencies as the Treasury and the Civil Service Department. These can be arranged along a continuum with procedural at one end and substantive at the other. Though both departments deal with both types of objective, the Civil Service Department is concerned much more with procedural matters and the Treasury with substantive ones.

The Treasury's function of central co-ordination is now performed solely in relation to finance. First, there is financial control for the purpose of substantive co-ordination, that is, to ensure that policy objectives are achieved. All central departments are required to submit their expenditure plans to the Treasury each year in the form of estimates before presentation to Parliament. Incidentally, this provides the Treasury with some influence on other public bodies in as far as financial provision for them is included in the estimates of a central department.

Civil estimates must be presented to Parliament by a Treasury minister and the Treasury may even veto expenditure, which it has earlier approved and for which Parliament has voted the money. The estimating procedure enables the Treasury to scrutinize the general level and pattern of a department's expenditure plans, and it is also a rule that certain types of project involving new expenditure require Treasury sanction. Control of the estimates is one of the ways in which the Treasury can 'keep a grip on the never-ending sequence of new policies, changes in policy and other events which give rise to new expenditure'.[9]

In addition to the Treasury's role in the supply cycle above there is the rule that no legislation requiring expenditure can go before the House of Commons without the support of a Treasury minister. A further rule prohibits the submission of departmental proposals requiring additional expenditure to the Cabinet without prior consultation and discussion with the Treasury. Together these rules lead the Treasury 'to concern itself with every important aspect of government policy'.[10]

Treasury control extends well beyond the annual supply procedure and the day-to-day consultations over variations in financial policies. In recent years it has been developed to cover more areas of expenditure and longer time periods. Departments have to submit five-year expenditure forecasts to the Treasury, thus giving it a central role in long-term planning. Not only has the time span been lengthened but Treasury scrutiny has been extended to cover expenditure not included in the estimates, the most important being spending by local authorities, the nationalized industries and other public corporations. The annual 'forward looks' analyse expenditure by function (for example, defence, health or education) and by economic category (for example, wages, goods and services, fixed capital formation). Departments submit their forecasts to the Treasury which, after discussion, reports to the Public Expenditure Survey Committee on which sit the principal finance officers of the major spending departments. This is chaired by a Treasury deputy secretary.

The next important area of financial control is over the investment programmes of the nationalized industries. The Treasury's role here arises from the corporations' practice of funding capital investment by borrowing from the Exchequer or with Exchequer backing. The Treasury scrutinizes their long-term investment plans to ensure that they are likely to produce an adequate rate of return and that they are in line with the Government's economic policies.

The second objective of this type of co-ordination involves the maintenance of agreed procedures and methods of working. In the field of public expenditure the Treasury controls the form in which departments keep their accounts, the use of savings on one sub-head of a vote to cover overspending on another (*virement*), and the form in which estimates are drawn up for presentation to Parliament. The Treasury also prescribes how departmental contracts shall be made and instructs departments on the implementation of recommendations made by the Public Accounts Committee of the House of Commons. The above does not exhaust the Treasury's role but the other aspects will be discussed under later headings.

The other main example of a centralized co-ordinating agency is the Civil Service Department. Here the balance of co-ordinating responsibilities is tilted in the opposite direction to the Treasury. The Department is more concerned with the standardization and development of personnel and management functions within departments than with service manpower policy, although this is not a negligible part of its responsibilities.

The creation of the Civil Service Department in 1968 brought within one organization the Treasury's responsibilities for civil service pay and management, the co-ordination of government policies for public sector pay and pensions and the recruitment functions of the Civil Service Commission. The functions of the Department and the Commission, which forms an independent unit within it, are organized in divisions responsible for the three broad areas of work: personnel management, administrative and managerial efficiency, and terms of service.[11]

In the control and co-ordination of departmental activities with respect to policy objectives the Department is concerned with administrative expenditure generally and the manpower requirements of government in particular; and with government policy for pay and pensions throughout the public sector. It is directly responsible for the control of manpower expenditure through the establishment of annual manpower ceilings for all departments. This control is carried on in parallel with the Treasury's annual survey of public expenditure to which the Department contributes data on the manpower implications of expenditure forecasts. Thus an individual department, in submitting its estimates, has to satisfy it of the reasonableness of its staff and administrative costs as well as the Treasury on all other aspects of its proposed expenditure. The basic instrument of manpower control is a system of staff inspection through which the Department scrutinizes blocks of work in the departments to see whether staff are being used economically and efficiently.

Co-ordination in the sense of directing the diverse agencies of government towards agreed policy objectives (e.g. manpower ceilings) has been distinguished from co-ordination in the sense of ensuring conformity to general practices of administration (e.g. recruitment, training, improving managerial efficiency). In practice, of course, the two areas overlap. The Department's task is to develop methods of manpower control which contribute to the increased efficiency of the department and not just to keep staff numbers within an overall ceiling. Also its responsibility for ensuring uniformity in pay scales throughout the service includes the application of any incomes policy which a Government might have to the public sector.

Moving further along the continuum we eventually come to a pure form of procedural co-ordination found in the organizations set up to provide a common service for the Government as a whole. Here administrative uniformity is provided by handing the task to special agencies so as to avoid wasteful duplication of effort. The activity is centralized for the sake of economy. The Central Office of Information and Her Majesty's Stationery Office are obvious examples.

In local government the classic example of an organization for co-ordination is the clerk's department. The tendency has been for local authorities to move away from procedural towards substantive co-ordination, and to do this by changing the role of the clerk to that of some kind of chief executive.

Traditionally the clerk to a local authority acted as legal adviser to ensure that the authority did not exceed its powers. This inevitably gave the office a measure of importance which other heads of departments did not enjoy. This led to the clerk assuming administrative functions, particularly the co-ordination of departmental work within the authority as a whole, subject to the professional judgement of a particular chief officer. The emphasis tended to be on communications and the role of the clerk in ensuring that the council was fully informed of technical and professional advice and that its decisions were carried out efficiently. His function in the administrative process was to ensure adequate communication between committees and departments.

In the last ten years or so the trend in local government has been towards the establishment of a chief executive officer who not only has unambiguous authority over other principal officers but who also has a more positive role in policy formation. The substantive content of the chief officer's co-ordinating function has increased as responsibility for securing a corporate planning approach to the authority's services has been delegated to him. As head of the administration the chief executive officer is also responsible for developing the authority's personnel policies and for ensuring that these are implemented in all departments. Increasingly the chief executive's job has come to be defined in terms of the more efficient uses of the authority's resources generally. Each of the new authorities established under the *Local Government Act, 1972,* has been advised to appoint a chief executive to act as leader of the officers of the authority and principal adviser to the council on matters of general policy.

Like the Treasury in central government, the treasurer's department of a local authority performs both substantive and procedural co-ordinating roles. One of its most important tasks is the preparation of the authority's budget in consultation with the spending committees and departments. Unlike the Whitehall Treasury, however, the local authority treasuries are also responsible for audit, both in the traditional sense of preventing fraud and enforcing financial regulations, and as a management process for improving efficiency and economy. On the procedural side the treasurer's department is responsible for keeping expenditure in line with the authorized budget, ensuring payments are according to financial regulations and managing the consolidated loans fund.

CO-ORDINATION OF POLICY MAKING

We have considered the Treasury and the Civil Service Department as central co-ordinating agents and have suggested that the above type of co-ordination is designed to integrate the policies and decisions of other functional agencies for the achievement of established objectives, whether these be policy goals or administrative procedures. We think it useful to distinguish another kind of co-ordination in order to examine another type of central co-ordinator – the interdepartmental committee.

The existence of a committee structure at the apex of government is itself suggestive of the particular concept of co-ordination which we have in mind. This concept stresses the harmonization of efforts to produce goals and objectives for the future, rather than the backward-looking co-ordination of the line manager and central agency, concerned with ensuring the implementation of agreed policy.

Co-ordination in our second sense, then, entails the seeking of agreement over the development of new plans, new political strategies and new methods of working through the collaboration of roughly equal decision makers who individually control interdependent parts of the central government machine. This is co-ordination by consultation and agreement rather than by control, and the committee-type mechanisms used reflect the social interaction required for effective communication. The committee is a medium for horizontal communication and this is more appropriate for problem solving or planning inter-related lines of action than the vertical communication typical of the line manager or control agency.

Clearly the Cabinet is the outstandingly important example of a policy planning committee. The definition of Cabinet functions given by the Haldane Committee in 1918 is still authoritative and emphasizes the strategic planning objective of Cabinet co-ordination:

(a) the final determination of the policy to be submitted to Parliament;

(b) the supreme control of the national executive in accordance with the policy prescribed by Parliament; and

(c) the continuous co-ordination and delimitation of the activities of the several Departments of State.[12]

Most of the work on planning new policy is done outside the Cabinet system in the parties, in departments and in interdepartmental committees, although in recent years the administrative apparatus serving the Cabinet has been strengthened in this direction. The Cabinet ensures that departmental planning is consistent with government policy as a whole. 'The main task of the Cabinet is to co-ordinate the work of the various departments and committees and thus ensure that the activity of the government has a certain coherence'. To perform this function the Cabinet may have to act as a court of appeal resolving conflicts between ministers, particularly concerning the pattern of public expenditure. Disagreements between departments and the Treasury over the estimates are often resolved in this way. Cabinet co-ordination consists of ministers defending the interests of their own departments against the threatened encroachments of others.[13] The Cabinet is thus the place where disputes are settled, where major policies are endorsed and where the balance of forces emerges if there is a disagreement.[14] The Cabinet co-ordinates by a process of review, supervision, adjudication and formal approval.

In other circumstances Cabinet co-ordination may involve ministers in taking decisions which override departmental interests in order to do something which was in the interest of the nation as a whole, or consistent with the Government's overall strategy. Here co-ordination means 'that departmental views and concerns are woven into a unified and dominant Government policy and that Ministers consider their major duty to be to partake in the formulation of this policy'. Patrick Gordon-Walker has described how, as Secretary of State for Education, he did not always feel it his sole or even primary duty to fight an all-out battle in defence of his department's expenditure proposals when faced with a need to cut back on government spending.[15] Evidently not all Cabinet ministers are likely to adopt the same concept of co-ordination at the same time. Whether the emphasis of co-ordination is on conflict resolution or a unified strategy depends on the issues and personalities involved.

The size of the Cabinet has been a constant problem. A group of twenty or so leading members of the majority party and heads of the most important departments of State is not the most convenient forum for planning policy. Hence the delegation of this aspect of the Cabinet's functions to Cabinet committees and moderately successful attempts in recent years to reduce the size of the Cabinet by amalgamating departments under secretaries of state.

Cabinet committees are more involved in the detailed work of policy planning than the Cabinet itself and enable non-Cabinet ministers and junior ministers to be involved. Our knowledge of contemporary Cabinet committees is inevitably thin because of state secrecy. But we do know that they provide a system of policy planning surrounding the Cabinet with the necessary qualities of specialization, expertise, urgency and coherence of policy-making in functional areas such as defence, economic affairs, the social services and foreign affairs. Subject to the importance of the issue, the type of problem involved and the way in which the Prime Minister and senior Cabinet colleagues decide to use the system, Cabinet committees perform an important role in policy-co-ordination.

Another method of reducing the size of the Cabinet and increasing its co-ordinating power is the appointment of co-ordinating ministers or 'overlords' as they have been known since an experiment of this kind was tried by the Churchill Cabinet of 1951. The 'overlord' idea involves the appointment of non-departmental ministers of Cabinet rank with the task of co-ordinating the work of departments whose ministers are not in the Cabinet.

The difficulties inherent in this method of co-ordination are that 'overlords' as policy makers are remote from day-to-day administration. Ministerial responsibility for the department's activities is blurred. The creation of an élite within the Cabinet can create resentment among other members of the Government, particularly those who head departments but do not have full control over them. But perhaps more than anything these difficulties indicate the inappropriateness of the 'line manager' type of co-ordination in a policy planning situation.

It is much more common to use the non-departmental ministers in the Cabinet (Lord President of the Council, Chancellor of the Duchy of Lancaster, Paymaster General, Lord Privy Seal) in more modest co-ordinating roles, such as taking responsibility for special projects which may or may not cut across departmental boundaries (e.g. negotiations on Britain's entry into the European Economic Community) or as chairmen of Cabinet committees. Sometimes, too, a senior departmental minister is given responsibilities extending beyond the functional boundaries of his department. In 1967 Mr Crossman was made Secretary of State for Social Services responsible for the new Department of Health and Social Security and for co-ordinating the whole range of social services, including those outside his department, such as the Children's Department, then part of the Home Office. More recently, however, the practice has been to keep the size of the Cabinet down and increase co-ordination by merging departments under secretaries of state assisted where necessary by ministers of state of non-Cabinet rank responsible for functional wings of the 'giant' departments.

An impressive bureaucracy has grown up around the Cabinet to assist it perform its function of policy co-ordination. The parts of this bureaucracy together constitute the Cabinet Office. The most important part is the Cabinet Secretariat consisting of about twenty-five administrative personnel, a dozen professionals and some two hundred subordinate staff. In addition to providing the usual secretariat services to the Cabinet and its committees by helping chairmen with agendas, ensuring papers are presented, preparing special reports and recording decisions, the Cabinet Secretariat provides the Prime Minister with policy advice. It records decisions in the form of instructions to departments. It thus assists the task of co-ordination by creating the link between the decisions of the Cabinet and the individual departments.

The latest addition to the body of administrative and technical expertise supporting the policy co-ordinating function of the Cabinet and its committees is the Central Policy Review Staff. This unit was set up in the Cabinet Office in 1970 after the publication of the White Paper on *The Reorganization of Central Government*[16]. It is a relatively small group (about twenty) of temporary and established civil servants under the ultimate supervision of the Prime Minister and working for the Government as a whole, supporting the collective responsibility of ministers for policy analysis, review and development.

Colloquially known first as a 'central capability unit' and more recently as a 'think tank', it is a multi-disciplinary research team. It reflects the government's attempt to develop an integrated strategy and policy framework. The aim, as set out in the White Paper, is to achieve a degree of policy co-ordination hitherto absent from British Government. Its task is to enable ministers to take better policy decisions by assisting them to work out the implications of their basic strategy in terms of policies in specific areas, to establish the relative priorities to be given to the different sectors of their programme as a whole, to identify those areas of policy in which new choices can be exercised and to ensure that the underlying implications of alternative courses of action are fully analysed and considered.

These very ambitious aims tell us very little about what the Central Policy Review Staff might achieve in practice. It would seem inevitable that the approach be a selective one – government research and development, regional policy, the computer industry, Concorde and industrial growth and decline in the 1970s and

1980s were its original projects – if only to avoid the danger of replicating the policy planning and co-ordinating work of the spending departments and of the Treasury. But this could defeat the object of providing ministers collectively with a comprehensive strategy. Yet it is difficult to envisage how an intelligence function could operate to encompass all the activities of government as a whole. The ongoing work of the Central Policy Review Staff, on such topics as the social needs of the community in the next twenty years, the effects on taxation of a transfer of investment from manufacturing to service industries or the significance of foreign control over parts of industry, illustrates the needs of ministers for intelligence which relates the policies of their own departments to the broader sphere of government strategy. In this sense it supports co-ordination at Cabinet level by intensive research, reviews of progress, informal advice and *ad hoc* briefings on pressing issues.

Equally important to the co-ordination of policy initiatives are the interdepartmental committees at official, as distinct from ministerial, level. Committees are now thought to have almost constitutional significance in British government and to reflect an aspect of our political culture. Certainly it is a phenomenon which dominates any scene involving interaction between officials, especially when they represent different departments. Again little is known of current practice, either because committees of officials are linked to Cabinet committees and are therefore drawn under the same veil of secrecy, or because they are subject to normal departmental confidentiality, or because they are informal and *ad hoc* and therefore receive little or no publicity.

Co-ordination is but one of the very many uses to which committees may be put. Committees may legislate, administer, control, inquire and advise.[17] The distinctive feature of the interdepartmental co-ordinating committee is that it is designed to produce uniformity in some aspect of the behaviour of the organizations represented by the committee members, even if this is achieved mainly by an exchange of information and not by the taking of formal binding decisions, perhaps after a conflict of interests. For example, R. J. S. Baker has described how British official delegates at international conferences adopted attitudes consistent with one another after attending committee meetings organized by the Foreign Office mainly for the purpose of exchanging information.[18]

Generally, however, co-ordinating committees do not exist for an exchange of views and information or to explore a problem through joint effort, although these things will occur during the committee's deliberations. Indeed, interdepartmental committees naturally have the characteristics, virtues and vices of any other kind of committee. They are to be distinguished by the fact that they do one of two things. First, they may produce a submission to ministers, probably sitting on a Cabinet committee. This submission will embody the points of agreement and disagreement between the officials concerned and will reflect a consensus on the nature of the problem if not on its solution. In this type of committee preparatory work is carried out by the representation of departmental interests and by exchange of information prior to the co-ordination proper – the decision of the ministerial committee taken on the basis of the submission. These committees may present opportunities to resolve conflict and reduce opposition before Cabinet discussion. They prepared the ground for the Cabinet committees by setting out clearly the issues which could be settled out of hand and those which required discussion and decision.[19] An example of a major committee of this type is the Public Expenditure Survey Committee.

This is an interdepartmental committee about which we do know something, mainly because of attempts by Parliament and those interested in Parliament to monitor the results of its deliberations. The Committee is composed of the principal finance officers of all the main spending departments and is chaired by a senior Treasury official. Its job is to produce a document each year for submission to ministers setting out the costs of continuing existing policies over the next five years on the basis of forecasts of future demand – for unemployment benefits, hospital beds, university places, grants for road improvements and so on. Much of the argument in this committee is about the rates of increase in their levels of expenditure which departments think are indicated by their forecasts and estimates of demands for their services. When the Committee is agreed on the implications of current policies for the next five years it is then up to ministers to decide, in the light of the medium-term economic assessment of growth, consumption, investment and the balance of payments over the next five years, whether the projected level of public expenditure has to be cut and whether the allocation of resources between programmes is in line with the Government's overall strategy.

The second function of an interdepartmental co-ordinating committee is to produce guarantees of some action or decision by the members of the committee or the organizations they represent. Such committees exert control over the member organizations by extracting commitments to act in a way which is consistent with the committee's plans.

Examples of such a committee are the regional planning boards. These were set up between 1964 and 1965 in each of eight English economic planning regions, and in Scotland and Wales. Their membership has varied from time to time under the influence of departmental reorganizations in Whitehall. Basically they are interdepartmental committees of the senior representatives of the regional offices of government departments concerned with regional planning. In the English regions the chairmen are the regional directors of the Department of the Environment with the rank of under secretary. In Scotland and Wales the chairmen are senior officials of the Scottish and Welsh offices.

The job of each planning board is to assist an advisory commiteee, the regional planning council, to produce development strategies for the region and to give advice to ministers on the implications of central government policies for the economic potential of each region. They also have a function in the execution of regional programmes, although the individual officers acting in their capacity as departmental officials are probably more important to effective policy execution than the interdepartmental committees on which they serve.[20]

Nevertheless, the boards have a number of co-ordinating roles. First there is the problem of integrating the research and information functions carried on by the regional offices of the departments. This is one of the ways in which the boards service the planning councils. The boards commission studies of aspects of the regional economies, such as transport, agriculture, population and manpower trends. Board meetings are particularly important when research and information projects cut across departmental boundaries. The co-ordination of this research effort has been found to reveal gaps in official sources of data and to produce new ideas and approaches to planning.[21]

Secondly, membership of a board introduces a new element into the work of regional civil servants. They become more aware of the implications of their work for the region as a geographical and economic entity and for the administrative efforts of their fellow officials working in hitherto self-contained departments, linked vertically with headquarters in London rather than horizontally with other decentralized offices.

Thirdly, the boards provide a forum for the resolution of conflict and development of co-operation between departments concerned with interrelated projects and policies, such as the demands made on land by housing, industry and agriculture. However, the officials on the boards are not given discretion to vary their department's policies according to their assessments of their region's needs. Any discretion which an individual committee member might enjoy is determined by the policy of his department.

Despite these co-ordinating functions the very sparse evidence we have on the regional planning boards suggests that they may suffer from some of the disadvantages commonly associated with committee work. They are sometimes regarded as an unnecessary and time-wasting addition to existing informal methods of liaison and communication between regional officials. In this connection it must be remembered that they came into being as part of a political exercise designed to produce regional machinery with an image of expertise and effective executive power. As such they are not typical of interdepartmental committees designed for purely administrative purposes.

In local government each department or group of departments is mainly responsible to one committee, and not to a political office-holder, as in central government. Committees thus have administrative functions in that they supervise the executive work of departmental staff. Local authority committees illustrate perfectly the appropriateness of committees for policy making and their disadvantages as executive co-ordinators. In the former activity 'a committee enables decisions to be taken by a number of people after discussion and it can be argued that there is a better chance of the decisions being right if many minds contribute to them . . . They ensure that the interests of a variety of people are represented and heard; they can provide safeguards against bureaucratic and unresponsive administration and keep officers in close touch with political and public opinion.'[22]

In administration, however, the shortcomings of committees in supervising the work of departments increase as the volume and technical complexity of the work grows. 'The system wastes time, results in delays and causes frustration by involving committees in matters of administrative detail.'[23] Instead of controlling and directing the department, committee members become pre-occupied with petty details.

The importance of the committee in producing the co-ordination required for policy formulation is further illustrated by recent developments in local government. As local authorities increasingly adopt a corporate approach to the planning of services the need for a policy committee analogous to the Cabinet in central government has become apparent. Like Parliament, the local council is the final decision-making body. But within it there needs to be a committee, sometimes consisting of senior members of the majority party, sometimes a 'coalition' of senior councillors, to initiate policies. Within local government, opinion and practice varies on the issue of policy committees. However, further changes in structure are likely in response to the latest report on the subject, that of the Bains Working Group, which recommended that 'Each authority should establish a Policy and Resources Committee to provide co-ordinated advice to the Council in the setting of its plans, objectives and priorities. The Committee should also exercise overall control over the major resources of the authority and co-ordinate and control the implementation of the Council's programmes.'[24]

Again as in central government, local authorities are witnessing the creation of specialized staffs and interdepartmental committees of officials for policy analysis and review in support of the policy committees, such as the corporate planning and management teams of principal chief officers also recommended by the Bains Report. Practice varies from one authority to another but the general idea of the planning unit is of an interdepartmental working group for the identification and review of objectives and priorities, the linking of objectives, programmes and budgets, and the monitoring of progress. Management teams, under the leadership of chief executives, should prepare plans and programmes for the long-term objectives of the Council and should be responsible for their general co-ordination and implementation.

Co-ordination is not achieved purely by the exercise of authority by a central co-ordinator, such as the Cabinet, Treasury or interdepartmental committee. Behind the array of formal co-ordinating mechanisms, and assisting their functioning, lies a set of informal relationships through which interdependent agencies adapt their behaviour and decisions to each other. Lindblom has called this process co-ordination by mutual adjustment, having in

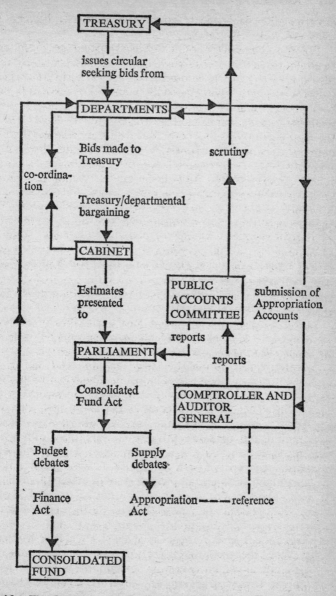

Fig. 13. **The Sequence of Financial Planning**

mind the kind of co-ordination effected between consumer and producer by the market mechanisms. In principle there can be co-ordination without controls or specific devices for achieving it. Lindblom applies his concepts to the governmental process as a whole. But if the idea of mutual adjustment between interdependent decision makers is applied to the relationships between agencies in central government then it is possible to add another dimension to the structure of formal co-ordination described so far. Mutual adjustment can operate through a number of different kinds of relationship which may be present when the formal methods of central co-ordination are at work.

Thus it is clear that some participants in co-ordinating processes work through adaptive adjustments, altering their own behaviour in response to circumstances but without seeking to change the actions of other decision makers. For example, a Prime Minister may influence policy by keeping matters off the Cabinet agenda or by taking decisions with little or no reference to colleagues. The Chancellor of the Exchequer draws up his Budget with reference to no one but the Prime Minister. He is aware of his colleagues' views and has to fit in with the Government's economic policies. But he does not have to negotiate and bargain to produce action from others. Another minister's position may be weakened by being outside the senior group. He may take decisions influenced by deference to others.

Alternatively, co-ordination may be accompanied by, and achieved through, manipulated adjustment when decision makers try different ways of producing desired responses from others. There will be negotiation, as between the Treasury and spending departments over the Estimates, or bargaining, when decision makers threaten or make promises to get their own way (a minister threatening to resign, for example). In all forms of co-ordination there is discussion, and the mutual review of arguments, evidence and assessments of possible lines of action (as in the case of the Public Expenditure Survey Committee, discussions about the reliability or reasonableness of forecasts of future demand for a service under existing policies). The natural authority exuded by a committee member or agency image (e.g. the British Treasury in the eyes of the rest of the civil service) may exert great influence.

We do not, as yet, know very much about the informal relationships between central government departments either as factors influencing the operation of the formal machinery of co-ordination or working independently of it. But we do know it is only part of the picture to describe central co-ordination in terms of hierarchy and control. It must also be described in terms of adjustment, adaptation and manipulation.

Notes

 1 Cmnd. 4506, 1970, p. 4
 2 Mackenzie, 1950, p. 82
 3 Bains, 1972
 4 Cmnd. 6502, 1944
 5 Select Committee on Nationalized Industries, 1967
 6 Simon, 1945, p. 9
 7 Simon, 1945, p. 134
 8 Simon, 1945, p. 10
 9 Bridges, 1964, p. 34
10 Bridges, 1964, p. 41
11 Civil Service Department, 1970
12 Haldane, 1918
13 Walker, 1972, p. 125
14 Mackintosh, 1968, p. 529
15 Walker, 1972, p. 25–6
16 Cmnd. 4506, 1970
17 Wheare, 1955
18 Baker, 1963
19 Jennings, 1969, p. 143
20 Smith, 1969; Petersen, 1966
21 Cross, 1970
22 Maud, 1967, para. 127
23 Maud, 1967, para. 128
24 Bains, 1972, p. 124

Chapter 5
The Public Service

A distinctive feature of the British system of government is that the organizations that constitute it are not staffed by a single body of public servants. In fact, the phrase 'the public service' is hardly ever used; the student of public administration is much more likely to speak of, and study, the civil service, the local government service, the staff of the national health service, National Coal Board employees, etc., and to treat them as quite separate subjects. The reason for this is that the personnel of government do not form a homogeneous group but may be easily differentiated in many important respects according to the particular part of the government machine in which they are employed. Each type of body, and indeed many individual bodies, has its own method of recruitment, training, discipline, grading, pay scales, pension systems, and more generally, its own definition of the role, scope and significance of permanent employees.

We have chosen to refer to the totality of public employees as 'the public service' rather than the 'bureaucracy' for two reasons: as mentioned above, public servants in Britain can not be organized in a single, unified hierarchical structure, and many of the individual services within the whole depart considerably from the ideal-type 'bureaucracy' set out by Max Weber.[1] But it is a consequence of our general approach that we regard it as important that the whole of the public service should be considered within a common framework; in other words, the comparative approach should be adopted here as well as in the other chapters.

There are certain broad general principles of conduct which apply across the board, such as the need for impartiality in decision making and the absence of nepotism in recruitment and promotion procedures, but the divisions within the public service tend to correspond to the divisions in the system of public administration described in the previous chapter.

The public service of Britain is generally less unified than other countries in Western Europe, where the state itself takes a greater interest in recruitment and training, but even so it is much more homogeneous than the public service of America where the federal system and the generally greater freedom for local authorities in these matters combine with the fragmentation of the federal executive to produce a situation almost unintelligible in its diversity.

Our first major concern is to look at the place of the main categories of public servant in the system of government and their distinguishing characteristics. Much of what is said in the later sections of this chapter refers mainly to the civil service, as this is the part of the public service that has been most investigated and documented, but we shall use comparative material from the other parts whenever possible.

The public service, therefore, consists of the employees of central departments (the civil service), employees of local authorities (the local government service) and the employees of the diverse collection of public bodies that we described as 'non-departmental organizations'. But there are several doubtful categories of personnel which might be included in the public service but which we shall not consider, except in passing references. These are the employees of judicial and military organizations, the staff of legislatures where these are not civil servants, and temporary appointments where these are made to politically sensitive roles or key linking positions in the system of government, often on partisan grounds.

In 1971 the civil service accounted for some 700,000 public servants, nearly half a million of whom were non-industrial (industrial civil servants are those employed in factories, dockyards, ports, depots and stores). The local government service contained over 2,000,000 people, including nearly half a million teachers, nearly 100,000 police and a large number of manual workers, about ten per cent of the working population. The nationalized industries, not including the other non-industrial public corporations such as the British Broadcasting Corporation, accounted for almost as large a number. Finally, there was the national health service of that time employing or in contact with half a million doctors, dentists, nurses, technical, professional, administrative, clerical, manual and domestic staff.

Public servants as individuals can be distinguished in terms of the type of work that they do, and the proportion of each type of employment in a public organization serves to characterize it in comparison with other bodies in a way that is important for understanding the problems that arise in managing the public service in the processes of government. The civil service is predominantly non-industrial and administrative, in that only 28 per cent of its non-industrial staff are employed as professional architects, lawyers, scientists, etc., rather than as administrative, executive and clerical officers carrying out policy formation and management functions. The industrial and commercial nature of many of the public corporations, as well as their constitutional status, has produced many contrasts between their staff and the civil service. With some important exceptions, the employees of public corporations are analogous to those in the private sector. At the time of nationalization a deliberate decision was taken not to make the staff civil servants. They may, therefore, be contrasted with the civil service both in terms of the proportions in industrial and commercial occupations and by the fact that no overall statutory provisions regulate their staffing.

Contrasts may also be drawn between civil servants and local government officers. Most of the services and functions of local authorities require professional and technical skills. Thus an important difference to the civil service is that senior personnel in local government are specialists rather than generalist administrators. 37·8 per cent of local government staff were employed in professional or technical capacities, compared with 24 per cent in administrative and 29·9 per cent in clerical work. If policemen and teachers were included the specialist nature of the local government service would be underlined further.

The national health service, in so far as it was an integrated public service, was different again, in that its foundation consisted of the relatively autonomous medical and allied professions. The health service was in fact a combination of individual services working under different managerial control – the executive councils, the regional hospital boards and local health authorities. The staff of the two former were neither civil servants nor local government officers, but the latter's employees in personal health services were part of the local government service. The reorganization and unification of the diverse structure of the health service under the new area health authorities will be a fundamental redeployment of three-quarters of a million public servants. Although the majority of staff are in occupations requiring medical and allied skills and training, and related technical roles, there will be special problems associated with the recruitment, training, career development and status of administrators in health service administration, especially the professional hospital administrator.

There are many other characteristics of individual public servants which may be important in distinguishing different types of public body and different roles in the overall governmental system. Some of these we consider at length later in the chapter, but it is worth mentioning some of the characteristics that we cannot consider properly for lack of space.

Some of these relate to the working life of the individual. Public servants may be *full-time* or *part-time*, *permanent* (often = established) or *temporary*, and *career* or *non-career*. Others relate to their empirical attributes rather than legal or contractual position, i.e. their sex, religion, age, social class origins, place of birth, etc. Only a few of these have been properly considered in research and we are forced to follow the conventional choice in our later discussions.

The Public Service in its Constitutional Setting

Permanent officials have considerable political power, sometimes as individuals but more usually collectively. This has long been a recognized feature of private organization, such as political parties and trade unions, who are formally governed by elected committees, but the traditional writers on public administration have been curiously loth to look at its significance in public administration. We mentioned in an earlier chapter one aspect of this subject – the political roles of field officers – and also mentioned that only left-wing critics of the 'bourgeois state' have paid much attention generally to the political consequences of the existence of elaborate organizations of public servants.

Yet in the countries with which we are familiar it would be quite wrong to describe the political system as 'government by the bureaucracy'. The question is therefore in what ways is the power of the public servant restrained so that responsibility is placed on those who are answerable to the general body of citizens and chosen by it to take political decisions; in other words, what is the constitutional position of the public service, particularly in a democratic state?

THE MERIT SYSTEM

It is accepted as part of the British theory of responsible govern ̄
ment that employees of public institutions should be recruited on
the basis of merit, to be demonstrated through some form of competitive, open selective system, rather than by political patronage,
nepotism or tradition. This is of course done partly to try to
ensure that public servants are competent in the work that they
have to do, but it is also intended that political blame and praise
should only be levelled at those who can be removed from office
by democratic procedures. This would not be the case if members of
the civil service, the military and the judiciary were dependent on
political favours.

This idea has been much less readily accepted in the United
States, and many states and localities still have partisan public
services. In Britain, as we shall see later, there are some occasions
when the principle is rejected, and it has been suggested that these
are growing. In other countries, revolution or major changes in
the political system are associated with the dismissal of civil
servants and their replacement by others, even though in times of
'normalcy' this would be rare or non-existent.

Service to the Crown means for practical purposes service to
the minister appointed by the Crown. As such, the actions of the
civil servant are taken in the name of his minister. The neutral
position of the civil service is further reflected in the code of
conduct which imposes the duty of giving individual allegiance to
the State at all times but excludes taking an active part as private
individuals in any matter of public and political controversy.

MINISTERIAL RESPONSIBILITY

This aspect of democratic theory in Britain is embodied as far as
the civil service is concerned in the constitutional doctrine of
ministerial responsibility. This prescribes that a minister of the
Crown shall be held accountable to Parliament for his decisions
and the decisions of his department. Accountability means in
theory that the minister explains and defends the actions of his
officials before Parliament, and also that he may be held culpable
for faults in his personal conduct and errors in departmental

administration. The doctrine thus includes the sanction of enforced resignation for departmental mismanagement.

This concept of responsibility may be contrasted with some foreign constitutional systems, such as the French and American. In the United States constitutional prescription on legislative-executive relations is clearer in theory than in practice. In theory the doctrine of the separation of powers clearly distinguishes the executive from the legislative and neither the President nor the heads of executive departments sit in Congress. The responsibility of all parts of the executive branch for administrative actions is exercised through the President whose responsibility is more directly to the people than to elected representatives sitting in Congress. There is no concept of individual ministerial answerability to the legislature.

However, Congress is extremely active and effective in subjecting the administration to scrutiny. This power is based on the concept of 'legislative oversight' which is seen as a necessary condition of Congress's legislative role. In effect this means that the United States Congress can go much further in investigating administration than the British Parliament is able to because Congress is not restrained by the doctrine of ministerial responsibility which in Britain protects the civil service against direct accountability to the legislature.

France demonstrates yet another model of responsible government under the constitution of the Fifth Republic which has swung the balance of power in favour of the executive branch. The separation of powers prevents ministers from sitting in the National Assembly, although they may appear before it. Constitutional rules limiting the sovereignty of Parliament reduce its effectiveness in controlling the executive. The power of investigatory committees has also been reduced. As in the United Kingdom ministers are responsible to Parliament, but collectively more than individually. As in the United States they are not members of the legislature. But unlike Congress Parliament has lost its power of legislative oversight and scrutiny. In so far as the executive is responsible to the legislature it is for broad policy, not administrative detail. The significance of this for responsible government in France is even further reduced by the important part played by the President in policy-making.

ANONYMITY

In Britain the civil servant is protected by ministerial responsibility from political criticism and attack. He remains anonymous. His opinions and decisions are regarded as those of his minister. The civil servant is not identified as being concerned with a particular area of policy. Should he find himself in a position of speaking for his minister, say to a Select Committee, he can explain but not justify, describe but not defend. The part he plays in the formulation and execution of policy, and the advice which he gives, remain hidden from public view. The civil servant is neutral, not only in the sense of being politically uncommitted but in the sense that he is not to be judged as right or wrong. Responsibility in the ethical sense rests with the minister. Theoretically it is not for the civil servant to judge what is in the public interest.

Anonymity is regarded as a necessary condition of impartiality. How, it is asked, could a minister work with a civil servant known to be in sympathy with a predecessor of a different party? And how could such sympathies avoid being known? Thus, if civil servants say too much publicly, their loyalty to their ministers is inevitably at risk. They would begin to rival ministers as the focus of political accountability. 'Once they became publicly identified with particular views on policy, their usefulness as members of an objective, non-political service is at an end.' The logical corollary of such identification is sometimes thought to be that top posts become political appointments.

IMPARTIALITY

In exchange for the protection of anonymity the civil servant offers political impartiality. He is not identified with any partisan interest, although this does not mean he has no political role in the sense of contributing to the policy-making process. Instead, the permanent official is expected to administer and manage the policies of his political masters regardless of their party attachments. Governments of different party complexions can with reasonable confidence expect loyal and efficient service from the same administrators who served their predecessors in office. From time to time there are signs of stress between ministers and civil servants which may or may not be based on partisan differences.

But there is not sufficient evidence to suggest that the basic principle of political neutrality on the part of permanent officials has been significantly eroded.

PRESSURES FOR CHANGE

The constitutional position of the civil servant as described above represents a constitutional model which is qualified in reality and subject to pressures for change in the contemporary political environment. A number of factors influence the practical role of the civil service in the constitution.

First there is the greatly weakened concept of ministerial responsibility at present operative in British politics. Culpability has virtually disappeared from the working of this principle. Ministerial resignations for departmental failure are extremely rare – some twenty in over a century.[2] Given the reality of British Parliamentary politics the reasons for this development are not difficult to find. Finer identified four: the collective responsibility of the Cabinet combines with an appeal to party solidarity to change a threat to a minister into a threat to the Government; Cabinet reshuffles which simply move the offending minister from one office to another; the power of individual ministers which may enable them to hold on to office; and the practice of reinstating a minister in a different office after a 'decent interval'. MPs now recognize that it is unreasonable, in the conditions of modern government, to expect ministers to have knowledge of every decision taken by their often enormous departments. If ministers can only be said to 'take' decisions in the most theoretical and legalistic sense, they can only be said to be responsible for them in similar terms. Ministers are simply not thought to be responsible for decisions which they did not know about and would not have approved. Similarly the time-span of government projects is often long enough to cause problems for a minister arising from the decisions of his predecessor for which it would be unreasonable to hold him responsible. While ministers remain answerable to Parliament in the sense of having to explain and justify the actions of their departments to the House of Commons (which may include the repudiation of a predecessor), the realities of administrative and political life combine to protect ministers against the ultimate form of Parliamentary censure.

In relation to the anonymity of the civil service it is important to distinguish between different types of official. The constitutional rules about anonymity are much more operative in relation to administrators than to professionals and specialists of various kinds, and to officials based at headquarters in London than to those working in the field in regional and district offices.

It is more likely that professionals will be called on to identify themselves publicly, even to the extent of defending a particular policy, than their counterparts in the administrative grades. As policy advisers, often one stage removed from contact with ministers, they have a degree of freedom to offer their expert advice publicly which is not enjoyed by the administrator who is more concerned with the choice of policy options and their political implications for his minister in Parliament, in the Cabinet, in the party and in the eyes of the public or sectional groups closely concerned.

The formal model of individual ministerial responsibility needs to be further amended to take account of a growing willingness to identify civil servants as responsible for certain decisions when mistakes are made – to name and blame. This of course undermines the anonymity of the civil service and suggests that civil servants could become directly accountable for departmental policy.

Instances of the public identification of civil servants tend to be *causes célèbres* and therefore perhaps exceptions which prove the still important constitutional rule. The cases are certainly few as yet. Officials were identifiable or identified in the Ferranti case when excessive profits were made on the Bloodhound missile contract; in the navy spy scandals of 1961; and the Vehicle and General Insurance Company case of 1972.[3] Cases such as these clearly reduce the anonymity of the civil service. They may also involve public expressions of disapprobation by some form of public inquiry.

Recent trends in British government have also tended to increase the visibility of civil servants to aid Parliamentary scrutiny of the administration. There is a long history of direct communication between MPs and civil servants through the media of the Public Accounts Committee and Select Committee on Estimates. This has only taken on a new constitutional significance with the change in the role of such committees from a concern with checking administrative detail to the investigation of policy and policy formation in which the contributions of officials could become more easily identifiable.

So far reductions in the anonymity of civil servants have not constituted a significant departure from this part of the constitutional convention. So long as Parliament does not attempt to impose sanctions and discipline directly on civil servants that it judges to be at fault, less anonymity should only mean less secrecy, a development which would be widely welcomed.

Anonymity and neutrality clearly imply that it is not for the civil service to decide what is in the interest of the community. However, it may well be that senior civil servants would be willing to assume such a responsibility. Indeed they may already have seen themselves as having a duty to protect the public interest. Members of the First Division Association (representing the interests of the old administrative class) have suggested that civil servants not only have responsibilities to their ministers and the administration of which they form part, but also to Parliament, the democratic system and the rights and interests of individuals and groups that make up the community as a whole.

From time to time politicians drop hints that senior officials have exhibited strong biases towards certain kinds of policy, even to the extent of thwarting the wishes of ministers. Other high office holders have publicly stated views leaving no doubts as to their opinions on certain policy issues. Even the expression of strongly held convictions on individual policy issues, however, does not imply a permanent party or ideological attachment. To this extent constitutional doctrine is undamaged.

The 'Whitehall irregulars' are more likely to be closely associated with the politics of the ministers they are brought in to advise. These are businessmen, trade unionists, academics or others seconded to government to provide specialist advice on aspects of policy in areas in which they have achieved some eminence. Such advisers, like the industrial advisers brought into the Department of Economic Affairs in 1964 have access to Ministers and officials at all levels[4] and help to strengthen the links between government and the private sector.

The appointment of 'outsiders' to permanent posts that civil servants would normally expect to fill does have greater constitutional significance than the appointment of temporary advisers. There have been some instances of this recently in connection with the units of accountable management set up in the form of departmental agencies for various executive functions. Businessmen have been brought in or transferred from the team of Government advisers in order to take charge of the Defence Procurement Executive, the Property Services Executive (for the management of government buildings and property) and the Professional & Executive Register within the new Employment Services Executive in the Department of Employment. In the last case the Executive itself is headed by a senior civil servant. The fact that the other comparable organizations are not suggests a new development in the use of 'outsiders' which may have a greater effect on the permanence of the service than the 'irregulars'.

The Local Government Service

It is not so easy to describe the 'constitutional' position of local government officers because it varies considerably from authority to authority, and perhaps also between different types of officer. This is a sphere in which the 'conventions of the local constitution'[5] are extremely important. Factors such as the size of the local authority, its legal responsibilities and the nature of partisan or non-partisan conflict have produced differing styles and forms of elected member-officer relations. There are, however, two major points of contrast with the civil service.

First, there is no concept of ministerial responsibility in local government. Administrative responsibilities are delegated by the 'legislature' (the local council) to committees, not individuals. Some committees have a statutory existence of their own. The heads of the local authority departments, its chief officers, serve these committees. They are thus in much closer and more frequent contact with elected representatives than are civil servants. In some authorities a committee chairman, perhaps because of seniority or party position, may emerge with much greater power than his members and appear as almost a ministerial figure. However, officials are, strictly speaking, servants of the authority working under the direction of committees, not individual councillors. Responsibility and accountability are thus more diffuse in local than in central government, although there is a clear understanding that responsibility rests in the majority of cases with elected members. And unlike civil servants, local government officers have to combine service to the council which is responsible both legally and politically to the electors and by whom they are employed, with responsiveness to a committee which supervises local administration.[6]

Second, chief officers of a local authority are much less anonymous than civil servants. They are more likely to be known to the electors and easily accessible to them. It is much easier in local government than in central to identify officers in the areas of policy and policy decisions, mainly because responsibility for a technical service rests clearly with the professionally qualified chief officer at the head of the relevant department. What is important for the purpose of contrast with central government is that the senior local government officer is not inhibited to the same degree that the senior civil servant is from being publicly identifiable with a particular policy, or from expressing values relevant to policy choices, by the fear of embarrassing a minister. This in turn leads to less secrecy and confidentiality in local government, even to the extent of admitting the press and the public to committee meetings. One only has to imagine official reactions to the suggestion that meetings between ministers and their senior civil servants should be made open to the public to see the contrast between local and central government in this respect.

In fact in the towns and countryside outside the largest urban areas, and sometimes within these, senior local government officers are often members of the local upper class in terms of salary, occupation and family background and enjoy a visibility in the local community not only directly from their work but also indirectly because they will be in demand for public speeches and as expositors of council policy and actions.

There are, however, other local authorities in which the public involvement of local government officers is thought to be undesirable and efforts are made to avoid openness of decision making by restricting admission of press and public to committee meetings to the legal minimum. In some areas there has been a running battle between the central government and local community groups on one hand and council members and officials on the other over the extent to which committees should be open.

Yet in other respects the parallels between central and local government service are much closer. Local government officers do not in general have a special responsibility to protect the public interest by standing between their councils and their ratepayers. There is one important exception to this in the treasurer's duty to disobey orders to make illegal payments. The general rule is that officials obey their councils and are responsible to them, not to the electorate.

In one sense the local government service differs from the civil service in that there is no single employer; each local authority in formal terms has the power to recruit its own staff. Thus the individual does not join the local government service; he is recruited to work for a particular authority. But in recent years several factors have combined to make employment in local government more like that of the civil service than it was before the Second World War. One of these is the intervention of the central government through the prescription of qualifications for certain posts and the regulation of superannuation arrangements. The creation of special agencies such as the National Board for Prices and Incomes, the Conservatives' Pay Board and the Local Government Staff Commissions have reinforced this intervention.

But perhaps more importantly the local government world itself has taken action to unify the local government service. On the employees' side both professional associations and trade unions have been active in promoting more uniform conditions of service and personnel policies. On the employers' side, the local authority associations have been active in creating standardized patterns of staffing and grading, and have formed joint organizations at the national level to deal with matters of common interest, the most significant of which is the Local Government Training Board.

The result is that there is now a uniform system of grading and pay structures which individual local authorities adopt (with necessary local variations), and a general acceptance of the norms of recruitment by merit rather than nepotism and patronage. Though no doubt some authorities have partisan or social biases and prejudices when selecting staff at the most senior levels, there is no spoils system. The vigilance of the unions and the professional associations often now prevents even small (and overtly justified) departures from national recruitment and appointment standards.

Officers are precluded from membership of their own councils and so cannot combine political and administrative office as is done in some other countries such as Germany.[7] Chief officers are expected not to participate in party politics, as are other senior officials who are concerned with policy formation and the management of executive activities. Some authorities do not object if the partisan involvement occurs in another area and officers can legally serve on councils other than their own. At the present time there is trade union pressure to permit low-level employees to serve on their own councils, but this is being strongly resisted, rightly so in the authors' opinion, by the central government and the local authority associations.

Within the council itself officials are usually debarred from advising, working for, or meeting with, private party organizations such as the council caucus. In some strongly organized partisan authorities, such as the Leeds City Council described by Wiseman,[8] the party groups held meetings to discuss and determine the line that all its members would follow in council and committee, and it was considered improper for officials to attend such meetings. But this principle is not always easy to maintain. For instance, if in effect the majority caucus meeting is the ultimate decision maker in the authority, the non-attendance of officers means that their technical and professional advice is absent from some of the most significant parts of the process. In a one-party system, also, each committee meeting is in fact a party meeting, and there is nothing to stop a majority party creating an official committee and putting only its members on it. Generally, however, local government officers will try to deal with elected personnel in their capacity as councillors rather than party members, just as civil servants deal with members of Parliament and members of the government, rather than with party groups within Parliament.

If the reader can imagine the variety of situations that can be created for the local government officer by different political and social factors he will begin to appreciate the importance of the 'conventions of the local constitution' we mentioned above.

Finally, there is a code of conduct applicable to all local government officers written into the *Scheme of Conditions of Service* worked out by the national negotiating machinery. This code requires that official conduct should never be influenced by improper motives, such as the subordination of public duty to private interests, and should always be of the highest standard to ensure public confidence in the integrity of officials.

At the time of writing the local government service is the subject of an investigation by a committee chaired by Lord Redcliffe-

Maud into the rules of conduct of both council members and officers. This is a consequence of the Poulson Affair and the growing number of prosecutions of both for offences particularly in the field of planning. The present malaise, however, is not restricted to the local government service as the offences so far revealed have involved many different branches of the public service and lay personnel as well as employed.

As one moves away from the service of governments to the service of managerial bodies which have been set up free from direct political control and interference, the political role and status of the public servant declines in significance. The pre-occupation tends to be with professional standards (where appropriate) or codes of conduct relevant to public service.

When we come to the public corporations we find staff who are comparable in almost all respects to employees in the private sector. The relevant statutes setting up the corporations contain no general staffing provisions and leave the boards free to manage their staff in the same way as any other employer, with two important exceptions. Joint consultative machinery must be set up to negotiate terms and conditions of employment, including health, welfare and safety; and provision must be made for advancing the skills of employees. Apart from this the staff of the nationalized industries have no special status other than that they are employees of public bodies, not private, but are not civil servants. This is more a reference to the employer than to any special duty imposed on the employee by virtue of public service. In fact employees of the public corporations do not form a public service. Their links are with trade unions and professional bodies which cut across the line between the public and private sectors of employment.

The Public Service in the Political System

The importance of the public service is not only to be found in its size and diversity, or in its role in the provision of public services as prescribed by law. A few public servants on occasion may be politically important as individuals, but for the most the political role of the public servant is performed collectively. In this section we are concerned with the significance of public servants in the operation of the political system, in effect with political roles in the widest sense, which are not recognized by formal theoretical accounts of the constitution or by most public servants themselves.

The traditional view of how far in a democratic system public servants affect policy making and the distribution of power within a society was that this was not and should not be the case at all. The civil service, for instance, was seen as essentially concerned with the 'outputs' of the governmental system, with implementing the decisions of politicians in the executive and legislative branches. The official's task was to advise politicians on the means to achieve whatever ends the latter deemed desirable; and to execute the consequent decisions effectively and efficiently. In this picture the civil servant had no political role.

It has become widely accepted that the pure theory of representative and responsible government as presented by the constitutional lawyers is, and always has been, unrealistic. This has been brought home to the student of the political system partly through comparative research and partly through more penetrating studies of domestic policy formation and implementation.

The political significance of senior public servants can best be understood by an examination of their work within the overall decision-making processes of modern government. Their political role is not something over and above their technical roles but a necessary aspect of them, embedded in their daily working life.

Obviously it is impossible to draw a clear line between the activities related to the development of policy, in which outsiders play a considerable part, and those related simply to execution. Though managing a large group of clerical staff is distinct from preparing a memorandum on the feasibility of a new policy initiative, there are many activities which seem to combine elements of both.

In fact, it is the decision-making process itself which mixes up the elements of policy and administration and creates the political roles of civil servants. Basically policy implementation 'feeds back' into policy formation so that the administrator can comment authoritatively on the practicability of different policy options. The knowledge and experience of specialized areas of public activity that senior administrators have gives them, if not a near monopoly of legitimate opinion, at least a more authoritative view of policy making in those areas. Organizational experience impinges strongly on policy formation. New policy often emerges as difficulties come to the notice of senior administrators dealing with the old, and their ideas are brought to bear on problems that politicians wish to solve. The closeness with which senior administrators, especially in the central departments, control access to information strengthens their position both in relation to outsiders and other insiders when policy changes are under consideration.

There is another factor which strengthens the position of the senior administrator relative to the politician. This is the permanence of civil servants compared with the mobility of ministers. The 'turnover' amongst ministers in central government has often been contrasted with the civil servant's longstanding familiarity with the affairs of his department. The experience of the most senior officials at the hub of government, such as the Treasury and the Cabinet Office, gives the higher civil service a unity and *esprit de corps* which is reinforced by the complex system of interdepartmental contacts through committees and less formal devices. This facilitates the emergence of consensus on policy issues at the official level, often before proposals are put before ministers. Indeed it is established practice in central government to seek agreement among departments affected by a possible policy change before a decision is made at the political level. In one sense a civil servant may be performing a great service for his minister by getting his point of view accepted in negotiations with officials in other departments and in the Treasury, before matters reach the Cabinet or a Cabinet committee, but at the same time departmental points of view act as a powerful counterbalance to new ideas brought in by politicians.

The increasing complexity of government and, at the centre at least, the size of some of its organizational units, combine to strengthen the influence of the most senior administrators over policy making. With the emergence of 'giant' departments such as Health and Social Security or Environment, the truth of H. E. Dale's statement that 'more is now decided and done without reference to ministers but on their responsibility' is even greater at the present than it was in 1941.[9]

The situation in local government presents some contrasts with the above, but there can be no doubt that there are many features of similarity. The equivalent of the higher civil service in each local authority is composed of the heads, and some of their deputies and other assistants, of the separate departments. Unlike senior civil servants, these are for the most part not generalists but professionally qualified in one of the technical specialisms relating to the work of their department. However, once the authority rises above a certain (quite small) size, with a consequent increase in the volume of work, their role ceases to be professional in the strict sense and becomes managerial, administrative or organizational in the literal meaning of these words. They also become very obviously part of the leadership of the authority in the widest sense.

But there are some differences between senior local government officers and senior civil servants, which derive from the different nature of decision making at the two levels. One of these is the consequence of different structures to the local government service as opposed to the civil service. Because of the absence of a unified local government service career advancement and promotion are much more the initiative of the individual officer who must decide whether or not to seek posts in other authorities in order to better himself. For many, promotion is to be found in a move to another authority, not within the same authority. The result is that senior ranks tend to be more mobile than civil servants; indeed, in some authorities council members are more permanent than the officers who advise them. Probably the least mobile local government officers are those who serve as generalists in the lower levels of each department's hierarchy. Sometimes innovating chief officers are caught between the conservatism of the elected member and the conservatism of long-serving section heads and administrative and technical staff.

Secondly, because the actual problems that local authorities face do not divide themselves up nicely into the categories used in creating departmental organization, many decisions involve several specialisms, and therefore several departments and several committees. Decision making is thus not completed in one place and several officers may be deeply involved. This is of course also true of central government, but civil servants operate in private and under the constraint of collective responsibility, which makes it more important for them to reach definite agreement than does the local authority committee system.

Thirdly, chief officers in local government are as bound by the limitations placed on local authority decision making as are council members. Though they may be influential in relation to the sphere of local authority powers and duties, they may find that this sphere is itself restricted, particularly by the central government itself.

Fourthly, local authority departments have also tended to increase in size through mergers of distinct, though related, operations. This process has rather different consequences in local government; it tends to put the chief officer more in the hands of his subordinates than before. No one can be an expert in several professions and thus the head of the department may do little more than preside over a collection of distinct activities.

Similar analyses could no doubt be undertaken of the relations, say between the senior officials of the National Coal Board and the Board itself, or between British Broadcasting Corporation controllers and the Board of Governors. The higher civil service and chief officers in local government are only two important and well-documented examples of the ways public servants may have political roles as a necessary consequence of their position in the decision-making process.

A Profession of Government?

As we have seen public servants in Britain are expected to conform to a code of conduct to ensure their independence of partisan attachment and their pursuit of efficient and effective government. As many of them can point to a rigorous recruitment and training programme, and sense of unity or 'belonging' among officials in different departments, they have sought recognition as a profession, particularly in the higher civil service.

To be a profession it is not sufficient merely to believe it oneself; it is necessary to secure wide social recognition of the claim. There is some disagreement about the essential characteristics of a profession, but it is widely accepted that it should be based on a code of ethics and on the possession of specialized knowledge that outsiders do not have. Related to these are organizational factors, such as self-recruitment or co-option, control of membership, monopoly of pursuit of the activities and a corporate body to manage the above.

Many public servants do not need to claim to be professional 'governors' as they belong to one of the traditional professions such as law or medicine; the demand for the recognition of administration as a profession in its own right is therefore particularly important to generalists. This has occurred in local government where a special examination body, the Local Government Examinations Board (now part of the Local Government Training Board), was created to help raise the educational standing of the administrative officer. The latter have now formed their own association, the Institute of Local Government Administrators, to look after matters of common interest.

However, the fact that administration is not as clearly defined or recognizable a skill as the older professions has meant that another important group of generalists – the higher civil service – has had difficulty in securing wide recognition of its claim to professional status.

Critics of the present status of generalists often confuse the professional administrator in Etzioni's terminology – an adaptation often found in professional organizations – with the administrator as a professional. However much an administrator learns about medicine through experience or attendance at courses he will never become a doctor. For administration to be a profession it is necessary that there be a body of knowledge relevant to administration the activity, which is acquired by special training and which offers a guarantee to the outside world that the person who has acquired it will be better at the occupation than those who have not. There is also a problem of defining the ethics of administration as a profession.

The reason why the two above points are difficulties can be found in our analysis of the role of the senior administrator in the civil service (and by implication in local government), a role which differs in that it does not allow scope for full professionalism. This role involves political functions performed in support of a minister and requiring the knowledge of the governmental process and a power of judgement of which, as we saw earlier, the administrative class of the civil service claimed a near-monopoly. As facilitator, mediator and arbiter the higher civil servant could well perform his role less well if his vision and impartiality were narrowed by a greater stress on the dictates of a specialism. To a considerable extent the word 'administrative' in 'administrative class' has always been something of a misnomer, for its members have been engaged in the substantive tasks of government rather than in managing or organizing the work of others. The analogy with line managers in industry is misleading for this reason, and the lay administrative officer in Mallaby's terms[10] in local government is much more a manager than is the senior administrator in central government.

Because of this political function the most important problem for the development of strict professional ethics is the possibility of a conflict of loyalties between the demands of the profession and the demands of the minister. A responsive and loyal service would be difficult to maintain if an individual became preoccupied with the external standards of his profession. If, as in other professions, a high degree of self-government, or colleague control, were to develop, reinforced on the one hand by self-education, or the process of developing the specialized knowledge, and on the other by internally applied ethical standards, the civil servant would find it very difficult to reconcile these factors in his working life with the traditional politico-administrative functions which basically derive from his position as a servant of the Crown.

Some of the characteristics of professionalism, such high qualifications on entry and relations of trust between the administrator and those with whom he deals, are relevant to the senior civil service. There is also a lively interest in ordinary ethical principles of allegiance, honesty, integrity and impartiality which are expected of public servants. Like the traditional professions public servants are expected to show higher standards of personal behaviour than those common in everyday life or in many private organizations.

The Management of the Public Service

The discussion of the professionalism of generalist public servants leads naturally to our final subject in the consideration of the personnel of systems of public administration. The question of whether the traditional model of professionalism can serve to guide recruitment, training and control in any part of the public service requires an analysis of the tasks actually performed. This itself is one of the managerial functions of those responsible for any organization and in recent years has had as one of its aims the creation of foundations for the more professional administrators demanded by the Fulton Committee.

These managerial functions are also used to try to deal with the many other problems encountered in the public services, for instance, in creating service-wide structures from the various occupational groups and specialisms which make up the service, and in keeping the service running at a satisfactory level of efficiency through the systematic employment of recruitment, training, career development, promotion, and 'exit' processes. The study of these is in fact a consideration of the basic processes of *personnel management* in government, including the structural framework within which the official's career is planned with both his own satisfaction and the organization's efficiency in mind. Job satisfaction and morale thus play an important part in the managing of the public service.

RECRUITMENT

The first facts that those responsible for civil service recruitment need to know before they can plan how best to obtain good recruits for different levels and types of work from the educational system or other occupations are the government's future manpower requirements.

Estimates of these are usually made over a five-year period by individual departments. This is an extremely difficult business. Political demands change and affect the need for manpower. Projected levels of government expenditure are prone to fluctuation. There is also variation in the growth rates of different categories of civil servant (for instance executive officers and clerical assistants). Wastage rates also have to be estimated. The size of the non-industrial civil service can itself become a political issue and manpower forecasting can be affected by political decisions.

In the past as a general rule the clerical class was recruited from school leavers with 'O' level passes in the General Certificate of Education. Executive class officers were traditionally recruited from among school-leavers with 'A' levels. Recruitment from these sources has become increasingly difficult as more students with GCE qualifications go on to seek university degrees. The executive class has tried with reasonable success to recruit graduates in place of its former eighteen-year-olds. But it had to be recognized that graduate entry into the executive class had to be made more attractive by improved career prospects. The administrative class had always relied on university graduates but here again there had been increased competition from other types of employment. This, together with the acceptance of a need for more graduates in the service generally, and problems encountered in recruiting graduates to the administrative class, contributed to the pressures for change in the structure of the service which would enable graduate recruits to compete more equally for the top posts.

One of the main factors conditioning the process of recruitment into the public service is the need to prevent patronage and ensure a fair system based on merit. The methods of selection in the civil service vary, with different combinations of written examinations, interviews and psychological tests being used. But the aim is always 'to assess each candidate's intellectual ability, personality, potentiality and, where relevant, his professional or technical skill in relation to the requirements of the post to be filled'.[11]

The civil service is not alone in finding difficulty in recruiting the calibre of staff which it wishes to employ. Local authorities have great difficulty in recruiting and retaining officers of good quality. Like the civil service, local authorities have been adversely affected by the increasing proportion of eighteen-year-olds going on to higher education thus reducing the traditional source of lay administrative officers. Graduate recruitment runs at a very low level, the majority of graduates in local government going into professional or technical occupations. The problem is aggravated by the limited prospects of the generalist in local government as compared with the professionally qualified officer, and the large number of individual recruiting authorities, many of which are unable to offer competitive financial inducements. However, it is hardly meaningful to compare the lay administrative officer in local government with administrators in the civil service because of the very different types of work which the two public services perform and the different ways in which required qualifications are obtained. Nevertheless, it is strongly felt in local government that recruitment for both administrative and professional posts should be more closely related to the new educational pattern and that this means taking in more graduates.

The greatest point of contrast with the civil service is the absence in local government of a central, independent recruiting authority comparable to the Civil Service Commission. The objectives of local government selection procedures are of course comparable: to secure the ablest candidates in a strictly impartial way. But some individual authorities recruit their own staff, especially senior ones, through an establishment department and an establishment committee, often with very little delegation of responsibilities to heads of departments. This procedure dates from a time when favouritism was a serious problem. It is also explained by the closer relationships in local government between councillors and officers at all levels of their hierarchy: 'it is understandable that members should be concerned about the appointment of officers with whom they will work closely.'[12] Whatever delegation may now be practised, particularly as a result of the Mallaby Committee report, it is still to be noted in contrast to the civil service that public servants in local government are recruited often either by a committee of councillors or their principal officers according to the seniority of the post to be filled.

TRAINING

The volume and variety of training in the public services reflect the different types of personnel and organization involved. Some of it is very extensive, well-established and closely related to the needs of individual groups of public servants. In the state-owned enterprises, for example, training is a statutory duty imposed on the public corporations by law. The coverage is very wide and geared to the needs of the particular industry or concern. The record of the public corporations in training is a good one, but the training task is to some extent made easier by the fact that the industrial and commercial skills needed are clearly defined and relatively easily taught. This is not the case in other areas of public administration.

The training situation in local government is also relatively straightforward since most senior staff, being professionals, either have to obtain their professional qualification and therefore their training before they can be appointed, or pursue them through professional institutions when appointed. There is, however, an internal training need which has to be met through *ad hoc* arrangements drawing on various types of educational institution. Much induction training is given on the job and opportunities for being granted release for training vary widely from one local authority to another. Management training is of particular importance in organizations where professionals occupy managerial positions at the heads of departmental hierarchies. There is no local government staff college – it is generally thought that this kind of training is best acquired from diverse sources selected according to the needs of the officers concerned. There is however a Local Government Training Board responsible for evolving long-term plans and policies to meet the training needs of local government as a whole, and for promoting and co-ordinating training programmes. It operates a system of training levies and grants which spreads the costs fairly among all local authorities. A major proportion of the Board's efforts have been towards developing management and administrative training for local authority staff.

The civil service runs an extensive system of central, departmental and external training programmes. The main interest, growth and development in recent years have been in central management training, but it is important to understand that this forms only a small proportion of the service's total training effort – less than ten per cent. Its importance may, however, be considered greater when measured by other criteria such as the seniority of the staff being trained.

The main bulk of training, organized by departments, is specialized and vocational. It ranges from background courses in economic aid (for officials administering the aid programme) and exporting (for those on Board of Trade promotion work) to taxation law and practice for tax inspectors. The great variety of training has been brought about by the implementation of the Assheton Committee's recommendation (1944) that all new entrants should receive training of various kinds and to the development in recent years of new techniques such as automatic data processing. All this formal training is of course supplemented by a strong civil service tradition of training at the desk under the supervision of a superior officer.

Central management training through a staff college responsible for a wide range of courses of varying types and length for different grades of civil servants now seems a firmly established part of the total civil service training programme. But the period of transition has not been one of smooth continuity but of great change, not least because of the structural changes in the service which had fundamental implications for training, and the renewed emphasis on management training for specialists. Three issues will predominate in the planning of training programmes.

The first is how best to teach the many disciplines relevant to the practice of management and administration in a way which makes them relevant and applicable to the public sector. The second major problem in central training policy derives directly from the first and concerns the assessment of training needs in the service. Research into the needs of staff in different groups cutting across individual departments, whether generalists or specialists, should precede decisions about courses which tend to be made on more *a priori* educational assumptions. This in turn leads to the third major problem. Assessment schemes need to be instituted to test whether the training courses have had the required effect on the administrator's performance in his department.

The distinguishing characteristics of central training in the civil service show up more clearly when compared with the French *École Nationale d'Administration* (ENA). The effects of French administrative methods on the *École* have produced a training system which contrasts strongly with the British.

ENA is both a recruiting agency and a training college. Unlike the Civil Service College it holds competitions to admit entrants to the higher civil service from both graduates and existing civil servants. At the end of the training course the successful trainees are able to choose, in order of merit, the vacancies in the service. Those with the top marks inevitably chose the *grands corps* or élite groups within the service which dominate the most important posts in the French ministries.

Preference for relevance is given in the recruitment process in that the competition is so specialized in the relevant social sciences and other subjects that candidates need to have prepared themselves by taking post-graduate course at an institute of political studies. In fact 90 per cent of the candidates hold diplomas from such institutes, 80 per cent of those from the Paris *Institut d'Études Politiques*.

The training programme at ENA lasts two and a half years, just over a year of which is spent working in a prefecture or embassy and (very briefly at the end of the course) the private sector. The training is very much career-orientated in the sense of giving a general education in administrative and legal processes, international relations, economics, public finance and social policy. Unlike the Civil Service College it does not cater for a wide range of civil servants at different levels of middle and higher management requiring both specialized courses and more general management training and development relevant to different stages of their careers.

In recent years criticisms of ENA, notably by its own trainees, have intensified, particularly of its social and administrative élitism, the poor opportunities for internal promotion through

ENA and the lack of direct relevance of the training programme to departmental functions. A Commission was set up in 1968 under the chairmanship of M. Francois Bloch-Lainé which ranged widely over civil service recruitment, structures and career opportunities as well as training. If implemented, its recommendations would make the training given at ENA and at the Civil Service College much more comparable at least as far as direct entrants and internally recruited members of the higher civil service are concerned.

GRADING STRUCTURE

The many different tasks which the personnel of large organizations perform must be classified and graded for the purposes of personnel management in all its forms. Broad types of work must be identified and assigned to groups which are recruited to provide the required levels and kinds of ability and expertise which the duties and responsibilities to be performed require. A hierarchy of grades thus emerges into which people are recruited at different levels and through which they move as their careers progress. The overriding objective of those who manage such a personnel structure is that it should maximize efficiency in the organization by ensuring that every position is filled by the best available employee. The classification of different levels of responsibility should not obstruct the best use of the organization's human resource.

As the civil service developed over the last century in response to the increasing demands of the state its structure became correspondingly complex. New tasks have emerged as the role of government has expanded into the economic and social fields and as new technologies affected the ways in which decisions are made. The relatively simple structure of a hundred years ago, when the service was divided into two classes of clerks, in the 'higher' and revenue departments, has become much more differentiated as more refined distinctions between clerical, executive, managerial and policy-making work was required. New grades and classes have also been created for the scientific, professional and other specialists that the work of government has increasingly come to need.

SPECIALISTS IN THE CIVIL SERVICE

It is important to remember that almost every branch of every profession and skill is represented in the Civil Service and that the specialists constitute over 28 per cent of its non-industrial manpower. At the higher levels of the service some two-thirds are in the professional classes. Their role is 'to bring expert knowledge, skill and experience in specialist fields to bear on the determination and execution of government policy'.

Industrial organizations traditionally distinguish between production or 'line' personnel involved in executing decisions and day-to-day management, and 'staff' units performing auxiliary professional services such as legal advice, economic and statistical analysis, scientific research and production design.

It is not always the case, however, that staff are advisory to and controlled by line people – that the experts are 'on tap and not on top'. In many organizations the professionals form the line organization and generalists or administrators perform supporting services. This is obviously the case in institutions such as hospitals and universities. In other organizations professionals span both line and staff categories. This is a distinctive feature of English local government, where the heads and senior members of departments tend to be professionally or technically qualified in disciplines relevant to local government services. Most local government services and functions require professional and technical skills and experience. Senior officials thus combine the exercise of their professional expertise with the administrative functions of planning the development and execution of services, advising committees and supervising the execution of council and committee decisions for the provision of services.

Britain is almost alone in subordinating specialists to generalists in its central civil service or in even making such a distinction. Elsewhere it is common for all public servants to be regarded as specialists in some aspect of government work and to have relevant qualifications before appointment. Britain's rejection of 'preference for relevance', which we have already noted, is quite unusual and stems from an educational tradition which has maintained the leading role of the 'gentleman amateur' in politics and administration. In France, however, 'virtually all higher Civil Servants have prescribed qualifications'. Both administrators and *tech-*

niciens hold managerial posts and there seems less likelihood in France than in Britain of conflict between professional and organizational loyalties. In France 'there is no underlying theory that there are two sorts of people, specialists and generalists, suited by their different backgrounds for different sorts of career'.[13] In the USA, too, the picture is 'one of specialized, technically competent persons administering activities in which their specialist competence is regarded as a prerequisite to administrative efficiency.'[14]

Changes are being made in Britain in this area where very little is known, through an absence of appropriate research, of the likely effects of giving professionals managerial and financial responsibilities. Research into private sector organizations suggests that there may well be conflict between the goals of the organization and the professional standards of the specialist manager. Loyalty to the profession and commitment to universalistic standards may outweigh loyalty to the employing organization. While it is common to find managers in industry who have moved into management from a professional occupation, there have also been cases where management has had to revert to line personnel because professional standards made unreasonable demands on organizational resources.

PERSONNEL MANAGEMENT POLICY

In this section we are concerned with the way in which the careers of public officials are managed by those responsible for the efficient deployment of staff – the establishments divisions, as the personnel sections of departments are known. The policies which have been developed here extend beyond those which have to do with what traditionally are known as 'conditions of service', such as pay, pensions, tenure, discipline and so on, to include career planning and development which, in the civil service means 'enabling each person to realize his or her potential as fully as possible in line with the interests of the Service'.[15] As such, personnel management in government can be summed up as securing the most efficient performance from staff by effective, humane and equitable management.

An important element in effective and equitable management is remuneration, in so far as it attracts the required staff and rewards them fairly. Civil service pay is based on the principle of 'fair comparison' with the remuneration of staff employed on comparable work outside the service. This was established after acceptance by the official (employers') and staff (employees') sides of the National Whitley Council of the recommendations of the Royal Commission on the Civil Service 1953–5.[16]

Civil service agreements on pay and conditions have been reached which cover all grades regardless of the kind of work performed or the department in which personnel are employed. The task of personnel managers is largely one of applying centrally formulated rules. A standardization of personnel procedures is in fact characteristic of civil service establishments work as a whole.

At the end of the official's career retirement comes after a long period of job security supported by national agreements between the Treasury and the staff associations. The general aim of retirement policy has been 'maximum retention' – employing all fit and willing officers for as long as is practicable and with the highest possible degree of uniformity in age of retirement. The effect of this policy was inevitably to strengthen the security afforded by a civil service career, and retirement cannot be regarded as a punitive instrument of personnel management.

Concerted efforts have been made in recent years, especially since the publication of the Fulton Committee report, to improve personnel management both in the interest of a more efficient deployment of staff and the job satisfaction of individual employees. Improved arrangements for assessing staff performance by the development of 'appraisal interviews' have been introduced to improve communications between line managers and their staff. Through these interviews supervisers and subordinates agree on the objectives of a particular block of work, the results achieved and possible improvements in individual performance.

In all respects the approach of the service to the problems has been very cautious. The possibility of making pay arrangements more flexible as a means of increasing incentives and rewarding merit has been investigated amid considerable scepticism of the advantages of change. Administrative specialization has been studied through a sample survey of 2,000 middle-range administrators. It was found that the division into two groups proposed by Fulton was unworkable. The unique features of each department made such a broad division meaningless. Thus, specialization continues to be related to departmental activities and therefore not interchangeable with other departments in the same broad policy field, even when the specialism is functional such as automatic data processing, statistics, training and establishments work.

Just as the civil service has had to modernize its conception of the personnel function so too local government is finding it necessary to bring personnel management into line with the best practices in industry. Traditionally local government has adopted a rather narrow view of personnel management, or 'establishments', seeing it as being concerned primarily with recruitment, with the administration of rules about pay and conditions, and with the control of staff numbers.

More recently, however, a broader approach to the management of local authority personnel has been adopted. Authorities increasingly recognize the positive aspects of personnel management and its relevance to the effective functioning of the organization, especially in a changing environment. More attention is gradually being paid to what the Bains report called the 'supply' side of manpower planning, that is, to improve the quality of the organization's human resources by more sophisticated processes of recruitment, training, career development and staff appraisal. In order to encourage this trend the Bains Report urged the new local authorities to substantially develop their personnel functions on the grounds that 'In a highly labour intensive organization like local government the major scope for improvements in efficiency must come through more effective use of human resources'.[17]

CHANGE AND MORALE

As might have been anticipated, the civil service resisted some of the pressures to introduce a more competitive personnel system. Admittedly, much of the evidence to the Fulton Committee from the world of private business asserted a positive relationship between efficiency and morale, and a system in which rewards and penalties, in terms of pay, promotion and security, followed from stricter assessments of performance. The Committee's acceptance of this line of reasoning was reflected in its report and recommendations.

However, there are two fundamental issues which have to be considered when dealing with the relationship between personnel practices and efficiency in the public service. One concerns the features of work which contribute in a particular occupation to the satisfaction of the individual's needs. The second and broader question is whether efficiency in the organization can always be assumed to be increased by improved morale and job satisfaction. If it can be shown that efficiency and morale are linked in this way, and if the factors contributing to job satisfaction can be revealed, it should be possible to predict the likely effects of making fundamental changes in personnel practices such as those recommended by the Fulton Committee.

The available evidence on job satisfaction in the civil service is fragmentary and not always consistent, but what there is does not seem to support the view that public servants seek a working environment which stresses economic rewards and keen competition. R. G. S. Brown analysed the evidence and found that feelings about economic rewards and penalties, such as pay, career prospects, security and sanctions do not seem to be related to job satisfaction, even though individual features, for instance, pay, might be a source of dissatisfaction for certain grades. Satisfaction with civil service work seems to arise from social factors, such as congenial colleagues, the status attached to the job and good relationships with superiors; and psychological rewards, such as the intrinsic interest of the work, the scope given for initiative and the opportunities for the development of individual potential. Whether individual civil servants feel satisfied or dissatisfied, the source of their feelings would seem to be in the social and psychological effects of their work rather than in the material rewards or sanctions which it might afford.[18]

The Fulton Committee seemed to think that a more competitive system of man management would increase both efficiency and morale in the civil service. They may well have been wrong, in view of what civil servants appear to look for in their work. The successful introduction of such a new system would depend on new recruitment methods and the projection of a new image to attract people with different motives and values. However, if efficient administration is not dependent on high morale it may be possible to increase the efficiency of the organization while at the same time damaging morale (assuming this to be a real option). Similar information was obtained from a survey of local government officers' attitudes towards their work carried out in 1966 for the Committee on Staffing in Local Government. The main factors attracting people to local government as a career were found to be a belief that the work would be satisfying, the security and pension, and 'prospects'. The main sources of dissatisfaction were too little scope for responsibility and initiative. However, over 60 per cent of the sample felt that prospects had turned out as they thought they would.

From the evidence that is available it would seem that the relevance of morale to efficiency depends on the level and type of work concerned. At the lower levels of the career hierarchy, whether people like their work seems to have an insignificant effect on personal efficiency, wastage and absenteeism. There are also many officials in Government who like their work but who are below average efficiency, and many who are above average but who dislike their jobs.

At the higher levels in the organization, however, it may well be more functional to improve job satisfaction and so increase the sense of commitment which the employee feels towards his job. But here we are brought back to the first problem: is a sense of identity with a job increased by material rewards and incentives or by other, psychological, rewards such as opportunities for self-realization? Fulton assumed that civil servants wanted a system based more strictly on the assessment of achievements, and a number of changes have been made in personnel structures and methods as a result. What the final effects will be remain to be seen. Civil servants generally appear to welcome the new opportunities for career advancement on merit, but at the same time the changes have been absorbed into the traditional methods of civil service management and consequently are not having such an abrasive effect as they might have had. So it will be extremely difficult to establish whether any changes in overall performance, however these might be measured, can be explained in terms of a new system of man-management, or of other factors.

Any difficulties encountered in implementing reforms in person-nel management or in achieving the desired results from change are likely to be caused by conflict between the assumptions made about employees' attitudes and values on the one hand, and reality on the other. One social psychologist has written that 'if the organization expects its members to be committed, flexible and in good communication with each other for the sake of overall organizational effectiveness, it is in effect asking them to be *morally* involved in the enterprise, to be committed to organiz-ational goals and to value these. And if it expects them to be involved to this degree, the organization must for its part provide rewards and conditions consistent with such involvement'.[19] A crucial question for the public services is how far the assumptions made about motivation and rewards are consistent with the attitudes of different types of employee to their work. If these assumptions are wrong the features of civil service life which are most conducive to organizational effectiveness could be damaged by new methods of career development.

There are strengths in the old system, as the Fulton Committee recognized. It was impressed by the calibre of staff in the service, the training schemes, the areas of sound line management, enlightened employment practices, the pains taken to be equitable and conscientious in dealings with the public, the care taken with public money and the benefits of Whitleyism to staff relations. The Committee was in fact surprised that the non-incentive system had 'called forth the dedication, conscientiousness and enthusiasm that we so often saw'.[20] It may even be the case that these qualities are dependent on the existence of a non-incentive scheme. As R. G. S. Brown has commented, 'It would be a pity if these advantages were lost as a result of trying to assimilate the service to a more industrial career pattern'.[21] To this we would add that not only might it be a mistake to adopt an inappropriate model of management from private industry but also it is wrong to assume that the latter contains only one pattern of organization-employee relations.

Notes

 1 Weber, 1947; Gerth and Mills, 1948
 2 Finer, 1956, p. 386
 3 Gunn, 1967; Gunn, 1972
 4 Adamson, 1968, p. 184
 5 Mackenzie, 1951
 6 Hart, 1962
 7 Jackson, 1967, pp. 132–4
 8 Wiseman, 1963, 1967
 9 Dale, 1941
10 Mallaby, 1967
11 Civil Service Commission, 1968, p. 297
12 Mallaby, 1967, p. 143
13 Ridley, 1968, p. 98
14 Ridley, 1968, p. 177

15 Armstrong, 1971, p. 15
16 Priestley, 1955
17 Bains, 1972, p. 127
18 Brown, 1971, 1972
19 Schein, 1965, p. 104
20 Fulton, 1971, p. 195
21 Brown, 1971

Chapter 6
Control of the Administration

We have noted, in our discussions of organization and personnel, the difficulties which the 'managerial' approach to public administration finds in accommodating the need to hold public officials accountable for their decisions and actions, and the importance of ensuring that they behave impartially and properly in their dealings with members of the public. Part of the difficulty arises from the fact that management techniques derived from the private sector deal more effectively in those values which are easily measured, such as economy and technical efficiency. But public bodies are also expected to have regard for the imperative of equality, as we explained in Chapter One.

The consequence of this is that Britain still relies on traditional methods of holding the administration accountable for their interpretation and execution of public policy. The process is dominated by Parliamentary procedures and institutions. These also deal with individual grievances, but a recognition of their inadequacies has led to a gradual extension of quasi-judicial machinery to deal with individual cases.

The responsibility of government to the representatives of the people is an essential feature of the British political system. As we explained in Chapter Two, this system is executive-dominated in that the government controls and influences the rest of the machinery of administration. Any form of public control must therefore include ways of holding the executive branch accountable for its actions. 'Responsibility' in representative government means not only responsiveness to public opinion but also accountability to the organ of government which confers legitimacy on the decisions and actions of the executive.

It is still a controversial subject as to what the power of Parliament should be today. However, it would probably be generally accepted that Parliament legislates in the sense, for the most part, of legitimizing Cabinet decisions; that it grants supply, i.e. authorizes expenditure by the departments of state; that it makes possible the appropriation of resources; and that it tries to maintain continuous supervision of administrative activity.

The supervision of administration expresses itself in three ways: in the seeking of redress for individual grievances felt by members of the public arising from administrative actions for which ministers may be held responsible; in ensuring that public expenditure conforms to policies authorized by Parliament; and in seeing that ministerial powers are exercised in the most efficient and economical way.

Ministerial Responsibility

The constitutional doctrine on which Parliamentary oversight of administration rests is ministerial responsibility (see Chapter Five). In recent decades, however, reality has undermined theory in a way which has affected the relations between a minister and Parliament, between a minister and his civil servants, and therefore between the citizen and the administration.

However, the part of the doctrine which remains usefully intact, and around which recent Parliamentary developments revolve, is the concept of answerability. Parliament is able to induce a degree of self-control on the part of the executive by the practice of requiring ministers to answer for and defend the actions of their departments publicly. The knowledge that a serious error in administration may not incur the resignation of one's minister but could well cause him discomfort and embarrassment in Parliament and within the government, a government which is generally accepted to be waging a continuous battle for electoral success, is obviously a restraint limiting irresponsible action.

QUESTIONS TO MINISTERS

The traditional method of holding ministers accountable for acts for which they are responsible is at Question Time, which is the first main item of Parliamentary business each day in the House of Commons. Subject to certain procedural rules, Members may put questions orally to ministers seeking information about administrative actions or raising grievances brought to their attention by constituents. Members who merely seek factual information may not feel it necessary to have their question answered orally and may seek only a written reply from the minister concerned.

Question Time is still considered 'a very important element in the doctrine of individual ministerial responsibility' and is especially important as 'one of the last procedural devices at the complete disposal of the back-bencher'.[1]

Question Time undoubtedly carries with it something of a threat to ministers. It also places a considerable administrative burden on departments. The number of 'starred' questions (that is, for oral reply) runs at a daily average of about 70 to 75. The difficulty due to pressure on time in obtaining verbal replies has led MPs to seek more written answers and the daily average has risen steeply in recent years to about eighty. Of course this figure conceals wide variations. The fact that there is always the possibility of awkward supplementaries means that departmental officials must be at hand to 'provide the minister with defensive ammunition'. The administrative burden of Parliamentary questions is very heavy, and the preparation of answers and information to cover the minister in the very likely event of difficult supplementaries is one of the senior administrator's most important tasks.

The administrative costs of having so many questions dealt with, often only after considerable time has been spent collecting information and checking responses with all the branches of the department involved by relatively senior officials (mainly principals or assistant secretaries), are obviously high. Dealing with questions, often at short notice, breaks into administrative routine and the long-term consideration of policy issues. Even though some Parliamentary questions may appear trivial, they are nevertheless taken seriously.

It is probably true to say that Parliamentary questions still keep departments sensitive to the possibility of public scrutiny and perhaps political embarrassment for their ministers. They thus serve to ensure to a considerable extent that departments are prepared to defend their actions and only take decisions which can be justified by current policy. Faults in the administrative process are detected and remedies effected. The power which the Parliamentary question gives Members to challenge decisions taken at all levels in the organization by direct confrontation of ministers can be an important safeguard against abuse of authority or carelessness in executive action.

However, as a device for the effective scrutiny of administration, Question Time has serious limitations. It is extensively used for other purposes, such as to score partisan points off the government, to present statements of policy to the House or to raise matters simply to draw attention to them as part of the Parliamentary conflict. Questions rarely produce 'pure' information about the administrative process. Indeed, they are hardly appropriate instruments for probing the immense variety and complexity of administrative actions for which ministers are only nominally responsible.

The period of about an hour set aside for Question Time has remained constant over the years, despite the large increase in the number of questions put down for verbal reply. This has led to the use of a rota system to limit the number of questions remaining unanswered. In this way ministers take it in turns to head the list on a particular day and this in turn means that an individual minister heads the list infrequently.

Finally, developments in the machinery for administration, especially in relation to publicly-owned enterprises, have enabled ministers to avoid Parliamentary investigation through questions in the House. Ministers cannot be questioned about areas in which they have no powers, or decisions for which they are not responsible, which in principle excludes from scrutiny the actions of local authorities and the nationalized industries.

CORRESPONDENCE WITH MINISTERS

One response to the growing difficulty experienced by Members in getting individual attention through Question Time has been an increasing use of personal correspondence between MPs and ministers. This device has become more and more popular so that it is now of greater importance than questions as a means of revealing deficiencies in administration. Something like 50,000 letters are thought to pass between MPs and ministers each year.

The idea that correspondence substitutes for questions may be valid in the context of constituents' grievances, which may well be satisfactorily dealt with by letter. But it is doubtful whether this sort of exchange between an MP and a minister can duplicate the kind of control which is implicit in a publicized criticism, which can then be met with defence and explanation on the floor of the House or even simply published in Hansard.

Correspondence with ministers may nevertheless keep civil servants alive to the possibility of public accountability for specific decisions. For one thing it involves greater numbers of administrators at lower levels in the hierarchy than questions. It can also be a more effective form of scrutiny, requiring detailed explanation and justification set out in a document which might well, if found unsatisfactory, form the source of a question or adjournment debate and hence difficulty for the minister. A letter from a Member can bring the minister quickly into close contact with his officials. Thus a relatively simple expedient can be a potent agent of public accountability.

ADJOURNMENT DEBATES

As a kind of follow-up to a Parliamentary question a Member may initiate an adjournment debate in order to probe executive action. The opportunity occurs at the completion of public business each day and Members ballot for choice of subject. Such debates must be into matters for which the government is responsible. They receive little publicity and cannot be used to probe issues requiring legislation. The fact that their impact on the executive is likely to be slight means that 'debates tend to be formalized occasions and, apart from the opening and the winding-up speeches, are attended only by the handful of MPs who wish to speak'.[2] Constituency matters usually dominate this part of the Parliamentary day.

Adjournment debates provide added opportunities for examination of the nationalized industries and have been used to raise matters for which ministers are not directly responsible. The subjects covered range from the future of the Grimsby–Peterborough railway line to the action of the British Overseas Airways Corporation in curtailing services to Israel. Railway matters tend to predominate as does the fact that the issues raised are mainly local.

NATIONALIZED INDUSTRIES

One of the most important areas of government theoretically excluded from the type of Parliamentary investigation provided by Question Time is the provision of goods and services by publicly owned industrial corporations.

Apart from the opportunities provided to Members to examine the industries during debates on borrowing powers bills, annual reports and accounts and select committee reports, Question

Time permits a limited form of Parliamentary scrutiny. It is limited by the fact that legal powers are vested in the boards and not ministers, and that it has always been thought necessary to preserve a measure of independence from normal Parliamentary control in order to allow the industries concerned to act on the basis of commercial rather than political considerations (see Chapter Four). Thus the intention, when the main bulk of the public corporations in the industrial sphere were set up, was to combine Parliamentary control with managerial autonomy. To do this the minister's role was not extended to 'day-to-day' management. Parliamentary accountability was further limited by the fact that the expenditure of the corporations was not borne on the estimates.

However, ministerial intervention into different areas of corporation decision-making has varied enormously. This in turn has led to a lack of consistency in the relations between Parliament and the relevant ministers. Because of the appropriate rules of Parliamentary procedure, what has come to determine answerability is not whether a question concerns day-to-day administration or general policy (a distinction later framed in terms of 'commercial interests' and 'national interests'), but whether ministers have been prepared to answer questions on matters outside their statutory powers. Also, the statutory powers provide pegs on which Members have been able to hang questions by, for example, asking for a 'general direction' to be given by a minister to a board on a very detailed matter. As a result, a great deal of work falls on civil servants and board officials arising from Parliamentary accountability. The Select Committee found that in one year 500 questions were tabled in both Houses about British Railways alone. The Board had to provide information on 246 of them. This represented an increase of 35 per cent on the previous year. In addition the Chairman of the Board received over 1100 letters from MPs.

Obstacles to Parliamentary Scrutiny

A number of factors obstruct effective Parliamentary scrutiny of the executive. This is a reflection of the executive domination mentioned earlier; in this case the 'rules of the game' in Parliament are weighted heavily in favour of ministers. For instance, the MP does not have access to detailed information about administrative action in which he may be interested. Ministers on the other hand do, and they are not obliged to give access to files, papers or other documents or to provide more information than they think necessary.

Secondly, delegated legislation (the rules and orders made under laws laying down broad principles and policies) has increased in volume faster than parliamentary scrutiny can keep up with. Thus a device designed to free parliamentarians to consider the essential principles of legislation has the accompanying disadvantage of excluding much of the technical and administrative details embodied in such rules and orders from effective Parliamentary scrutiny.

Thirdly, government has not only increased in scope but in complexity, particularly in economic and financial terms. Effective Parliamentary control of the details of public expenditure, which is now roughly 200 times as large as it was 100 years ago, is extremely difficult. As the technological complexity of government projects increases, particularly in the fields of electronics, weapons systems and aerospace, so the problems of costing, negotiating contracts and control of research, development and production increase correspondingly.

This factor has another side; civil servants, particularly generalists, are as likely to experience difficulty in dealing with these complex technological questions as are MPs. The result is that they are more likely to make mistakes and the advice that they give to ministers will be less authoritative, and therefore the information that ministers give to Parliament will be less reliable.

Fourthly, the House of Commons has become less and less satisfied with the existing arrangements for examining the government's proposals for public expenditure. The fact that on the executive side new techniques for planning expenditure have been developed has been an added incentive for the House of Commons to amend its procedures to match such developments.

It can be argued that any improvements in new techniques of Treasury control and departmental financial planning will in the long run enable Parliament to carry out its traditional role more effectively in the changed circumstances. This is because, if the techniques are applied correctly, they generate information relevant to decisions so that the problems are more clearly understood and the choices more clearly articulated.

Fifthly, managerial practices in Whitehall further change the problem of Parliamentary control and investigation. Attempts are being made, under the impetus given by the Fulton Committee, to extend the use of 'management by objectives' or 'accountable management' in government departments (see Chapter Seven). If the information needed for such purposes is made available to Parliament, it will enable the House to 'assess the performance of Departments, or of units within them, in a way which is not possible at present'. Similarly output budgeting, which is being developed by a number of departments should give the House further insight into departmental planning. In addition, the House should also be in a better position to measure the efficiency of departments in terms of their success in meeting objectives within the limits of costed programmes.

Nevertheless the kind of opportunities provided for general Parliamentary investigation and control by elected representatives are limited, given the operation of the doctrine of ministerial responsibility and current trends within the executive. The role of the individual MP as a 'watch dog' must be seen in the context of majoritarian government, strong party discipline and civil service anonymity. As a member of the whole House the MP has had to reconcile himself to the fact that the government's policy is likely to be little affected by Parliamentary debate, with the possibility of defeating the government on an adverse vote being very slim indeed. As a result of the political reality of Parliamentary politics it is now generally recognized that a different sort of activity is required, which would be conducted in a subtly different atmosphere to the partisan conflict which characterizes the relationships between MPs and the administration in the chamber. As a result the House has increasingly turned towards specialization in small groups for the effective supervision of administration by Parliament.

Select Committees

It now seems to be widely accepted, despite some powerful expressions of dissent, that the most effective means of 'controlling' administration, in the sense that this is possible within the British political context, is the device of the select committee. This is a committee of up to about fifteen Members appointed to investigate and report to the House on specified matters. They obtain evidence by the power which they are given 'to send for persons, papers and records' and receive assistance from the Clerks of the House and, in some cases, specially appointed advisers. Some, such as the Public Accounts Committee and the new Expenditure Committee, are set up under the House's standing orders. Others are appointed each session, such as the Select Committee on Nationalized Industries and, more recently, Science and Technology. The view supporting this development is that Parliament as a whole is an ineffective means of controlling administration and needs to be supported by informed and expert groups who have made specialized studies of areas of government in an atmosphere free from partisan conflict. It is not necessary to describe the composition and activites of these committees in detail, as such information is easily available in sources listed in the bibliography. The objective here is to explain the issues raised by developments in this field, particularly in relation to parliamentary control as part of the setting for administrative decision making.

Many of the significant developments in select committee work are mainly of interest to students of Parliament, although they may have some importance for public administration. As far as the administrative process is concerned, however, the most interesting development has been the emergence of committees with new terms of reference which give them wide powers to examine government policy, once considered beyond their legitimate scope, as well as the administrative and financial aftermaths of policy decisions.

Select committees originated as a method of confirming that departmental expenditure had been authorized by Parliamentary approval and had given value for money. Their present terms of reference, non-partisan methods of working, their educational, objective and informative reports, and their use of outside experts as advisers, are an indication of a change of emphasis in their purposes.

The Public Accounts Committee's work is generally more closely related to routine administration than that of other committees. We have already mentioned the importance of the concept of the accounting officer in departments, which arises from the responsibilities of the Committee working through the Comptroller and Auditor General.

However, like the other committees the Public Accounts Committee has had grafted on to its original concern with financial regularity and propriety an interest in financial policy and the future implications of current expenditure. The extension of the Public Accounts Committee's activities into the fields of financial policy is supported by developments in government auditing by the Comptroller and Auditor General and the Exchequer and Audit Department. This institution requires a special mention in a discussion of accountability.

The main task of the Comptroller and Auditor General like any state auditor, is to further the accountability of public authorities by checking their financial transactions. This entails 'certifying' the accounts of government departments. The accounts are scrutinized to ensure that they are technically correct and that there has been no fraudulent transaction. At the same time, the auditor ensures that expenditure is in line with Parliamentary authorization.

For this purpose the Comptroller and Auditor General acts as an officer of Parliament, receiving the reports of the audit sections of government departments, certifying them and submitting them to Parliament. To this control of regularity must now be added the increasingly important function of investigating the reasonableness of expenditure measured against criteria of efficiency and economy. The Comptroller and Auditor General is now concerned with the financial policies of the spending departments. While checking that particular payments are properly accounted for and conform to authorized expenditure, he looks for ways of improving the financial soundness of projects and the efficiency of their execution. State audit in Britain is now only minimally concerned with regularity and is much more interested in procedures for ensuring that the prices of goods and services obtained by public authorities are fair and reasonable. His investigations of financial estimating and controlling procedures in connection with defence contracts have been of particular importance, not least because of the immense sums of public money involved.

INFLUENCE ON THE EXECUTIVE

It is extremely difficult, if not impossible, to measure the precise impact of select committee scrutiny on decisions and policy making in departments and other parts of the executive. But first there are quite high administrative costs involved in this and related forms of Parliamentary accountability, expressed in terms of the time spent by high-level officials in producing written memoranda and giving oral evidence. The administrative burden is nevertheless borne willingly and often with enthusiasm by civil servants, board officials and other public servants.

Secondly, it is usually agreed that the threat of possible select-committee investigation acts as a restraint on arbitrary and ill-conceived administrative action by public officials who know that their own block of work or area of responsibility might be what a select committee will choose to study next. This particularly applies to the Public Accounts Committee. This latent threat has become all the more real with the appointment of an Expenditure Committee able to examine the policies behind the presentation of public expenditure proposals relating to the whole field of government spending.

Thirdly, select committee scrutiny may force a salutary reappraisal of policy and administration on the organizations which are singled out for investigation, even if no significant change follows. The activities of the Public Accounts Committee, supported by the Comptroller and Auditor General, have also served to improve managerial efficiency.

Indeed, it could be argued that select committees are now more involved in the process of policy formation, as one of the formative influences, than with ensuring that administrative decisions conform to predetermined policy. The norms by which administrative effort is evaluated are by no means always those of established policy. The Select Committee on Science and Technology influenced official thinking on nuclear reactors, coastal pollution and carbon fibres by approaching these subjects knowing that they were of national importance, involved heavy public expenditure and required change to keep public policy in line with technical developments.[3] The standards by which current policy in these areas was evaluated were of the Committee's own making. Indeed the work of select committees is the clearest evidence available of how inseparable the policy planning process is from the implementation of established policy.

Finally, there is the enhanced competence and expertise which select committees are supposed to bring to the House as a whole, making it a more informed and therefore more efficient forum for the scrutiny of government policy. Unfortunately, while debates may be better informed as a result of exhaustive committee investigation the evidence suggests that the vast majority of MPs do not take the opportunity offered to use the intellectual weapons so painstakingly forged for them. A frequently voiced criticism of debates on committee reports is that the only debaters are the committee members themselves.

From Parliament's point of view the methods open to it for holding the executive accountable for its actions may not appear to go very far towards changing the balance of power in favour of the legislature. Indeed, it has been convincingly argued that additions to the volume of information demanded from administrators through 'explanatory dialogues' carried on in the non-partisan atmosphere of the committee rooms, adds nothing to the power of the House to control or check departments.[4] This argument would perhaps have less force if MPs, through select committees particularly, were not seen in the negative light of checking and restraining within the context of sanctioned policy but rather as more positive forces in the policy-making process, contributing to the multitude of influences from the interaction of which political and administrative policy emerge.

On the administrator's side Parliamentary devices impose considerable burdens which must be seen as keeping the executive accountable, even if nowadays this principle has lost the element of Parliamentary sanction that has at one time associated with it. The impact of legislative scrutiny on administrative action must be seen in the context of party government. It is thus unlikely to deflect the government significantly from its chosen course. At the moment such choices are likely to be conditioned more by pressure group influences than Parliamentary scrutiny.

On the negative side, of course, the threat of Parliamentary exposure is a real restraint on arbitrary action, negligence and other kinds of administrative misconduct. Defects in policy may be protected by the government's majority in the House, made an issue of confidence or otherwise defended as being in line with the minister's assessment of the public interest. But administrative error, or maladministration, is not so easily disguised or defended. Parliament's scrutiny by questions, adjournment debates and, more recently, the Parliamentary Commissioner still acts as a latent threat of exposure and embarrassment for ministers. While the revelation of such error will almost certainly not bring about a minister's resignation, it can cause discomfort and harm the government's image. The civil servant thus has to be on his guard.

Other Political Influences on the Executive

Administrators are subject to influences other than the controls exercised by Parliament and the machinery for the redress of grievances over the executive. Much of the sensitivity of senior officials to politically contentious issues is caused by factors in the political environment outside Parliament. This political environment is a structured one consisting of the press and organized groups which attempt to influence the administrative process in two ways. These organizations may act on behalf of an individual in attempting to change an administrative decision. Or they may act on their own initiative to change an aspect of the administrative process which affects some matter in which they have an interest.

As far as the press is concerned, it is unusual for it to campaign successfully against the administration on behalf of an individual. Cases like that of Crichel Down, which eventually led to the resignation of a minister, are rare. But there have been a few important instances when the press has drawn public attention to individuals whose civil liberties appear to be threatened by administrative action, such as cases of evicted families or deported immigrants.

However, the press has become considerably more active in recent years in the investigation of faulty administration. Newspaper investigations have revealed cases which have subsequently caused public concern, such as conditions in mental hospitals. Civil servants and other public officials are very sensitive to press reports likely to embarrass their political masters. They often have to provide ministers with information and arguments to counter press criticism.

Nevertheless, we should not exaggerate the impact which the press has on Whitehall. On the whole the national newspapers do not look very closely at administration. It is unusual for press reaction to a policy issue to result in any major changes. At neither central nor local government level does the press appear to have a great deal of influence on public opinion. There are many constraints on the amount and quality of local government news which the local press can report. These constraints, including shortages of official information and the sparse resources of the local press, also reduce its scope for discussing issues and probing administration. With a few exceptions, the local press is neither a medium for the redress of grievances, nor an influence on the administration of local services.

In order to make some impact on the administrative process the individual needs to mobilize not only the support of the press and his MP, but also an organized group or association which can represent his interests. Organized public opinion is in a much more powerful position than, for example, individual consumers who may be affected by government policy. Pressure groups, particularly of the promotional or 'cause' type, are increasingly active in supporting individuals in their dealings with the administration, thus adding to official sensitivity to the effects of the administrative process on the client and on the implementation of policy generally. An example is the aid given by the Child Poverty Action Group and the Claimants' Unions to applicants for various Social Security benefits. Trade unions assist their members in appeals to tribunals. A local branch of the National Union of Teachers may take up a member's case arising from conflict with the local education authority, and the ministry may be involved. Trade associations help individual businesses in their applications to departments for assistance and sponsorship under the government's industrial or commercial policies.

However, departments are more responsive to organized interests when those interests are being represented collectively rather than individually. Pressure groups have a particularly important part to play in decisions relating to the administrative details of policy implementation. Consultation with the leaders of organized interests ranges from the creation of hundreds of formal advisory bodies of different kinds, on which representatives of 'outside' interests sit, to *ad hoc* meetings with ministers and senior officials.

The influence which such groups can have on the executive is a function of government's dependence on the co-operation and technical expertise of organized interests in the administration of public policy. Governments, central and local, also use private associations extensively for the actual administration of some public policies. Leading members of representative organizations serve on the managing bodies of many state concerns. Such is the extent of inter-dependence and co-operation between public and private officials that the boundaries between public and private decision making are becoming increasingly difficult to define and less and less relevant to an understanding of the administrative process.

The relationships between public and private officials at the local level are less significant for administration than in national government. But the importance of pressure groups in the formulation and administration of policy should not be neglected. In the case of the nationalized industries the point of contact between the consumer and the board is usually at the district or area level. Special machinery of doubtful efficacy, in the form of consumer councils, has been created to protect the consumer's interests.

In local government, organized groups are becoming increasingly effective, particularly in the provision and protection of local amenities. Local organizations commonly seek the support of local authorities for privately initiated projects. Contacts tend to be made with politicians, rather than officials, at the local level. Although the processes of influence are different from those at the national level, the result is a similar one of composite or corporate government. This aspect of local administration certainly deserves more attention than it has received in the past from political scientists or than we are able to give it here.

Justice in the Administrative Process

As we have seen, Parliamentary action may be inappropriate or ineffective for the protection of individuals in conflict with the state. Consequently, other devices have been invented. Administratively, this means that decisions may have consequences which extend beyond the organization initially responsible.

The administrative process may be continued by review and revocation by a judicial or quasi-judicial body. The administrator's act may be contested by the individual and controlled by supervisory organs of the state. In some areas of decision making, procedures for the review of decisions in the interest of the citizen are built into the administrative process. The final outcome of the administrative process in matters which affect the rights of the citizen may be one to which parties other than the administrator have contributed.

The approach adopted here is intended to assist in the understanding of a complex subject. It should not be taken to mean that there is a systematic adjudicatory process which gives a comprehensive coverage and protection against administrative defects.

A.B.   H

Administrative law in Britain is not like this. It is by no means always clear what method of securing redress the individual should choose. In some cases his rights of appeal are extremely limited. But institutions exist and they cannot be entirely separated from administration as a process of decision making, the object of which is in some way to affect the rights and interests of the individual.

The administrative decisions which directly affect the individual and give rise to grievance and conflict are many and varied. They range from the refusal of an agricultural grant to the refusal of compensation for losses incurred by dealing in treasure trove; from assessment of liability for value added tax to errors in pay-as-you-earn codings; from a refusal to back-date a war pension to a refusal to make a payment for good maintenance under housing legislation; from a decision about places in secondary schools to the dispensing of drugs under the national health service; from the expulsion of a student from college to the refusal of admission to an immigrant. No list can adequately convey the immense variety of private and corporate affairs which may be affected by the decisions of the authorities.

By risking oversimplification, it is possible to classify such diverse decisions under two broad headings. There are those which infringe the rights of the individual and there are decisions which threaten the interests of the individual. The rights which an individual may feel have been infringed are very numerous. Conflict over rights generally arises from claims which a 'client' of the administration might make on a minister or public servant for some benefit, in the broadest sense of that term, to which he feels entitled.

The other broad source of grievances are decisions which are thought by the individual to impose some unfair hardship or to affect adversely his private interests. Such decisions may be the result of faulty administration or the proper application of public policy. In both such circumstances the citizen may feel that he is being made to suffer by an unjustifiable administrative act. Such cases do not arise from claims to some commodity, to which the citizen thinks he has a right. They are largely the result of clashes between public and private interests or a sense of having been wronged. Often such powers operate so that they restrict the individual's freedom of action. Thus there is often a blurred line between grievances arising from claims to rights and those which arise from harm to interests.

Having seen something of the sources of grievances, we can now turn to the different types of administrative fault about which the citizen might complain, and the machinery which exists for their redress. For explanatory purposes each major type of grievance and the administrative defects which lie behind them will be followed by an explanation of procedures for appeal and review. However not all problems fall into neat categories or are immediately subject to adjudication by an appropriate body.

JUDICIAL REVIEW

One very fundamental objection to an act or decision of the administration is that it is not sanctioned by law, but is *ultra vires*. In such cases the citizen is likely to be making one of three broad types of complaint. First, that the administrative authority is in excess of its statutory powers: this particularly affects local authorities. But the powers of central government are also subject to judicial review. In many cases, especially those affecting property, both local and central powers are involved, such as when a minister makes a decision on appeal from a local planning or housing authority.

Second, an aggrieved citizen may wish to force an authority to do something, which it is reluctant to do, but which the citizen thinks it has a statutory duty to do. Experience has proved that it is difficult to enforce a duty in law,[5] especially when many duties imposed by statute on ministers (such as a duty to promote a comprehensive health service) can only be enforced politically.

Finally, the citizen may discover a remedy against a public authority because there has been some defect in the way in which the decision complained of was made. Some statutorily prescribed procedure may have been neglected, such as when a local authority serves notice for slum clearance without giving details of a right to appeal. Administrative action must also be taken without negligence. The power to take such action may have been delegated to someone not entitled to it, another type of legal defect in the administrative process. A more common failing is to neglect to act according to the rules of natural justice when fairness demands it. A citizen may wish to challenge the exercise of administrative power if it appears to him that he is being 'condemned' unheard or that the administrative agency is acting as judge in its own cause. The administration may also be challenged for acting unreasonably, in bad faith or from ulterior motives.[6]

When it is alleged that an administrative authority is *ultra vires* it is likely that the individual will seek redress through the courts. As one leading authority on administrative law has pointed out, 'recourse to the courts of law is the normal remedy for the citizen in this country who suffers from a grievance at the hands of some other person'. When that other person is acting in the name of an administrative agency the citizen is protected by the common law doctrine that governmental power must be within the law.

The effects of the rule of law on the administrative process are far-reaching. First, central departments contain units staffed by lawyers to advise on the legal aspects of the formulation and implementation of policy. Nearly 600 members of the legal class in the civil service are organized in the Treasury Solicitor's Office or in branches of the large departments for 'the giving of advice, both on the implications of major policy questions and on day to day business; the preparation of Government bills and the drafting of subordinate legislation; litigation; and conveyancing'.

Another 200 are employed in departments concerned predominantly with specialized work, such as the Land Registry and the Department of the Director of Public Prosecutions. Their work is an indispensable part of the administrative process. 'Government business touches so closely and at so many points on matters of law that the contribution made by the lawyers is crucial.'

Administrators work in continuous anticipation of *ultra vires*. A distinguishing feature of administration is the concern with the strict application of the law, a factor which often leads to the charge of bureaucracy.

It may be necessary to build into the administrative process itself means by which disputed decisions can be reviewed at higher levels within the organization. This occurs in many administrative bodies where there is no provision for appeal to a tribunal or a hearing before an inquiry. But it can also be a feature of administration in departments where there is appellate machinery, but where many hundreds of decisions are being made each year by relatively junior officials in local offices, such as in the field of Social Security benefits. Here it may be necessary to institute internal review in addition to providing the claimant with a statutory right of appeal to a tribunal.

The research by the 'Justice' Committee revealed three significant features of administration in departments where discretion was exercised without a statutory right of appeal to a tribunal. First, some departments had devised their own non-statutory independent adjudicatory methods, such as by providing a right of appeal to agricultural executive committees or complaints committees for the hospital service. Generally the views of such bodies are accepted when they conflict with the department's, even though they lack statutory authority.

Secondly, a hierarchy of appeals within the organization may be established allowing the decisions at lower levels to be reconsidered and perhaps corrected by more senior officials. Complaints about postal and telephone services are dealt with in this way by the post office. Reconsideration at the regional level of decisions by local officials of the Supplementary Benefits Commission is an example of internal review linked with a right of appeal to an independent tribunal.

Thirdly, however, there is the less encouraging fact of the lack of any uniformity and consistency in administrative methods of appeal and review. The existence of such variation was felt by the 'Justice' Committee to be anomalous and led them to recommend an extension of the principle of impartial adjudication to all discretionary areas.[7]

In local government the factor of legality is even more present because of the way in which power is delegated to local authorities. This is especially the case in the budgetary process in local government where the finance officers work in close consultation with the district auditor to ensure that no proposed expenditure is likely to be ruled *ultra vires* (unless of course the council is determined to spend on unauthorized services, such as free school milk for certain age groups, going against the statutory provisions determined by the minister and his department). The leading role of the clerk to the council, who is usually legally qualified, in decision making in local authorities also testifies to the latent threat of judicial control.

TRIBUNALS AND THE REVIEW OF DISCRETIONARY DECISIONS

The second major type of appeal against the administration occurs when a citizen wishes to challenge the way in which a discretionary power has been used without necessarily contesting the legality of the decision. In many areas of public policy the application of general rules to individual cases requires the exercise of discretion after an evaluation of the circumstances. There is often room for disagreement between the individual and the official over the former's entitlement to some benefit, service or treatment, for instance, not over the legality of the official's decision but over the assumptions he has made in applying general policy to a particular case. Basically, what is involved in the exercise of such discretion is a decision as to whether the individual falls into a category to which certain rules apply. Clearly there is always the possibility of error in such decision making, and it may be necessary to establish some independent arbiter to decide whether the claimant's or the official's assessment of the situation is right. The citizen does not necessarily assert that the official is acting *ultra vires*, or even that his decision was motivated by bias, negligence or perversity. His contention is that the official's interpretation of the facts is wrong, when a correct one would entitle the complainant to what he considers his by right.

In many such areas of potential dispute between citizen and administration the latter has ceased to be judge in its own cause. It has delegated the power to adjudicate and, if necessary, substitute a new decision for that which caused the dispute. The final stage in the executive process is not the decision of an administrator or minister but of an independent body charged with the duty of carrying out an impartial review of the case and empowered to make a legally binding decision which may or may not support the administration.

These bodies are administrative tribunals and their object is to secure an impartial, open and fair judgement in cases of appeal against discretionary decisions of public authorities. They provide an alternative to the political weapon of appeal to one's MP or the press. Appeal to the Parliamentary Commissioner for Administration exists for a different purpose, although there are some overlaps. Tribunals are an acknowledgement of the difficulties, for the courts and the public, of loading disputes between the citizen and the authorities upon the ordinary courts of law. It is generally accepted that adjudication in disputes of this kind require continuity and expertise which only specially constituted courts can provide. As well as overwhelming the courts with many cases of a routine kind, making the appeals system unmanageable, this alternative to administrative tribunals would be undesirably expensive and formal. Tribunals thus provide informality, specialization and an opportunity to handle the many hundreds of disputes arising each year from the effects of legislation on the individual citizen.

Tribunals are neither purely administrative nor purely judicial. They constitute a special procedure prior to the taking of a decision which is not found in the ordinary course of administration. The procedure involves testing an issue by weighing up the relative merits of interests, both public and private. In recent years the judicial nature of tribunals has been increasingly accepted and they are now generally regarded as informal courts of law.

The procedures adopted by tribunals vary immensely and one of the tasks of the Council on Tribunals has been to try to bring about some consistency and regularity in tribunal hearings. It would be wrong to ignore the special requirements of the different policy areas within which tribunals work and insist on rigid uniformity, such as making all tribunal hearings public regardless of the personal details which have to be made available to the tribunal; or insisting on the enforcement of the rules of evidence and thus perhaps denying the tribunal an opportunity to consider relevant information in making its decision; or in creating such a formal atmosphere that appellants are overawed and intimidated. The diversity of tribunals is so great that 'there is nothing as yet resembling a common code of procedure, and there are exceptions to almost every rule'. Because of the different requirements of different tribunals which modify what might appear to be universal rules of procedure, such as the giving of reasoned decisions, it is considered necessary to judge every tribunal's procedural rules on their merits. This is in fact the way in which the Council on Tribunals works.

TRIBUNALS AND THE ADMINISTRATIVE PROCESS

The decisions of administrative tribunals have a great significance for the administrative process in the departments concerned. Above all they constitute a body of precedent to guide the officials whose task it is to make the original decisions which may give rise to appeals. In the field of social security, for example, the national insurance commissioners, who decide appeals from the decisions of local tribunals, publish any decisions establishing new principles as precedents for the guidance of the other adjudicating authorities, including the insurance officers who first dealt with claims for benefit.

Where government policy establishes legal rights to which anyone fulfilling the necessary conditions are automatically entitled it may be necessary to make special administrative arrangements within the department concerned for dealing with the many thousands of individual cases on which decisions will have to be made. Thus in social security decisions civil servants in the Department of Health and Social Security and the Department of Employment (for claims to unemployment benefit) are statutorily appointed insurance officers. They have a special status in the department as part of the statutory authorities which include the local tribunals and the commissioners. This status gives the insurance officer an independence from interference in his work either from a superior officer (unless he also has the status of insurance officer) or the minister, and appeal against his decisions lies with a local tribunal.[8]

An interesting question is why some areas of administrative discretion are either subject to review by special tribunals or delegated directly to them, while others are kept firmly in the hands of ministers or departmental officials whose discretion is binding. When the Whyatt Committee investigated administrative discretion not covered by statutory tribunals it found a number of areas where the possible sources of grievances were comparable to those covered by tribunal machinery. Examples were the district auditor's power to surcharge local councillors, the power of the Registrar of Business Names to refuse registration, the power of the Comptroller General of Patents, Designs and Trade Marks, the power of a local education authority to allocate children to schools, the Department of Health and Social Security's discretionary decisions concerning special drugs and equipment, and decisions under the local employment acts. There appears to be as much variation in the procedures for reviewing decisions in the areas of administration which have not been 'tribunalized' as in those which have.

It would be taking the judicial approach to the administrative process too far to say that all decisions should be subject to some appeals procedure by an independent body, with the possibility of having all departmental decisions overruled by people not subject to ministerial control. There are too many decisions which raise major policy implications for such an approach to be possible. It must also be remembered that many decisions are in the hands of local authorities whose position would be made intolerable if they were continually threatened by tribunals substituting their decisions for those of the council. However, as the Whyatt Committee pointed out, some discretionary decisions are subject to appeal to an independent body of adjudicators and some are not. 'These and other areas of discretion have been omitted from the tribunal system possibly for reasons of administrative convenience or because of some historical accident or perhaps on account of some oversight, but whatever the explanation may be, inconsistencies have grown up and areas of discretion have become, in some instances, areas of friction.'[9]

The Whyatt report recommended the adoption of a Swedish institution, a general tribunal which would hear appeals against the miscellaneous discretionary decisions not covered by specialized tribunals. This proposal really defeats the main object of a system of administrative tribunals which is to provide specialized and expert appellate machinery. Such a general tribunal would have to be provided with so many people with specialized knowledge to deal with the varying classes of decisions from which disputes can arise, that it would virtually have to divide up into a set of separate tribunals, thus adding to the existing system in a piecemeal way.

A much more ambitious proposal is that Britain should attempt to adopt a system of administrative law and related institutions for the adjudication of disputes similar to the French *Conseil d'État*. This system is based on a set of special judges and courts administering a special body of law.

Broadly speaking, any dispute arising from the administration of a public service, defined as the action of a public authority satisfying a public need, comes within the jurisdiction of the *Conseil d'État*. However, cases are excluded from the jurisdiction of the *Conseil* and said to fall within the scope of the civil courts if a public service operates, say in the industrial and commercial field, under the same conditions and with comparable objectives to a private organization.

A French citizen can seek two basic defences against the administration through the *Conseil d'État*. First, he can appeal to have a decision of an administrative body annulled on the grounds of illegality. By invoking the principle of legality the appellant may claim that the administrative decision about which he feels aggrieved is *ultra vires*, contrary to the principles of natural justice or in conflict with certain philosophical assumptions about government embodied in the Declaration of the Rights of Man. The test of *ultra vires* has also been extended to include the abuse of administrative power rather than just excess. The court can render an administrative act void if it finds the principle of legality has been violated.

The usual grounds for such review of administrative decisions are first that the decision is outside the authority of the administrative body that has taken it, i.e. a clear expression of *ultra vires*. Second, breaches of administrative procedures, such as those governing the advertising of slum clearance orders, may be declared void if considered to be of substantial importance, Third, as an extension of the *ultra vires* and procedural aspects of legality, the *Conseil* may look at administrative decisions taken according to the required procedures and by a competent authority and yet declare it void on the grounds that it did not conform 'with the legal conditions set upon administrative action in the particular case'. Here the court is looking at the specific circumstances of an individual case to see whether the law requires more than a competent authority acting in accordance with correct procedures in order to acquire legality. It is appropriate as a remedy against an authority which neglects to perform a mandatory duty. Finally, the *Conseil d'État* may review an administrative decision from the point of view of the motives of the administrator. In such cases the court protects the citizen against decisions taken for an ulterior motive and contrary to the intention of the law authorizing the administrative body to act. In effect the *Conseil* can quash an administrative act on the grounds of bad faith.

Under the principle of liability or responsibility an administrative authority may be required to compensate an individual citizen for damages suffered as a result of administrative action, with perhaps the administrative decision annulled. Thus the citizen can claim compensation for harm suffered as a result of administrative error or for carrying an excessive burden in the public interest.

An administrative court based on the French *Conseil d'État* might seem quite appropriate for Britain, especially if it could enjoy the degree of confidence which the French administration and public place in the *Conseil*. The relatively simple remedies available in the form of annulment for illegality and compensation for hardship obtained by effective and straightforward procedures are also attractive to certain sections of British opinion.

Against this it can be said that the flexibility of the case law embodied in the decisions of the *Conseil d'État* brings the court perilously close to deciding on the merits of decisions and the needs of society, areas which in this country are jealously guarded by our ministerial and Parliamentary system of government. However, even with such a prestigious body as the *Conseil d'État* there is no guarantee that its decisions will be carried out by the authorities. All of this makes it extremely difficult to know whether an administrative court as powerful as the *Conseil d'État* would provide an effective substitute for 'the kind of ramshackle machinery of judicial control that tries to meet the needs of modern Britain, helped out by a toothless Council on Tribunals' and a closely confined Parliamentary Commissioner for Administration.[11]

THE COUNCIL ON TRIBUNALS

The Franks Committee found that tribunals were 'more the result of *ad hoc* decisions, political circumstances and historical accident than of the application of general and consistent principles'. Following the Committee's recommendations the Council on Tribunals (with a Scottish Committee) was set up 'to keep the constitution and working of Tribunals under continuous review', to report on any matters referred to it concerning any tribunal, and on administrative procedures involving statutory inquiries where some matter is either referred to the Council or is thought by the Council to be of special importance.

However, it is only an advisory body with no executive or

judicial powers. It is neither a court of appeal nor an appellate tribunal, although it has certain powers to investigate grievances (see below). The Council has over 2000 tribunals to supervise as well as a wide range of public inquiries.

Individual complaints and grievances about the conduct of tribunals or inquiries may be brought to the Council though it only examines individual cases in exceptional circumstances, such as when they are significant for the development of tribunals and inquiries generally. It receives about ninety complaints about tribunals and public inquiries from members of the public each year. It has no power to alter their decisions or recommendations. It can only make recommendations about procedures which have been drawn to its attention as a result of a complaint by a member of the public.

PUBLIC INQUIRIES AND THE PROTECTION OF INTERESTS

Two possible sources of grievance and injustice have been examined – legality and the use of discretionary powers. A third is the threat to private interests posed by public policies, particularly those which affect property, such as housing development and trunk road programmes, or the provision of basic services. Some policy decisions affect personal interests to such an extent that the citizen feels he has a right to express his views and have them taken into account in the decision-making process through a special procedure.

In cases of this kind the citizen claims that injustice or hardship might be caused by a proposed course of official action. He feels the need to protect his interests by being given a hearing before a decision has been made and a plan of action finalized. An example from the field of policy in which such hearings are most numerous, town and country planning, would be where a developer is refused planning permission and is entitled to appeal against the decision of the local planning authority to the minister.

More general interests may feel threatened when a major development project is proposed. People may wish to object to plans to build a road, designate a national park, build a new town, or compulsorily acquire land for some other purpose. Or there may be objections, not only from individuals but also from organizations like local authorities, to the central government's schemes for local government reform, police force re-organization, the establishment of rural development boards, the regrouping of water undertakings or the re-organization of sewage disposal.[12]

The commonest method of giving a formal hearing to interested parties before making a policy decision is the public inquiry. It takes many different forms and almost evades satisfactory definition. It is useful to start from the following conception: 'Public inquiries are constituted *ad hoc* to inquire into particular matters, and are for the most part concerned only to establish facts and to make recommendations'.[13] On to this can be built the notion that they are part of the machinery for the prevention and redress of grievances.

Public inquiries are held by representatives of a minister either adjudicating between an individual and a public authority, such as in the case of an appeal against refusal of planning permission, or in cases arising from a minister's own scheme, such as the designation of a new town or the acquisition of land for a motorway.

Inquiries are held under widely varying rules of procedure. Virtually anyone with an interest in the subject of the hearing may appear at the inquiry and express his views and give information. The proceedings are usually kept as informal as the circumstances allow; but formality has tended to increase as proceedings have become judicialized. Despite the inquisitorial appearance of the public inquiry it only results in a recommendation in the form of a report, and not an enforceable judgement. The final decision is made by the minister and does not necessarily follow his representative's recommendation. Public inquiries may thus be contrasted in this respect, as in many others, with an administrative tribunal which gives a decision which has the force of law.

INQUIRIES AND THE ADMINISTRATIVE PROCESS

Whenever a minister is required to adjudicate between the citizen and an administrative authority by way of a formal hearing the effect of his quasi-judicial position on the administrative process in his department is profound. A former permanent secretary to the Ministry of Housing and Local Government described the need to adjudicate in the conflict of private and public interest as one of two dominant considerations in the work of the department.[14]

This preoccupation is partly reflected in the organization of a special inspectorate, in the case of planning administration, and the appointment of outside inspectors in other cases to produce a special kind of information to be fed into the decision-making process. Again there is heavy dependence on lawyers in departments with quasi-judicial functions. As inquiry procedures have become increasingly judicialized so administrative processes have become more cautious and meticulous in respect to the rights of individuals and more sensitive to the demands of natural justice. For example, in the planning field (where most inquiries occur) the inspector's report has gained in importance because of the need to avoid too many reopened inquiries as a result of new evidence having been taken into account. The place of the inquiry in the administrative process inevitably brings conflicting pressures to bear on the department concerned from a public which both wants its cases dealt with quickly and wants to see the full principles of natural justice brought to bear on the proceedings. Due regard to the quasi-judicial position of the minister must also be paid by officials dealing with appeals by written procedures. About half of the planning appeals each year are dealt with in this way.

MALADMINISTRATION AND THE PARLIAMENTARY COMMISSIONER FOR ADMINISTRATION

Finally, we turn to the fourth type of complaint which the citizen may wish to make against the administration and have investigated – maladministration. Maladministration lacks any statutory definition, but it is generally thought to refer to a defect in the conduct of officials and their administrative procedures. So the gross forms of maladministration are malice, jobbery, bribery and corruption. In its lesser forms it means carelessness, negligence and inefficiency. In all cases maladministration arises when defects in conduct and procedure cause individual hardship or injustice. Although the line between a discretionary decision and maladministration is rather blurred, the latter gives rise to an accusation that an official has failed to observe proper standards of conduct in the exercise of his administrative powers, while the former gives rise to appeals against the decision and not the way it was reached.

The shortcomings of legislatures in the redress of grievances has increased the attractiveness of the concept of the ombudsman, citizen's defender or public grievance-man. This is a growing response to governmental power and discretion. Originally a Scandinavian concept (dating back to eighteenth-century Sweden) the idea of an ombudsman has spread not only to other Scandinavian countries but also to West Germany, New Zealand, Canada, Guyana, Mauritius, India and the United Kingdom.

In so far as it is possible to give a general definition of an ombudsman it might be in the following terms: a special commissioner appointed to receive complaints from citizens about official action; to investigate legitimate complaints; and to seek a remedy if the complaint is justified. The idea originated in the institution of the Swedish Chancellor of Justice who was empowered by the monarch to supervise the administration of law by judges and other officials. The Swedish Parliament became dissatisfied with the Crown's control of the judiciary and after unsuccessfully trying to sever the Chancellor of Justice from the Crown, created an ombudsman independent of the executive and elected by the legislature. Thus, the general features of the office of ombudsman as it has been adopted in other countries are that it provides an informal, impartial investigation into administrative action, undertaken on behalf of the legislature, but does not undermine the responsibility of the executive by substituting decisions for those of ministers or officials.

The British version of the ombudsman is the Parliamentary Commissioner for Administration appointed under the Act of 1967 'for the investigation of administrative action taken on behalf of the Crown'. The Commissioner is an independent official serving Parliament with status and powers conferred by statute. He is appointed by the Crown with a salary and pension charged on the Consolidated Fund and is secure from dismissal except by Parliamentary motion.

The title was chosen to convey that the Commissioner would not undermine the special relationship between MPs and their constituents. Thus he is only empowered to investigate a grievance when a written complaint is made to an MP by a member of the public claiming to have sustained injustice as a result of maladministration, and when the MP's reference of the problem to the Commissioner has the consent of the complainant.

This feature of the office has been criticized on the grounds that the citizen ought to have direct access to the Commissioner. Many people are unaware that they should not approach the Com-

missioner direct. When they do so, the Commissioner, rather than
return the complaint unanswered, looks into the case to see
whether it is likely to fall within his jurisdiction and advises the
complainant accordingly. Why then should the MP be involved
at all? Reference is often made to the Scandinavian ombudsmen
who not only receive complaints direct, but who undertake investigations on their own initiative. In Sweden, for example, the
ombudsman may be motivated by a newspaper report or by something seen on a tour of inspection of government offices, hospitals
and prisons. The Finnish ombudsman inspects courts and police
stations, as well as government departments. Compared with this
free-ranging power and close contact with the citizen, the Parliamentary Commissioner appears to some to be unnecessarily
shackled.

A more frequently-voiced criticism is that the jurisdiction of the
Commissioner is excessively restricted. He is basically subject to
two types of exclusion from his powers of investigation. There are
certain matters set out in the Act, such as hospital administration,
government contracts, personnel questions of public servants including members of the armed forces, and areas of administrative
discretion where there is a right of appeal to a court or tribunal.
Other areas of administration are excluded by not being listed in
the schedule of departments and authorities whose actions are
subject to investigation. The local authorities, the police and the
nationalized industries are the main bodies excluded from the
Commissioner's jurisdiction in this way. In 1974, however, the
idea was extended to local government.

Unfavourable comparisons with Scandinavian countries should
not be pushed too far, mainly because of the much smaller populations to be served. There are also special circumstances associated
with many of the administrative bodies excluded from the Commissioner's jurisdiction which either make this form of review
inappropriate or require specialized methods for the redress of
grievances. Thus complaints against the national health service
were thought to require a health service commissioner who can
fit into the existing machinery for the investigation of grievances
and this was done in 1973. In local government, too, special
arrangements are necessary in view of the number of administrative authorities involved and the special position of the
councillor in relation to both the public and the local administration. In the case of the nationalized industries, on the other

hand, it is argued that consumer representation on consultative machinery is sufficient especially since the industries are subject to the forces of competition and the operation of the market. Where there is a consumer-producer relationship, consumer choice is thought to embody sufficient sanction in cases of dissatisfaction with the service or product offered.

A significant extension of the Commissioner's power has come about as a result of difficulties in applying the terms of the Act to individual cases. The Act entitles him to investigate complaints of injustice as a consequence of maladministration. This term is not defined in the Act. As mentioned above, it is generally accepted as referring to the quality of administrative procedures prior to the making of a final decision, rather than to the merits of decisions made by the exercise of a discretionary authority. In the Parliamentary debate on the Act maladministration was said to mean 'perhaps neglect, inattention, delay, inconvenience, ineptitude, perversity, turpitude, arbitrariness and so on'.

The Commissioner, perhaps inevitably, has encountered difficulties in some cases when, despite impeccable administrative procedures, he has found that a decision has resulted in manifest hardship to the complainant. The distinction between the quality of administrative procedures leading to a defective decision, and the quality of a decision itself is sometimes difficult to draw.[15] The Commissioner was authorized by Parliament to investigate and comment on the quality of decisions taken without maladministration but nevertheless appearing to cause hardship or injustice. The Act specifically denies the Commissioner authority to question the merits of a policy decision. The problem of the borderline case can be partly solved by labelling a decision as 'perverse' when, though taken properly, it is such that no reasonable man could have taken it. This brings it within the catalogue of errors constituting maladministration. There appear to be relatively few cases where decisions appear so bad as to indicate bias or perversity on the part of the persons taking them. Nevertheless, the Commissioner has been able to draw attention to instances where the proper application of policy to individual cases has produced results which cause undue hardship and appear anomalous.

The Commissioner has also been encouraged to comment on departmental rules which, though applied without maladministration, produce decisions which bear oppressively on the individual citizen concerned. He can also inquire whether a department has reviewed a rule which caused hardship. Of course, in neither instance does he have the power to modify or cancel a rule. As an extension of his power to investigate reviews of departmental rules, the Commissioner was subsequently encouraged by Parliament to inquire into action taken by departments to review Statutory Instruments, the operation of which had caused hardship.

Inevitably, thorough and lengthy investigations into complex disputes between complainant and department impose administrative burdens on the officers concerned in addition to the normal internal follow-up and review of disputed decisions. The costs are fairly high in terms of the man-days spent of investigations, estimated roughly at $1\frac{1}{2}$ to $1\frac{3}{4}$ per case, and the seniority of the officials involved – all cases start with the permanent secretary. About 350 cases are fully or partially investigated each year. There may be additional costs, such as more cautious, and therefore slower, administration (which itself can give rise to complaints of delay), and the reluctance of departments to perform non-statutory duties, such as giving advice to the public on the operation of policy, lest that advice should provide grounds for a complaint. Finally, the increased risk of public accountability may impair delegation, forcing all decisions up to a higher level, thus making departmental management cumbersome.[16]

There are obviously benefits to be set against these costs. There is firstly the negative benefit of the unsuccessful complainant who, though disappointed, feels satisfied that his case has received full and fair consideration. Then, of course, there are the cases where maladministration is found and a remedy given. And like all other aspects of accountability there is what the first Commissioner called the 'tonic effect' of his presence and the latent threat of investigation which keeps the administrator on his toes.

Finally, there are the long-term improvements in departmental administration which may follow from an investigation, particularly one which throws light on the operation of departmental rules. In some cases the Commissioner's action leads to changes in departmental policy. Examples are a change in the date from which arrears of benefit are paid by the Department of Health and Social Security, and a modification of the rules governing the payment of tax arrears by the Inland Revenue.

On a much broader level, the office of Parliamentary Commissioner has had far-reaching implications for the anonymity

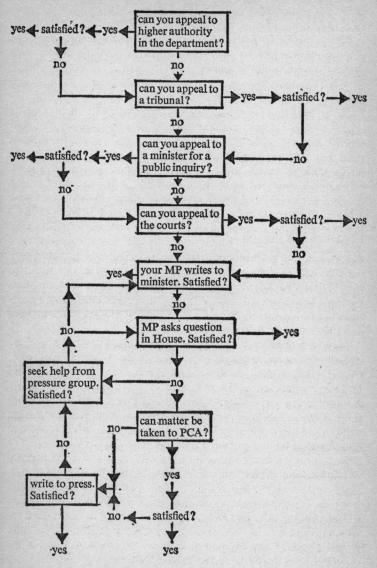

Fig. 14. The Redress of Grievances

of the civil service. This possibility became particularly apparent when the Parliamentary Select Committee sought to confirm that defects in administrative practices identified by the Commissioner had been put right by taking evidence from those directly responsible within the department. This appeared to some to involve the naming and blaming of civil servants rather than ministers and thus to be a violation of the convention of ministerial responsibility. If the Committee were to take evidence from subordinate officials rather than principal officers in order to check what changes were being made in a department it might well lead to a change in the relations between Parliament and the civil service, especially if the Committee found it difficult (as they would) to take such evidence without appearing to re-open the original case in order to expose and blame those responsible.[17]

The Pattern of Control

The main sections of this chapter have been devoted to discussing the individual methods or mechanisms of control of administration in the interests of individual citizens. It is worth concluding with a reminder that taking all these methods together creates a complicated pattern which many citizens find difficult to understand (see figure 14).

Some of the methods are obviously alternatives to each other; some are particularly relevant to a type of grievance, whilst others are appropriate when a case does not fall into a clear-cut category. They also vary in their effect on the general behaviour of public servants – the cost, speed and consistency of public decision making. Above all, they vary in their cost and availability to the ordinary citizen, and in their effectiveness in remedying 'wrongs' as the individual, as against the state, sees them.

Notes

1 Chester, 1970, p. 104
2 Mackintosh, 1970, p. 129
3 Morris, 1970, p. 21
4 Johnson, 1970, pp. 241–3
5 Wade, 1961, p. 143
6 Wade, 1961, pp. 63–80; Garner, 1961, pp. 118–21; de Smith, 1968, pp. 92–6

7 Whyatt, 1961
8 King, 1958, pp. 83–4
9 Whyatt, 1961
10 Brown and Garner, 1967, p. 122
11 Brown and Garner, 1967, p. 136
12 Wraith and Lamb, 1971, ch. 3
13 Wraith and Lamb, 1971, p. 13
14 Sharp, 1969, p. 25
15 Marshall, 1973
16 Compton, 1970, p. 6
17 Marshall, 1970, pp. 120–2

Chapter 7
Administrative Reform

In a sense the chapters on decentralization, public organization, the public service and control of administration have all been closely concerned with the problems of administrative reform. We have tried to give an impression of the forms, causes and consequences of changing patterns of public administration. We will conclude the book by considering this subject more systematically.

A system of public administration resembles a set of private bodies in that it is constantly experiencing *change* in a virtually infinite number of ways. Organizational change includes the adaptation of existing structures, expressed in terms of functions and responsibilities, to new objectives, technology, resources and environmental factors. Serving personnel die or retire and are replaced by new people who may subtly change the organization in the process of assimilation. Such adaptation may alter the allocation of work within the organization, change the size of managerial units and the methods of planning, co-ordination and review. It may be a process of clarifying organizational goals and adjusting procedures for the control and co-ordination of administrative procedures to meet new standards of efficiency and effectiveness. Organizational change is a continuous process; the hidden dynamic of government organization is a spontaneous response to feed-back from and reviews of the administrative process, including those of the new management techniques and supporting services.

However, not all change in government fits the above pattern. For instance, the demand for change may appear to originate in a belief that what is needed in government cannot be achieved given existing methods of recruitment or control, or some other characteristic of the system. This demand often appears to be associated with external political values, sometimes partisan ones, which the 'artificially' induced change seeks to serve.

It is obvious that the processes of reactive change are different in a number of ways from the sort of change that the local government system has recently seen in the conurbations, or from that which arises in the introduction of a fashionable new specialized administrative technique in a central department. It would be wrong to conceive of *change* and *reform* (as we designate the latter phenomena) as simply being two different categories. Rather they are at opposite ends of a continuum, at one end of which is the smallest adaptation to changing circumstances, and at the other the radical transformation which leaves a new pattern discernably and basically different from the old. In between there are varying combinations of change and reform, the exact mixture of which can be an important problem to unravel.

For instance, a post office may reorganize its delivery system, or a social security administration its local boundaries to accommodate the building of a new estate or a declining population. But it may encounter difficulties which it cannot solve with its existing intellectual resources (and organizational problems are always intellectual ones) so that it turns to outsiders or external ideas for additional help. It may not know how to organize community work in a declining slum area and so turn to a university for advice and perhaps research. It may also refuse to accept that there are organizational deficiencies, for instance, when a city's housing department evicts bad tenants who become the obligation of the social services department – at much greater cost – or when its planners are unable to prepare schemes for redevelopment which meet the current criteria of adequacy. In such cases the alternatives may be sometimes vigorously drawn to the attention of the public body.

The reform of the national health service, now in the process of completion, and the creation of the new water authorities is not of this order. There is nothing in the previous systems to which one can point as the origin of the changes, other than outsiders' perceived weaknesses.

But if one considers the post-Fulton 'reforms', it is necessary to ask how many of these arose from outside the civil service and how many were really changes that a substantial and influential body of opinion within the system wanted to make but needed some external authority as support. The interaction between change and reform is probably one of the significant features of recent years; to determine how far the changes made in some aspect of public administration result from the 'natural' processes of organizational adaptation and how far from externally imposed solutions is an important aspect of the understanding of re-organization and the work of commissions of inquiry and the like.

Both change and reform may also result from political conflict within the broad sector of government comprised of a variety of institutions dealing with related matters. Reorganization may change the power relations between different types of people within such a broad sector – for instance, those between specialists and generalists, or between doctors and politicians. Thus the demand for reform as opposed to change may be a political demand – for the recognition of special interests or the protection of a special status. But this aspect is most noticeable when the pressures for change are external rather than internal.

We have chosen to illustrate the problems in this area mainly from the work of the Fulton Committee, because this is one of the bodies that needs very careful interpretation if its role in administrative reform is to be understood. In doing so we are not giving any support to the view that the analyses undertaken and presented by that Committee are intrinsically valuable; on the contrary, there is much evidence that their importance arises from the fact that the opposite is true.

This Committee, in its review of the organization and working of the civil service, adopted a particular stance in its approach to departmental structures. This can best be characterized as a 'business management' approach but we believe that it is a mistake to think of a single model of managerial structure as the best one for all public administration. We also outline the important developments and changes in both structure and process currently taking place in the continuous search for increased efficiency in the administration of public policy.

THE FULTON COMMITTEE'S CRITICISMS

The major criticisms made by the Fulton Committee of the civil service can be grouped under the following headings: delegation of responsibility, budgeting, management structures, staffing, management services and policy planning. It should be noted that before these can command wide assent much more research is needed, but this is irrelevant from the point of view of the acceptability of the changes.

First, responsibility in central departments was said to be sparsely delegated. Because of political sensitivity and inter-departmental considerations, authority to take decisions may not be exclusively delegated to one official or unit within the organiz-ation. Decisions may be 'taken' only after contributions have been made by many levels in the hierarchy or after consultation through committees. It is argued that in place of such indeterminate auth-ority the principles of accountable management should be applied. This means 'holding individuals and units responsible for per-formance measured as objectively as possible'

Secondly, government budgeting methods do not provide the right kind of information for policy making. The measurement of performance implicit in accountable management requires new methods of financial planning and control. Traditional methods of vote accounting do not relate costs to the objectives of the organ-ization. Only when objectives have been clearly defined and costed can efficiency be measured. Accounting methods should be de-signed to measure output against costs. Where the 'output' of administrators cannot easily be quantified and costed, such as in reviewing the investment programme of a nationalized industry, or in studying and making recommendations on a proposed company merger, the principle of 'management by objectives' should be applied. The principle requires superiors and sub-ordinates to agree objectives and priorities and subsequently to review progress within their section of the organization.

Thirdly, and consequently, changes are needed in management structure; new organizational forms are required to complement new processes. The tall, thin pyramids with many levels, typical of government departments, should be replaced with 'flatter' structures with fewer levels in the hierarchy. Departments should be divided into budget centres or 'commands' to which clear responsibility and authority should be delegated and in which managers could be held accountable for objectively costed per-formance. Departmental structures have been contrasted un-favourably with organizational forms in progressive industries where more authority, it is alleged, is delegated to more flexible groupings of executives.

Central departments have also been criticized for the way in which work involving both administrators and specialists has been traditionally organized. Although joint and parallel hier-archies are acknowledged as having a number of advantages, mainly associated with the expertise of the administrator in financial control, co-ordination and political affairs, these are said to be outweighed by considerable disadvantages. The best kind of organization for technical projects is the 'single integrated structure under a single head', or 'unified hierarchy'. The head of the structure is chosen on the principle of the best man for the job regardless of civil service class or occupational group. Posts below this are also filled by administrators or specialists according to the requirements of the task.

Fourthly, departments have also been criticized for the limited authority over subordinate staff delegated to line managers. It has been noted that civil service managers cannot hire, promote, reprimand or dismiss, reward merit with extra payments or even stop annual increments. The value of annual reports on subordinates is reduced by civil service conventions against the use of extreme praise or censure.

The concept of a unified and politically neutral service means that recruitment and conditions of employment have been standardized, promotion is based more on seniority than on experience of managerial responsibility, and manpower controls and discipline have been centralized. Also 'the emphasis upon equity and fair chances for all deprives the line manager of what in industry is his main motivational tool'.[1] National agreements made through the Whitley machinery govern the allocation of duties to each grade and thus prevent line managers experimenting with the responsibilities of their subordinates.

Fifthly, management services need modernization. The promotion and maintenance of efficient organizations in central departments is the responsibility of the management services units in establishment divisions. These were criticized by Fulton as being too narrowly concerned with traditional organization management problems. It was recommended that the scope of management services should be widened to include efficiency audits; and the application of all relevant management techniques to departmental work. Staff should be more expert and specialized and should be equipped to operate at all levels in the department, including the highest.

Finally, deficiencies in long-term policy planning have been identified and changes recommended to improve this aspect of central departments' work. Policy planning is often crowded out by the immediate pressures from Parliamentary business, the legislative process, negotiations and day-to-day management. To rectify this it has been suggested that departments set up 'planning units' to identify and study the problems and needs of the future in specific policy areas and to analyse the possible means to meet them. The staff of such units would be relatively young, expert in their field and sometimes drawn from people outside the service. The head of the planning unit would be the minister's senior policy adviser. While the permanent secretary would continue to have overall responsibility for all the affairs of the department and particularly remain answerable to Parliament for expenditure, he would be mainly concerned with the day-to-day management of the department. The senior policy adviser would have direct and unrestricted access to his minister and would, after consultation with the permanent secretary and with ministerial approval, determine the work of his planning unit.

Central government is not alone in being criticized for its management structures and processes. Similar criticisms have been made of local authorities. A working party of senior local government officers even went so far as to say recently that 'The management structures of many local authorities remain those which emerged from the development of local government in the nineteenth century.'[2]

Specifically, management problems in local government are the result of their multifunctionality, and the direct relationships between the services provided by each authority and its environment, namely, the community which each serves. Like central departments, local authorities have been urged to improve the quality of their planning processes and to modify management structures to match those processes.

The processes of policy formation and management in local authorities have been criticized as:

1. lacking adequate data on community needs relating to particular services;
2. failing to test whether departmental objectives and programmes satisfy defined needs, and whether alternative programmes should be considered;
3. failing to cost out programmes in terms of results achieved and therefore value for money obtained; as in central goverment, local authority budgets are designed more to control expenditure than to plan policies;

    4. failing to evaluate the impact of an authority's activities on
the community's problems and needs.[3]

Local authority management structures have equally been found
wanting by critics conscious of the need for a corporate planning
approach to local authority administration. Criticism has been
levelled at:

1. the unclear relationship between councillors and officials,
producing mistrust and hostility;
2. the rigid departmentalism standing in the way of a corporate
outlook;
3. professional jealousies restricting the access of those with
management skills to senior posts (a reversal of the civil
service problem);
4. the proliferation of departments and committees so that
organization reflects the professional requirements of individual services rather than the objectives and programmes of
the authority;
5. the absence of a managing body (or political executive) for
the whole authority, in addition to the managing committees
for individual services.

By no means everyone deplores every aspect of these features of
local government organization, Neither is there a universally
accepted policy of managerial reform. But whatever form the
criticisms of local authority management take, they tend to focus
on factors which are very similar to those causing concern and
change in central government: the need for improved methods of
planning and budgeting; and the need for new organizational
structures to match new processes of administration.

The criticisms of organizational structures in both central and
local government appear to have had a considerable influence on
public administration. It is important, therefore, to have some
idea of how they might be approached, even though there is not
space here to undertake a full critique of either Fulton or one of
its counterparts at local government level, for instance the Bains
Committee Report.

One of the major considerations must be how far a committee of
inquiry such as the Fulton Committee has properly taken into
account the differences between industrial and public organizations, and whether it has been aware of the differences between

individual bodies within each category. It is not sufficient simply to say that civil servants work in a political environment that is absent from private business; it is necessary to spell out the differences between public and private that we discussed in Chapter One in a detailed form that is relevant to the particular organizations being examined.

First, departments operate within a political system which requires governments to act as impartial arbiters in the allocation of resources between competing interests in society. In so doing the government creates rights for and imposes constraints on different groups of individuals. The administrator is brought into frequent contact with his department's 'clients' – either individuals or interest groups and associations. His major concern is with equity and impartiality. Administrative procedures are built around the requirements of strict adherence to law and regulation. While private industry is expected to risk capital to gain profits, the civil servant is expected to maximize equity and minimize error. The government administrator must include a judicial element in his decision-making in order to avoid injustice or maladministration. Hence the appropriateness in much government work of bureaucratic organizations characterized by hierarchy, procedural inflexibility and limited authority delegated to particular individuals.

The administrator's need to take the interests and rights of different sectors of society in account also leads to the calculation of social costs which do not form part of decision making by the private entrepreneur. In no sense can the administrator simply look for the cheapest way of performing a given task. At the same time, however, the administrator works under pressure to economize and prevent waste or extravagance. Yet every social and economic interest wants to see expenditure increased in favour of its own cause. Professor Self has called the problem which faces the administrator one of 'market compression', in contrast to the business managers' imperative of market innovation.[4]

Secondly, the administrator is required to implement decisions which are in the public interest. Governments must not only take all interests into account in policy-making. They must perform an integrative function by pursuing the common interest. This is the yardstick by which politicians and the public evaluate administration and may be contrasted with the concept of profitability by which the market system tests the efficiency of management in private firms. In business, firms compete for resources on the open market. In government, departments compete for resources through the political system. It is consequently much more difficult for the administrator to quantify in financial terms the return on the investment of resources and to obtain a consensus within society about the value to be attached to the results of different government programmes, or on the question of how the welfare of society is to be maximized.

Even when the government is functioning in areas comparable to industry its special position requires it to act differently, such as by adopting special procedures for negotiating contracts or in maintaining stocks of defence equipment. It has to be mindful of social and political considerations, such as fairness and the 'national interest' which do not constrain private enterprise.

Thirdly, government departments frequently experience changes of political leadership and consequent changes in policy. Instability also results from changes in social conditions, public concern about a social problem or the *force majeur* of unforeseen circumstances or even disasters. Senior public officials have to adapt much more frequently and on a larger scale than senior managers in industry to new policy goals while maintaining an efficient organization.

Fourthly, the way in which governmental functions and statutory powers are allocated to ministers, local councils and other bodies often owes more to political factors than to bureaucratic rationality. This can mean that many issues can only be resolved through lengthy inter-departmental discussions and consultation which introduces a factor into decision making in government which has no counterpart in private firms.

Fifthly, top administrators spend a greater proportion of their time dealing with short-term issues and correspondingly less on long-term planning than do senior managers in industry. This factor arises from the day-to-day pressures of legislative scrutiny and the political work of ministers and councillors. The form taken by legislative control of finance has in the past also tended to engender a short-run concern with keeping expenditure within the limits of the correct votes rather than with forward planning to maximize efficiency. This feature has been linked with the preoccupation with avoiding mistakes (such as *ultra vires* expenditure), in contrast to private management's risk-taking in pursuit of success measured by profitability.

Finally, the factor which perhaps more than any other leads to doubts about the wisdom of transplanting management principles and practices from the private sector (even leaving aside the question: which part of the private sector?) is the variety of functions performed by government departments. There is not merely more variety of goals and tasks than in the private sector. There are functions which are exclusively governmental: defence, police, prisons, the regulation of private activity (e.g. factory safety), the provision of social services, taxation, the sponsorship of private activity (e.g. agricultural support), and the manipulation of the nation's resources through instruments and techniques of economic management and physical planning.

The force of the above argument is to show that the Fulton Committee (and also the Maud Committee before it) did not take into account some of the important detailed ways in which the public bodies they were studying differed from their private counterparts. The Committee might have produced a report which said that virtually the opposite policies should be adopted.

First, the introduction of a stress on *measurement* and *efficiency* in bodies whose performance or 'output' is basically not quantifiable in a direct manner can lead to a distortion of their activities towards those aspects which are most easily made numerical, at the expense of the 'intangibles'. This can be a form of 'displacement of goals' and is well discussed and illustrated by Etzioni.[5] Individuals and units should not therefore be held responsible for objectively measured tasks in the public service, and budgetary methods should not emphasize measurable costs against immeasurable 'outputs'.

Secondly, the management structures of individual public bodies should be fitted to the nature of the work undertaken, in effect the technology of the activities in its jurisdiction. Some bodies should have clearly defined hierarchical structures, with a well articulated division of formal responsibilities, whilst others should adopt a more flexible organizational pattern in which the lines of responsibility are blurred, and scope for independent action spread throughout the body. The research of both Joan Woodward and Burns and Stalker gives strong reasons for believing that an 'inappropriate' organizational form – one which is not suited to the technology of the body – may be a cause of organizational failure.

In addition the study of public organizations should distinguish clearly between professional and non-professional organizations as the management problems of the two types, though logically related, are in practice quite different. Thus local authority departments and hospitals face the reverse problems to those faced by civil service departments.

Thirdly, the public service should be careful how far it adopts a system in which line managers are given greater authority over their subordinates in recruitment, training, promotion, etc. It is easy to draw too strong a contrast here with private organizations, and there is much evidence that, as with the stress on measurement, the use of more direct reward/punishment oriented supervision can distort the activities of the organization. The usefulness of these powers in private industry is also limited by the fact that before they can be deployed successfully it is necessary to make a series of correct judgements which are beyond the intellectual capabilities of many line managers.[6]

Fourthly, the use of management services developed in private organizations should be undertaken only after careful investigation of their merits and defects. The field of specialized administrative techniques is one in which there is a great deal of intellectual trickery; many of the so-called modern methods are little more than profitable mystiques, promoted by those who make a good living out of the timidity and ignorance of those they serve. The most important task for those in charge of public bodies is to learn to distinguish between 'good and bad' in the management services field.

Fifthly, the sort of long-term planning that is necessary in building an oil refinery or a hydro-electric power station, with capital 'write-off' periods of twenty to fifty years, is inappropriate for many public activities. At worst it is undemocratic, because it tries to deny the right of electors to change their governors and their policies, and at best it is unrealistic, because the uncertainty of knowledge increases rapidly after only one future year has been considered. Long-term planning, if used at all, must be of quite a different sort in the public sector as opposed to some parts of private industry.

Despite the above criticisms it should not be thought that the work of the Fulton Committee has not been influential; as we show below, its report was the occasion to start a whole series of reforms in the British central civil service. The question that most concerns us here is whether if the Committee had produced the 'anti-report' above, this would have made any difference to the subsequent reorganizations.

Acceptance of the Fulton Committee's criticisms and recommendations was followed by an election which brought in a party committed to a 'new style' of government which was heavily dependent on managerial methods and techniques allegedly imported from private business. This factor, together with the continuous pressures for organizational change arising from changes in policies, appears to have stimulated considerable innovation in the machinery of central government. Some of the most highly publicized of these changes are described below.

The Fulton Committee's recommendations on *accountable management* have had a considerable impact on the organization of work in central departments. In the first place new structures have been created to which greater autonomy has been delegated for managerial efficiency. Secondly, new methods of financial planning have been introduced to relate costs more closely to performance and output. Obviously these experiments have occurred most in areas of government activity with commercial characteristics.

For example, a unit of accountable management has been set up in the Ministry of Defence for the procurement of weapons systems for the armed forces and the management of defence research establishments and the civil aerospace programme. An employment service agency has been created in the Department of Employment to provide a new model placement service. The Civil Service Department has a central computer agency. In the Department of the Environment the management of public buildings and works comes under a new property services agency.

Organizational details vary from agency to agency. Some of the chief executives are senior civil servants. Others are business men specially recruited by the Government. Not all agency chiefs have been made the accounting officers for their expenditure, this function sometimes remaining with the permanent secretary of the department. Similarly, not all are directly responsible to the minister. But in all cases the general principle of delegating responsibility for the management of the agency's budget and personnel (in the latter case within the limits of civil service procedures) has been applied.

These aspects of central government are the more obvious candidates for tests of cost effectiveness and individual performance. In other areas, where output and performance are more difficult to measure, where programme costs are more difficult to define and where, consequently, managerial performance is more difficult to assess, there will be greater problems in introducing accountable management.

Nevertheless, rapid changes are taking place in the way in which central departments plan expenditure. Any improvements in management accounting will inevitably make the introduction of accountable management easier. A method of growing importance to central government is output budgeting (or planning, programming, budgeting).

The aim of this method is basically to increase rationality in governmental policy planning. It requires a department to clarify its objectives and devise methods of costing the different ways of achieving them. The difference in accounting terms between this and traditional expenditure planning is that it relates expenditure to outputs and objectives and not inputs or the resources used by the organization, e.g. staff, buildings, debt charges, equipment. If the costs of departmental programmes are known it is possible to evaluate the effectiveness of alternative policies leading to the same objectives, and compare the real demands on resources being made by different objectives.

The Ministry of Defence was the first department to introduce output budgeting. The planning of defence expenditure is now based on forecasts of functional costs as well as the traditional estimates of men, materials and services needed for defence projects. Although it is not possible in this way to attribute costs to the overall objectives of defence policy, which can only be expressed in very general terms such as the avoidance of war, the protection of British interests abroad, or the fulfilment of treaty obligations, functional costing enables improved evaluation to be made of the resources used in individual programmes related to these objectives. Functional costing has enabled the Ministry to make a better estimate of the full costs of such programmes as the TSR 2 aircraft and the forces stationed east of Suez.

Programme budgeting is also well-developed in the Home Office and Department of Education and Science. The Home Office is helping police forces to introduce output budgeting by costing the activities of individual policemen and civilian employees which contribute to different programmes, such as crime investigation and control, traffic control, training and so on. This has provided very different patterns of expenditure than those obtained from conventional accounting methods, such as showing the programme cost of police dogs in one force as £37,900 instead of the £1,000 previously estimated.

Output budgeting in the police reveals some of the problems associated with this method of accounting. For example, it is very difficult to devise objective criteria of efficiency in the prevention and detection of crime. Criminal statistics do not give a reliable indicator of levels of success, nor do they provide a basis for assessing the contribution to effectiveness of different parts of a force, such as patrolmen, forensic scientists, police dogs, and so on. Indeed the problem of measuring the effects of marginal variations in costs on different programmes occurs in most departments.

Other complications arise from the introduction of output budgeting in government. Many functions for which some departments have a responsibility are administered by local authorities. In such cases there is no complete control over expenditure which ought to be included in the department's budget. The identification of costs relating to different programmes is made doubly difficult. A further problem is that functions overlap, as in the case of the contributions made to traffic control and road safety by the Home Office and transport sections of the Department of the Environment. Expenditure relating to linked functions must be broken down in such a way as to provide a complete and accurate picture of programme costs.[7]

Another important aspect of output budgeting is the systematic review of ongoing programmes of expenditure. A system of programme analysis and review is being extensively introduced in central government to produce annual reviews of existing departmental programmes in the light of changing circumstances, for instance, increasing unemployment or population change. This entails a review of objectives both from the point of view of their continued political acceptability and of the effectiveness of different programmes of expenditure in meeting them – a progress review.[8] The technique feeds into the annual public expenditure survey by providing information on alternative policy options to be considered by ministers in comparison with forecasts of future expenditure under present policies.

Accountable management requires not only the delegation of financial responsibility to autonomous units or agencies. It also implies greater control over the use of staff than is common among line managers in the civil service. The reasons for the limited powers to 'hire and fire' given to managers in central government together with developments in personnel management designed to create more flexibility are dealt with in Chapter Five. At this stage we examine a management method increasingly used in central departments as a performance appraisal and review system by which results can be compared with stated objectives agreed between personnel at different levels in the hierarchy. Management-by-objectives requires managers to think about the aims of their parts of the organization. These are then translated into objectives or targets to be reached within established time limits. These objectives are further broken down into a hierarchy of subordinate objectives. Great emphasis is placed upon the participation of managers at all levels in agreeing reasonable targets and priorities for the future. Managers' tasks have to be specified and methods of measuring performance have to be devised. Desired standards of achievement have to be set out and plans for improving performance agreed between superior and subordinate. Management-by-objectives schemes have been applied to such tasks as the management of a naval stores depot, placement work in the Department of Employment, and the organization of the Home Office Prison Department.[9] Management-by-objectives is the personnel equivalent of output budgeting in management accounting.

Management-by-objectives, like output budgeting, is subject to limitations when applied from private business to central government, arising from the distinctive features of government set out above. Nevertheless, in principle it should be as possible to determine aims and review progress in implementing legislation and general policy in departments as it is to test performance in private industry. But special control systems will have to be devised for central government. Executive operations will have to be costed in a way which relates to objectives. And performance will have to be measured by specially designed indices which are appropriate to the special, non-commercial activities of government. Management-by-objectives thus depends on effective output budgeting. A start has been made in the more routine aspects of departmental work and in the quasi-commercial activities of some departments.

A number of departments have created integrated units of professional and non-professional staff to deal with projects requiring both kinds of expertise. Examples are found in the development work of the Architects and Buildings Branch of the Department of Education and Science, the Works Directorate set up in the War Office in 1958, large parts of the Ministry of Technology in 1965 and the highways organization of the Ministry of Transport in the same year.[10] Another important example of a successful integrated hierarchy was the Polaris Executive created in 1963 in the Ministry of Defence for the management of the Polaris Missile Submarine Programme. The common and distinctive feature of these structures is that generalists and specialists share equally in policy formulation and execution. The administrative and managerial aspects of the work are not seen as the sole prerogative of administrators.[11]

These innovations have not been sufficiently researched to enable firm generalizations on their effects to be made. However, Regan's conclusions on the working of integration in the Ministry of Transport probably have wider application. The extension of administrative responsibilities to professional engineers had important beneficial effects. Relationships between administrators and professionals improved, communication became more informal and frequent, and morale was increased. The professionals' heightened awareness of financial and political factors widened their perspective and increased the usefulness of their specialist advice. Within the department there was a widespread feeling that the quality of work had increased. These advantages far outweighed the problems which such integration caused.

Policy planning and research units exist in all the major departments of state.[12] A number of these pre-date the Fulton Committee report. The arrangements which exist by no means all follow the Fulton recommendations on the structure and personnel of planning units. They tend to be composed of older officials than Fulton thought desirable. They are almost always staffed by career civil servants. And the heads of such units do not have the seniority which Fulton envisaged.

Apart from these factors there is great variety in the ways in which forward planning is organized. The problem of forward planning varies from department to department. In some multifunctional departments, such as Health and Social Security, there may be a need for more than one planning unit. Some departments see a closer association than others between policy formation and day-to-day managerial and political considerations.

It is not generally accepted that policy planning should be separated from executive work. It may be argued that the two must feed each other and that both activities must be equally sensitive to the political environment. The time scale of planning also varies as between, say, a hospital building programme and a weapons system. Finally, departments may find it necessary to separate research, information and forecasting from the review of general policy and the formulation of new options. In fact the diversity of policy research and planning arrangements reflects the many different types of activity in which modern government departments are engaged.

Much of the change taking place in central government has its counterpart in local government. It is risky to generalize about administrative practices in local authorities, but it is possible to discern some developments which appear to be widely supported if not universally adopted. As far as the processes of management are concerned the main developments, and those which are likely to be extended by the recent reorganization of the whole structure, are:

the introduction of planning-programming-budgeting systems; research and analysis of the environment within which the authority functions; the adoption of a corporate management approach to the relationship between the authority and the community; and the monitoring and review of programmes against defined objectives.

Most local authorities are taking the opportunity presented by the 1972 Act to restructure their internal organizations. In many cases structural changes have been introduced because they are fashionable, without there having been a significant change in management processes. As a consequence they have not had much impact on the working of the authority. Also, some changes are more relevant to some authorities than others, mainly because of variations in size. However, some structural developments represent more than a veneer on old processes. The changes which have been introduced in the past and which are likely to be seen increasingly in the future, are:

the creation of policy committees; the appointment of chief executive officers; reductions in the number of committees and departments, conforming to programme areas; increased delegation from councillors to officials; the creation of teams of chief officers for corporate management; and the establishment of central policy planning units for programme analysis and review.

Local government, like central, has in recent years been subject to severe pressures for change, many of which have been motivated, consciously or unconsciously, by the belief that management in industry is better than management in government and that the latter would benefit from a strong injection of management ideas and techniques from industry. It is perhaps worth ending this section with a quotation from the Bains Report which is applicable to all levels of government:

'As in other fields of management there are wide variations in the efficiency of local authorities, but we believe that at its best local authority management compares favourably with management in other fields . . . Neither are we convinced that it is possible to apply straight business concepts to management in local government. Local government may well have lessons to learn from industry, but one must be wary of attempting wholesale transplants from one to the other. To pursue the analogy, the rejection factor will be extremely high because of the different nature of the constraints within which management must operate in the two fields.'[13]

As we mentioned earlier, much of the main part of this book has been concerned with the changing pattern of public administration in Britain, and some evidence relating to the various problems we consider has been drawn from official inquiries into aspects of government – such as Maud, Redcliffe-Maud, Mallaby, Fulton, Kilbrandon – some of whom also commissioned academic research. There can be scarcely any doubt that the academic study of public administration is closely connected with processes within government itself. In fact, the latter are engaged in an enterprise which is itself partly academic.

The main evidence for this lies in the terms of reference of the committees and commissions themselves. Any person with only a little familiarity with the social sciences will immediately recognize in these a whole series of academic problems; by this we mean problems that are and have been studied systematically by professional students, and about which there is a varied literature. Thus, the terms of reference of the Redcliffe-Maud Commission relate to social geography, sociology and economics, as well as political science. The Fulton Committee was concerned with problems which have attracted immense attention from those researching in the social science of formal organizations. In each case the questions to be answered are defined as belonging to the social sciences, not by impertinent outsiders, but by the members of the organizations and those responsible for the machinery of government. Thus, fundamentally, reform is based on an academic exercise, to which political values and processes are added.

The above view, of course, contrasts with the usual cynical view of committees of inquiry, which sees them as delaying devices, or as methods of deceiving the public. We do not deny that this is probably the factually correct one; what is important is to see that there is a formal aspect to such investigations which holds out to those in and out of government the hope that decision making will be better – more reasonable, more strongly based on facts, more clearly reasoned and articulated, etc. It is the literal interpretation – the sort that examinees should give to questions.

The argument could be taken a stage further by looking at the nature of change rather than reform. For if an administrator or manager faces a problem, perhaps something that appears once or twice a week, or several times a year, to which he feels that organizational change of some sort is the answer, then he may also be engaged on an activity that is fundamentally academic. Suppose he wants to know whether it is worthwhile sending his section heads on a block release course in order that they may acquire a relevant professional or technical qualification. The evidence on which a decision can properly be made can never be contained solely within his experience, or the experience of those with whom he has personal contact. It involves a reference to facts that only emerge from the experience of other bodies, which have been systematically compared, from an analysis of employment trends, from estimates of the educational effectiveness of the particular type of course, etc.

An examination of reform (and of change where this is articulated sufficiently in a public manner) soon shows that the process scores very badly on the criteria of truth, relevance, coherence and consistency, comprehensiveness, etc. There are several possible reasons for this.

First, politicians and administrators may have decided on what they want to do before the investigatory and advisory stages are set under way (which is what the cynical view maintains) and therefore look for an 'authority' for what they are going to do regardless. If this is so then a short, clear and persuasive report will not serve their purpose, unless it agrees exactly with their original intentions.

For instance, the government might have photocopied page 242 of the New Universal Library edition of *Representative Government* and sent a copy of the following to the press, universities, top civil servants, etc., instead of appointing the Fulton Committee It reads:

> As a general rule, every executive function, whether superior or subordinate, should be the appointed duty of some given individual. It should be apparent to all the world, who did everything, and through whose default anything was left undone. Responsibility is null, when nobody knows who is responsible. Nor, even when real, can it be divided without being weakened. To maintain it at its highest, there must be one person who receives the whole praise of what is well done, the whole blame of what is ill.[14]

Though Mill was thinking largely of the heads of public organizations, that principle easily becomes, when applied to the large hierarchical organizations that he did not foresee, the Fulton Committee's 'structure in which units and individual members have authority that is clearly defined and responsibilities for which they can be held accountable'. In fact, 'there should be recognized methods of assessing their success in achieving specified objectives'.[15]

The passage from Mill would not, however, suit the purposes of civil service reformers. First, John Stuart Mill is not an acceptable 'authority' whose name legitimizes present-day proposals for reform in government. Secondly, he is too clear and uncompromising. The only qualification is the phrase 'as a general rule'; what is needed is a repeated hedging of any recommendation which will make it consistent with virtually everything that someone might want to do. The sort of expressions that will fill this role are: 'as objectively as possible'; 'the ways most appropriate to its own tasks'; 'whenever they can'; 'the availability of men and women with the right training and experience'.[16] One does not need to be a great sophist to reconcile a wide range of actions with these phrases.

The most striking example of this occurred in the report of the

Maud Committee. The positive proposals for a management board form of internal organization of local authorities were generally rejected in favour of the dissent by Wheatley, which proposed an alternative model. The amazing point about this is that Wheatley's scheme is literally inconsistent: it contradicts itself by requiring committees to be both executive and non-executive at the same time.

Neither the student of public administration nor the citizen (nor the public administrator, one would have thought) can be satisfied with the present state of affairs. The processes of investigation, analysis and advice about the machinery of government do not justify the words used to commend them when, for instance, a royal commission is created. The cynical view is undoubtedly realistic; reform arises from political demands or political expediency, and the language of rational discovery is a façade. The political demands need not be simply partisan; they may arise from power struggles within the system of government, and reflect the effort to assign the blame for defects in the performance of government to another body. This is the view that the Deputy Clerk of Pembroke County Council took of the centrally inspired (and English) reforms of Welsh local government. Criticisms of the shortcomings of small Welsh local authorities, he held, were attempts by Whitehall and Westminster to pass the buck.[17]

In order to improve the process of reform from the point of view of the citizen (and also, we believe, the administrator) several changes will have to be made.

First, some effort will have to be made to come to terms with the diverse literature on management – 'organization theory', 'administrative science', call it what you will. Unless it is possible to distinguish good and bad within this literature, it is impossible to use it in measures of practical reform. And there can be no alternative to it.

Secondly, those who report on administrative organization from the inside (who must remain a major source of relevant information) must be prepared to give up their reliance on intuition and impression and develop the ability to describe and analyse their own experiences within the proper framework; in other words, a framework which has been shown, independently of the particular investigation, to be a justifiable one. This may mean no more than it meets the ordinary standards of truth and reason.

Thirdly, and perhaps as a consequence of this, there must be a radical reform of the system of advisory commissions and committees. This is not the place to discuss at length the ways in which this should occur, but if the committee of inquiry is to remain as a method of investigating complicated social science subjects, then changes have to be made in the ways that members, particularly chairmen, are selected. It is fortunate for some that they are not football league managers for they would have been sacked after one season and never been offered a job again.

We are conscious that this short discussion of reform and change in administrative organization, procedures and personnel does not do justice to the importance of the subject. But to take it further is to raise the whole question of the status and usefulness of the study of government and politics generally. Economists, and to a lesser extent sociologists, now have a recognized place in the system of government – as experts in the subjects they have studied. This is not true of political scientists or of those who have specialized in the study of public administration. One of the urgent needs of our subject is to establish a more academic and professional status. This book is an attempt to contribute towards the foundations of such an endeavour.

Notes

1 Fulton, 1968, vol. 1, p. 89
2 Bains, 1972, p. 4
3 Stewart, 1971
4 Self, 1972, pp. 266–67
5 Etzioni, 1964, pp. 8–16
6 Whyte, 1956; Packard, 1962
7 Williams, 1967
8 Garrett, 1972
9 Garrett, 1972
10 Regan, 1966
11 Profitt, 1968
12 Fry, 1972
13 Bains, 1972, pp. 4–5
14 Mill, 1861, p. 242
15 Fulton, 1968, p. 50
16 Fulton, 1968, pp. 50–54
17 Rees, 1971

Appendix
Sources of Statistics Relating to Public Administration in Britain

The statistics relating to public administration in Britain are always changing and any up-to-date figures cited now would be out of date by the time the book appears in print. We have therefore generally preferred not to give exact figures for one point in time where quantification is appropriate but to indicate approximate proportions and relative sizes, which do not change so frequently.

In this appendix we list the sources for statistics relating to many of the headings used in the text, so that the readers who need to have more exact and up-to-date information will be able to discover it for themselves.

Britain, 1974: An Official Handbook, a factual account of the administration and national economy of Britain, published each year by the Reference Division of the Central Office of Information.

The Municipal Year Book, published annually by the Municipal Journal, Ltd. Many national public organizations, including central departments and non-departmental bodies, publish a report each year on their activities, including staffing, finance, organizational changes and developments in the services and functions for which they are responsible.

Some examples are: Department of Health and Social Security, *Annual Report, 1972* (published July, 1973), Cmnd. 5352. From 1972 the statistics will be found in two separate publications – *Health and Personal Social Service Statistics* and *Social Security Statistics*.

Welsh Office. *Cymru: Wales, 1972.*

The British Broadcasting Corporation. *Annual Report and Accounts.*

The National Coal Board, *Annual Report and Accounts.*

For statistics relating to the decentralized organizations of central departments and non-departmental bodies see the relevant annual report.

For numbers, types and names of local authorities see the *Municipal Year Book*, which provides statistical information and factual details relating to many aspects of local government.

Local government finance is covered in two joint publications of the Department of the Environment and the Welsh Office:

Local Government Financial Statistics, England and Wales, published annually;

Rates and Rateable Values, also published annually.

For the civil service see *Civil Services Statistics*, published annually by the Civil Service Department.

For local government staff, including teachers and policemen, see *Annual Abstract of Statistics*.

For the national health service staff see: Department of Health and Social Security: *Annual Reports*.

The *Annual Report* of the Civil Service Commission gives figures relating to many aspects of recruitment to the civil service.

A guide to the internal structure of central departments can be obtained from The Civil Service Year Book, published annually by the Civil Service Department (it is the successor to the British Imperial Calendar and Civil Service List), supplemented by Her Majesty's Ministers and Senior Staff in Public Departments, published five times a year.

For most aspects of public expenditure see the annual Command Paper on Public Expenditure.

Statistics relating to the work of the Parliamentary Commissioner for Administration are found in his annual report to Parliament.

Statistics relating to tribunals are found in the Annual Reports of the Council on Tribunals.

Bibliography

The first part of this bibliography is a list of general textbooks and collections of readings on public administration, and the second part contains the references cited in the text.

General Textbooks and Books of Readings
Baker, R. J. S. (1972). *Administrative Theory and Public Administration*, Hutchinson University Library
Brown, R. G. S. (1970). *The Administrative Process in Britain*, Methuen (reprinted in 1971 as a University Paperback)
Chapman, R. A. (ed.) (1973). *The Role of Commissions in Policy Making*, Allen and Unwin
Chapman, R. A., & Dunsire, A. (eds.) (1971). *Style in Administration: Readings in British Public Administration*, Allen and Unwin for the Royal Institute of Public Administration
Chester, D. N., & Willson, F. M. G. (1957). *The Organization of British Central Government*, second ed. 1968, Allen and Unwin for the Royal Institute of Public Administration
Clarke, R. (1971) *New Trends in Government*, Civil Service College Studies, no. 1, HMSO
de Smith, S. A. (1973). *Constitutional and Administrative Law*, second ed., Foundations of Law, Penguin Education
Dunsire, A. (1973). *Administration: The Word and the Science*, Martin Robertson
Etzioni, A. (1964). *Modern Organizations*, Foundations of Sociology, Englewood Cliffs, New Jersey, USA, Prentice-Hall
Hanson, A. H. (ed.) (1963). *Nationalization: A Book of Readings*, Allen and Unwin for the Royal Institute of Public Administration
Hanson, A. H., & Crick, B. (eds.) (1970). *The Commons in Transition*, Fontana Studies in Politics, for the Study of Parliament Group
Hanson, A. H., & Walles, M. (1970). *Governing Britain*, Fontana Studies in Politics
Hawley, C. E., & Weintraub, R. G. (eds.) (1966). *Administrative Questions and Political Answers*, Princeton, New Jersey, USA, Van Nostrand

Heady, F. (1966). *Public Administration: A Comparative Perspective*, Foundations of Public Administration, Englewood Cliffs, New Jersey, USA, Prentice-Hall

Hill, M. J. (1972). *The Sociology of Public Administration*, World University, Weidenfeld and Nicolson

Keeling, D. (1972). *Management in Government*, Allen and Unwin for the Royal Institute of Public Administration

King, A. (ed.) (1969). *The British Prime Minister*, Student Editions, Macmillan

Mackenzie, W. J. M., & Grove, J. W. (1957). *Central Administration in Britain*, Longmans

Morrison, H. (1964). *Government and Parliament*, third ed., Oxford Paperbacks, Oxford University Press

Raphaeli, N. (ed.) (1967). *Readings in Comparative Public Administration*, Boston, USA, Allyn and Bacon

Ridley, F. F., & Blondel, J. (1964). *Public Administration in France*, Routledge and Kegan Paul (second ed., 1969)

Robson, W. A. (1960). *Nationalized Industry and Public Ownership*, Allen and Unwin

Rose, R. (ed.) (1966). *Studies in British Politics*, Macmillan

Rose, R. (ed.) (1969). *Policy Making in Britain*, Student Editions, Macmillan

Self, P. J. O. (1972). *Administrative Theories and Politics*, Allen and Unwin

Simon, H. A., *et al.* (1950). *Public Administration*, Kropf, New York

Thornhill, W. (1968). *The Nationalized Industries*, Thomas Nelson

Thornhill, W. (ed.) (1971). *The Growth and Reform of English Local Government*, World University, Readings in Politics and Society, Weidenfeld and Nicolson

Thornhill, W. (ed.) (1972). *The Case for Regional Reform*, Thomas Nelson

Tivey, L. (ed.) (1973). *The Nationalized Industries since 1960*, Allen and Unwin for the Royal Institute of Public Administration

Wiseman, H. V. (ed.) (1966). *Parliament and the Executive*, Routledge and Kegan Paul

Wiseman, H. V. (ed.) (1970). *Local Government in England, 1958–69*, Routledge and Kegan Paul

References

The reports of official committees and commissions of inquiry are cited by the name of the chairman and the year of publication, and where relevant, the volume number. Other government publications are cited by their command number, and publications of Parliamentary Committees are listed under the name of the Committee.

Adamson, C. (1968). 'The Role of the Industrial Advisor', *Public Administration*, 46, summer

Almond, G. A., & Verba, S. (1963). *The Civic Culture*, Princeton, USA

Armstrong, W. (1971). *Personnel Management in the Civil Service*, HMSO

Assheton, 1944. *Report on the Training of Civil Servants*, Cmnd. 6525

Bains, 1972. *The New Local Authorities; Management and Structure*, Department of the Environment

Baker, R. J. S. (1963). 'Discussion and Decision Making in the Civil Service', *Public Administration*, 41, winter

Baker, R. J. S. (1972), *op. cit*

Blau, P. M. (1956). *Bureaucracy in Modern Society*, Studies in Sociology, New York, USA

Blondel, J. (1959). 'Local Government and the Local Offices of Ministries in a French Department', *Public Administration*, 37, spring

Brett, C. E. B. (1970). 'The Lessons of Devolution in Northern Ireland', *Political Quarterly*, 41, 3

Bridges, E. (1964). *The Treasury*, The New Whitehall Series, Allen and Unwin for the Royal Institute of Public Administration

Brown, L. N., & Garner, J. F. (1967). *French Administrative Law*, Butterworth

Brown, R. G. S. (1970). *op cit*.

Brown, R. G. S. (1971). 'Fulton and Morale', *Public Administration*, 49, summer

Burns, T., & Stalker, G. M. (1961). *The Management of Innovation*, Tavistock

Chester, D. N. (1953). 'Public Corporations and the Classification of Administrative Bodies', *Political Studies*, 1, 1

Chester, D. N. (1970). 'Questions in Parliament', in Hanson, A. K., & Crick, B. (eds.). *op. cit*.

Civil Service Commission, 1968. *Annual Report*

Civil Service Department, 1970. *Report for 1969*

Clarke, R. (1971). *op. cit*.

Compton, E. (1970). 'The Administrative Performance of Government', *Public Administration*, 48, spring

Coombes, D. (1966). *The Member of Parliament and the Administration*, Allen and Unwin

Cross, J. A. (1970). 'The Regional Decentralization of British Government Departments', *Public Administration*, 48, winter

Cyert, R. M., & March, J. G. (1963). *The Behavioural Theory of the Firm*, Englewood Cliffs, New Jersey, USA

Cmnd. 6502, 1944. *A National Health Service*

Cmnd. 4506, 1970. *The Reorganization of Central Government*

Dale, H. E. (1941). *The Higher Civil Service in Britain*

de Smith, S. A. (1968). *Judicial Review of Administrative Action*, Stevens and Sons

Edwards, W., & Tversky, A. (eds.) (1967). *Decision Making*, Modern Psychology Readings, Penguin

Etzioni, A. (1964). *op cit.*

Fayol, H. (1916). *General and Industrial Management*, translated by Constance Storrs and published in English by Pitman in 1949

Fesler, J. W. (1962). 'The Political Role of Field Administration' in Heady, H., & Stokes, J. L. (eds.). *Papers in Comparative Public Administration*, Prentice-Hall

Finer, S. E. (1956). 'The Individual Responsibility of Ministers', *Public Administration*, 34, winter

Franks, O. (1947). *Experiences of a University Teacher in the Civil Service*

Friend, J. K., & Jessop, W. N. (1969). *Local Government and Strategic Choice*, Tavistock

Fry, G. K. (1972). 'Policy Planning Units in British Central Government Departments', *Public Administration*, 50, summer

Fulton, 1968. vol. 1. *Report of the Committee on the Civil Service*, Cmnd. 3638

    vol. 2. *Report of a Management Consultancy Group*

    vol. 3. *Surveys and Investigations*

    vol. 4. *Factual, Statistical and Explanatory Papers*

    vol. 5. *Proposals and Opinions*

Garner, J. F. (1967). *Administrative Law*, Butterworth

Garrett, J. (1972). *The Management of Government*, Pelican Library of Business and Management

Gerth, H. H., & Mills, C. W. (1948). *From Max Weber*, International Library of Sociology and Social Reconstruction, Routledge and Kegan Paul

Gladden, E. N. (1961). *An Introduction to Public Administration*, Staples Press

Goodnow, F. (1900). *Politics and Administration*, New York, USA

Griffith, J. A. G., & Street, H. (1964). *A Casebook of Administrative Law*

Gunn, L. A. (1967). 'Ministers and Civil Servants: Changes in Whitehall', *Public Administration* (Sydney), 26, 1

Haldane, 1918. *Report of the Machinery of Government Committee*, Cmnd. 9230

Hall, R. H., & Tittle, C. R. (1966-7). 'A note on Bureaucracy and Its Correlates', *American Journal of Sociology*, 73, 3

Hanson, A. H., & Walles, M. (1970). *op cit.*

Hart, W. O. (1962). *Introduction to the Law of Local Government*, 7th edition, Butterworth

Hunter, G. (1967). 'Methods of Rural Development', *Journal of Local Administration Overseas*, 6, 1

Jackson, R. M. (1965). *The Machinery of Local Government*, Macmillan

Jennings, W. I. (1969). *Cabinet Government*, 3rd edition, Cambridge University Press

Johnson, N. (1970). 'Select Committees as Tools of Parliamentary Reform', in Hanson, A. H., & Crick, B. (eds.), *op cit.*

Keeling, D. (1972), *op cit.*

Kilbrandon, 1973. vol. 1. *Report of the Commission*, Cmnd. 5460
vol. 2. *Memorandum of Dissent*, Cmnd. 5460–1

King, G. (1958). *The Ministry of Pensions and National Insurance*, New Whitehall Series, Allen and Unwin for the Royal Institute of Public Administration

Kingsley, J. D. (1944). *Representative Bureaucracy*

Klein, R. (1971). 'Accountability in the National Health Service', *Political Quarterly*, 42, 4

Laski, H. (1938). *Parliamentary Government in England*, Allen and Unwin

Likert, R. (1961). *New Patterns of Management*, Mcgraw-Hill, New York

Lipman, V. D. (1949). *Local Government Areas, 1834–1945*, Blackwell

Lupton, T. (1971). *Management and the Social Sciences*, Modern Management Texts, Penguin

Mackenzie, W. J. M. (1950), 'The Structure of Central Administration', in Campion, E. *et al.* (eds.). *British Government since 1918*, Allen and Unwin

Mackenzie, W. J. M. (1951). 'The Conventions of Local Government', *Public Administration*, 29, winter

Mackenzie, W. J. M. (1961). *Theories of Local Government*, Greater London Paper no. 2

Mackintosh, J. P. (1968). *The British Cabinet*, 2nd edition, Methuen University Publications.

Mackintosh, J. P. (1970). *The Government and Politics of Britain*, Hutchinson University Library

Mallaby, G. (1964). 'The Civil Service Commission: its Place in the Machinery of Government', *Public Administration*, 42, spring

Mallaby, 1967. *Report of the Committee on the Staffing of Local Government*, Ministry of Housing and Local Government

Marshall, G. (1970). 'Parliament and the Ombudsman', in Hanson, A. H., & Crick, B. (eds.), *op cit.*

Marshall, G. (1973). 'Maladministration', *Public Law*, spring

Maud, 1967. *Report of the Committee on the Management of Local Government*, Ministry of Housing and Local Government, 5 vols.

Merton, R. K., *et al.* (eds.) (1952). *Reader in Bureaucracy*, The Free Press, Glencoe, USA

Mill, J. S. (1861). *Representative Government*, reprinted in Dent's Everyman Library, with *Utilitarianism* and *Liberty*, 1910

Mooney, J. D. (1947). *The Principles of Organization*, revised edition, New York, USA

Morris, A. (1970). *The Growth of Parliamentary Scrutiny by Committee*, Pergamon Press

Packard, V. (1962). *The Pyramid Climbers*, Penguin edition 1965

Petersen, A. W. (1966). 'Regional Economic Planning Councils and Boards', *Public Administration*, 44, spring

Priestley, 1955. *Report of the Royal Commission on the Civil Service*, Cmnd. 9613

Profitt, T. H. (1968). 'Great Britain' in Ridley, F. F. (ed.). *Specialists and Generalists*, Allen and Unwin

Rees, I. B. (1971). *Government by Community*, Charles Knight

Regan, D. E. (1966). 'The Expert and the Administrator: Recent Changes at the Ministry of Transport', *Public Administration*, 44, summer

Ridley, F. F. (ed.). (1968). *Specialists and Generalists*, Allen and Unwin

Schein, E. H. (1965). *Organizational Psychology*, Foundations of Modern Psychology, Englewood Cliffs, New Jersey, USA

Seebohm, 1968. *Report of the Committee on Local Authority and Allied Social Services*, Cmnd. 3703

Select Committee on the Nationalized Industries, 1967. *Report, 1966–7*, H.C. 340, *The Post Office*

Self, P. J. O. (1972). *op cit.*

Sharp, E. (1969). *The Ministry of Housing and Local Government*, New Whitehall Series, Allen and Unwin for the Royal Institute of Public Administration

Sharpe L. J. (1970). 'Theories and Values of Local Government', *Political Studies*, 18, 2

Simmons, H. G. (1971). 'The Planner's Dilemma', *Canadian Journal of Political Science*, 4, 3

Simon, H. A. (1945). *Administrative Behaviour*, second edition, 1957, Collier-Macmillan

Simon, H. A. (1959). 'Theories of Decision Making in Economics and Behavioural Science', *American Economic Review*, 49, 3

Smith, B. C. (1967). *Field Administration*, Library of Political Studies, Routledge and Kegan Paul

Smith, B. C. (1969). *Advising Ministers*, Library of Political Studies, Routledge and Kegan Paul

Speight, H. (1962). *The Economics of Industrial Efficiency*, Macmillan (Papermac edition 1970)

Steer, W. S. (1964). 'The Origins of Social Insurance', *Transactions of the Devonshire Association*, XCIV

Stewart, A. C. (1935). 'The Significance of "Public"', *Public Administration*, 13, 3

Stewart, J. D. (1971). *Management in Local Government*, Charles Knight

Udy, S. H. (1959). ' "Bureaucracy" and "Rationality" in Weber's Organization Theory: An Empirical Assessment', *American Sociological Review*, 24, 6

Urwick, L. F. (1935). 'A Republic of Administration', *Public Administration*, 13, 3

Urwick, L. F. (1943). *The Elements of Administration*, Pitman

Vile, M. J. C. (1967). *Constitutionalism and the Separation of Powers*, The Clarendon Press

Wade, H. W. R. (1961). *Administrative Law*, Oxford University Press

Walker, P. G. (1972). *The Cabinet*, Fontana edition

Ward, R. A. (1964). *Operational Research in Local Government*, Allen and Unwin for the Royal Institute of Public Administration

Warren, J. H. (1954). *Municipal Administration*, second edition, Pitman

Weber, M. (1947). *The Theory of Social and Economic Organisation*, translated by Henderson, A. M., & Parsons, T., Free Press Paperback, 1964, Glencoe, USA

Werlin, H. (1970). 'Elasticity of Control', *Journal of Comparative Administration*, 2, 2

Whalen, H. (1960). 'Ideology, Democracy and the Foundations of Local Self-Government', *Canadian Journal of Economics and Political Science*, 26, 3

Wheare, K. C. (1955). *Government by Committee*, Oxford University Press.

Whyatt, 1961. *The Citizen and the Administration: the Redress of Grievances*, a report by a committee of the British Section of the International Commission of Jurists

Whyte, W. H. (1956). *The Organization Man*, Penguin edition

Williams, A. (1967). *Output Budgeting and the Contribution of Micro-Economics to Efficiency in Government*, Centre for Administrative Studies, Occasional Paper no. 4, HMSO

Wiseman, H. V. (1963). 'Local Government in Leeds', I, II, *Public Administration*, 41, spring and summer

Woodward, J. (1958). *Management and Technology*, Problems of Progress in Industry, no. 3, DSIR

Wraith, R. E., & Lamb, G. E. (1971). *Public Inquiries as Instruments of Government*, Allen and Unwin for the Royal Institute of Public Administration

Index